MONOPOLY GAMES
By Steve Kahofer

Published by Pen It! Publications, LLC
812-371-4128
www.penitpublications.com

Published in the United States of America by Pen It! Publications, LLC
ISBN: 978-1-949609-64-6

Edited by Peggy Holt
Cover by Donna Cook

Acknowledgements

To Debbi Stanton and her staff at Penn It Publications, thank you for your hard work to make this a terrific novel.

Thank you to my friends at the Sourland Writers Group and Jackson Writers Group for all their suggestions, constructive criticism, and editing to writing a better story.

My thanks go to Luke Smithwick, friend and owner of Himalaya Alpine Guides, for his help with the chapter on mountain climbing.

Thank you, Flo and Buddy, for your creative efforts and support.

To all my friends who have given me characters and a lifetime of human emotions to write about, thank you. I hope you enjoy the ride as much as I do.

To Joanie, thank you for always being supportive, giving me encouragement, and just being there for me.

Last, Lauren and Greg, thank you for your inspiration to write and see the job through.

Prologue

RUSSIAN AIRBASE ZHUKOV, SIBERIA
Two-hundred kilometers from the Chinese Border, near the Arctic Circle

Opening one eye, the operator shook his head and groaned in response to the flashing red light on his monitor, "This is not good." His cold hands shivered as his fingers ran over the keyboard. The control room was the warmest room in the guardhouse. But the old building's concrete floor and peeling paint on military grey walls could not protect its occupants. Outside, winter's Siberian Express howled across the endless tundra. Inside, the red light continued to blink.

"Sergeant. I've got a warning light indicating a security breach at munitions bunker Ivan Three."

"Damn, that's the other end of the base. Is it another malfunction?"

"Everything checks out on our end."

"Run your diagnostics," the sergeant replied, but knew he was just putting off the inevitable. The event would have to be logged, investigated and reported.

There would be paperwork. Ivan Three was nuclear weapons storage.

"Already done. Sarge, I know what the hell I'm doing." the operator snapped. "I've been sitting at this damn control desk for three years. There wasn't a power failure or malfunction on my end. Go check for a power outage in the bunkers."

"Watch it, Corporal. Control your mouth or you'll be standing guard outside tonight, freezing your balls off." The Sergeant took a sip of his tea, frowned and turned his attention to the blinking light. He knew the young recruit was right, but strict discipline had to be maintained even if he wished the red light would go away. "This tea tastes like shit even with vodka. Where is our roving patrol?"

"Last time the goat (UAZ-467 jeep) checked in, they were by the control tower. They get hot food in the tower."

The sergeant appeared calm, but his deep voice conveyed a sense of urgency. "Send them over to investigate, and keep their communications open. I'll wake up the Duty Officer."

The Captain was awake and reading in his room. A large pile of books, some in English, sat on his desk. After a difficult tour in Kazakhstan, he welcomed the total isolation of a Siberian military post.

"Sir, we have a problem." The sergeant briefed him as they returned to the control desk. Men snapped to attention as the officer entered the room.

"Sir," the Corporal spoke in a nervous voice.

"At ease," the Captain replied. "What have we got?"

"Sir, I've lost contact with the roving patrol. I was talking to the driver. He said he could see something big by Bunker Three. Then nothing, the radio went dead."

The Captain shook his head and silently recited a soldier's prayer, "Dear God, please not on my watch." He didn't want to do this, but it was a restricted area. As a soldier, he had no choice. "Sergeant, load up the truck and tell my driver to bring around my goat." He leaned in. "Keep the men calm. I don't want anybody shooting themselves in the foot on a false alarm. When we stop, I want it by the book. Give me a quick deployment." The two combat veterans looked at each other and nodded. No more words were needed.

Two hundred meters from the bunker, the Captain ordered his driver to pull to the side of the road. The Ural-4320 carrying twenty-two men stopped behind him. Forty meters in front, he could see the roving patrol goat sitting in the ditch. It appeared unoccupied. As the Captain opened his door, his driver's head exploded.

The gate to hell was open. Grabbing his AK-74M, he dove for the ditch as machine-gun fire raked the two vehicles. Three soldiers died before they could exit the truck.

A second rifle shot ripped the jeep's radio from its mountings. The Captain could not call for reinforcements. He knew it was a sniper, an experienced sniper using a night-vision scope, and explosive rounds. He yelled into his hand-held radio, "Sergeant, lay down a base of fire with First Squad and start a flanking maneuver to your left with the Second."

The Captain jumped from the ditch, ran thirty meters, and dove behind the snow covered bushes. He continued rolling as another round detonated in the snow beside him. Machine-gun muzzle flash from the top of Bunker Ivan Two gave away the enemy's position.

"Sargent, concentrate fire on Bunker Two. I'm going to flank right. Don't shoot me in the back."

He ran another thirty meters, then ducked behind a streetlamp. Its light momentarily blinded the sniper's night scope. Racing to the next light, he saw the silhouette of a man on top of the bunker. Breathing slow to relax, the Captain fired his weapon until the clip was empty.

The silhouette disappeared as he charged forward. The machine gun fire stopped, and the Sergeant ordered his men to advance. Climbing to the top of the bunker, they heard a helicopter taking off, but could see nothing in the night sky.

At the Captain's feet was the sniper's weapon. He hit the ground and shouldered the M82A1 50 cal. rifle. It was wet with warm blood. Checking the ammo, there was a round in the chamber and one in the clip.

With the powerful night scope, he sighted the chopper running dark and fired. Nothing.

Time for the last shot as the target faded into night. Squeezing the trigger, the gun recoiled in his grip. He continued holding his breath as he waited.

A great ball of fire lit up the night sky, then fell to earth.

Rushing to the crash site, they found the bodies burned beyond recognition. The Sergeant smiled, "Nice shooting comrade, for an officer with an American rifle. You will be decorated for stopping their Imperialist attack."

The Captain shook his head. "The Americans will sell guns to anybody. I'm more concerned about those two metal boxes in the wreckage. They're storage containers for our RDS-37 Hydrogen bombs. Why would the Americans risk war for two of our H-bombs? They have over twenty-two hundred of their own.

"Care for the wounded and establish a perimeter to secure the area. Nobody touches anything. When the brass get here, the debriefing and paperwork will start."

"But sir, who else could mount such an attack?"

"I'm not sure, but twice we have worked with the CIA's Professor Hamilton to stop a nuclear highjacking. You may get to meet him before this is over. Someone is in the business of stealing nukes and they almost got away with it. They will try again.

Chapter 1

Greg Welch walked quickly through the LAX terminal. A Washington DC redeye waited at the next gate. The Association of Electrical and Electronic Engineers, or A3E, paid him (although not very well) to manage and promote its Standards Balloting Service. The West Coast trip was a weekend getaway with his girlfriend followed by four hectic days of business presentations, training and conflict resolution. Now, he was tired and wanted to go home.

Passing a crowded airport bar, he stopped and stared. He had a plane to catch but couldn't pull himself away. A well-tanned, surfer-dude sat spewing obscenities in his girlfriend's face while everybody looked the other way. Welch wasn't able to do that.

Welch was a lean six feet. This guy was taller and built like steroid man. His large hand shot out, hitting the woman on the side of her head. Using the heel of his right hand, it left no bruises on her face or marks on his knuckles. He knew what he was doing.

"Hey you, stop it!" Welch yelled in a burst of anger that surprised even him.

The startled bully looked up to find the threat interrupting his fun. Seeing only a man in a wrinkled business suit, he laughed. "You want some of me?"

Welch continued to stare. He hated bullies, having received more than his share of abuse growing up a Yankee in the South. Unable to back down, the memories of their cruelty and his little brother's mistreatment locked his brain in fight mode. An adrenaline rush charged his muscles. He breathed deep to relax and focus.

They were in an airport, and the bully didn't look like a cop, so no gun. Welch hoped. His opponent was alone, so it would be one-on-one. The troublemaker was right-handed and drunk, but he had size, ego, and a big beer mug. Welch knew it would be over if steroid man got in the first shot.

The drunk bully moved toward his new target as if sensing an easy kill of small prey.

Welch dropped his luggage at arm's length in front while stepping back with his right foot. *Cocky bastard. The element of surprise is on my side.*

The dude hesitated and gave a disarming smile as he looked past Welch.

Welch didn't fall for it. He watched the subtle shift of his opponent's weight. *Hope I've still got it.* The hand with the beer mug pulled back. His forward momentum telegraphed the start of a violent attack.

Welch fired a front thrust kick over his suitcase. A shockwave of energy ripped through the soft tissue of the man's midsection. *All's fair in love and war.*

Welch's trained reflex was faster and stronger than his opponent. The bully staggered backward to keep from falling in pain.

Muscles still tense and heart racing, Welch turned to the bartender, "Call security. This fight is over."

The bartender nodded. "They're on their way."

Thinking everything was safe, Welch exhaled and let down his guard. *Where's the girlfriend?*

She screamed as she jumped on his back, fighting to protect her man. Welch tripped over his suitcase, and they crashed to the floor. He kept her at arm's length as she tried to bite him by inserting his foot in her stomach and pushed her away. Jumping to his feet, he looked down in disbelief. "Why? I was trying to help."

There was no time for an answer. Her boyfriend, now recovered, attacked from behind in a raging charge. Looking over his shoulder, Welch shot a back thrust kick to the groin, followed by an elbow strike to the jaw. Welch grabbed his hair and swept the legs out from under the bully. Slamming the man into the floor, he stomped on his ribs in anger.

"Police, freeze! Put your hands in the air." Their weapons were pointed at the back of his head. He slowly raised his hands, praying they weren't trigger happy. *No good deed goes unpunished.*

Fortunately, several witnesses came to Welch's defense. As a distinguished looking gentleman explained to the officers, "he was a concerned, good citizen who stepped forward to stop that domestic abuse." But Welch knew it was his own inner demons that had gotten out of control.

The police took statements and ran names while medics determined their patient would recover. The bully refused to press charges, and the police didn't want more paperwork. Welch was able to catch his flight and get his upgrade.

First Class was a comfortable place to contemplate the meaning of life, or at least the events of the day. The fight flooded his brain with excitement and fear. He couldn't even daydream about last weekend's Napa Valley bed & breakfast with Linda, and that was the best weekend ever. Trying to relax in his large reclining seat, he obsessively replayed the fight in his mind while he indulged in a variety of free cocktails. *God, I love upgrades.*

Reliving the victory helped put his deep anxiety to sleep. It was the first real fight since his military service many years ago. Even if he didn't save the world, he felt proud of himself, knowing he had done the right thing. Welch pushed his seat back and surrendered to the alcohol. He thought of Linda and closed his eyes.

The plane banked right, and Welch grabbed his armrest. The whine of the engines and vibration of the aircraft sent his imagination into panic mode. *Why is everyone sitting so calmly while the plane is falling out of the sky?*

He wanted to be with Linda.

"Sir." He opened his eyes. A smiling flight attendant placed a reassuring hand on his shoulder. "Good morning. Please return your seat to the upright position as we prepare for landing."

He tried to relax as he got ready for the new day's struggle— a quick meeting in Virginia with the Association's engineers in the electrical utility industry. Then it was back on a plane to New Jersey and home for the weekend.

The constant business travel had earned him a frequent flyer gold card, and he considered himself entitled to its benefits. Sitting in coach for five hours was like being in Dante's ninth circle of hell after one had tasted the delights of an upgrade to First Class heaven. The landing was smooth, and he breathed a sigh of relief. *If you walk away from the plane, it was a good flight.*

As the Boeing 737 taxied to Reagan National terminal, he looked out the window at the private luxury jets shining in the morning light. The largest jet, a sleek Gulfstream 550, taxied to a private terminal reserved for those privileged few. Nose to the window, he saw a Mercedes Maybach waiting on the tarmac.

What is that like? A private jet had to be a quantum leap above what Welch could only indulge in for five hours before returning to his lower station in life. *What's it like to have so much money that all you have to worry about is self-actualization…and where the next party is?* He tried to picture himself in the world of private jets, the elite one percent—a world of celebrity status with yachts and orgies. *But after a decade of playing corporate games, I'm back on the bottom rung of the management ladder with a bad attitude. I've got to find a better way.*

Chapter 2

"Let the games begin." It would be war and Charles Claiborne Shields III considered himself a great general. Sitting in his high-top leather chair, he glanced at his Rolex while rearranging the family pictures on his antique, mahogany desk.

Shields had been working on his company's financials all morning. The numbers didn't look good, but his new product was ready. He knew his superior intelligence and negotiating skills would win this financial deal for his company, and his family.

The Shields Communications Corp. specialized in military aviation networks, and he had won the Navy's X-47B drone contract. The deal would pay off his Gulfstream 550, his kids' college, and his wife's tennis lessons.

"Mr. Shields, we have an ETA of five minutes for Nassau Airport. Please prepare for landing." His pilot interrupted on the intercom.

The remainder of the military production was in system upgrades for the Air Force F-15 and Navy Super Hornets. This significant modification allowed secure ground control of the aircraft's weapon systems, similar to what was being used on the drones. Shields could lose money at his non-military

Mississippi and Taiwan sites, as long as production was strong on his fat government contracts in Ohio.

Shields fastened his seatbelt then picked up his favorite picture. It was an old photograph of his father and him with his young son. He stroked the gold frame as he admired the picture.

Today, the rollout of his civilian, two-way radio would start with Step One: Secure project financing with the sale of the Taiwan location. Step Two: Manipulate the quality standards of the Association of Electrical and Electronic Engineers, A3E, to create a monopoly. Step Three: Use the Congressman in his pocket to deregulate the target market. His new blockbuster service would give him a financial windfall.

The Gulfstream 550 touched down at 9:30 pm local time. Parking in front of a private hanger, its powerful engines went to sleep. As soon as the plane was secured by the ground crew, the door opened downward into a staircase. The pilot descended to the tarmac, turned and waited for his only passenger.

Shields was Basketball tall. He stood at the top of the staircase in his bespoke pinstripe suit, letting the world know he had arrived. After surveying the area to ensure he had the largest private jet on the ground, he smiled as he descended the stairs then turned to his pilot. "Be ready. If my schedule changes, I'll call."

They were met at the hangar by Thomas Dumont. "Thank you, Mr. Shields, for flying down to meet with my clients. I know this appointment will be worth your time."

"Call me Chuck."

"Chuck, I've been in meetings all week with the parties interested in the acquisition of your Taiwan facility.

"So, tell them not to waste my time. The name you gave me is just a shell company. Who are the money people? Are they serious?"

"Let me assure you, Chuck, these men are very serious, but they're also gracious hosts. So relax, play a little golf, and enjoy their island hospitality. If you like what they have to say, your people can wrap up the details. You are still interested?"

He weighed his response, "I would prefer to be home with my family for the weekend, but I'm here now, and I'm ready to listen. Then I'll decide if I want to proceed."

"Excellent. Timing is critical. They're only staying a few more days before one of their key investors is sailing back to Europe. They love their Bahamian registered yachts, and the island is one of their financial centers. After all, this is where we all do our banking."

Shields' heart skipped a beat as he struggled to maintain his composure. *God, do they know about my offshore accounts?*

There was a long pause before Dumont continued. "You and I want to make this deal. Now, a car is waiting to take you to your suite at the Atlantis Hotel. I've taken care of all the details."

"But I still don't even know who the hell I'm meeting with."

"Mr. Shields, I never would have set up this meeting if I didn't know this consortium has the capital. You'll be meeting with the decision makers, not some flunkies. They're ready to deal."

"We'll see." As they walked to the terminal, Shields knew he got the meeting he wanted, but for some reason, it didn't feel right. He was not in control.

After going through customs, they were met at the car by Miss Hall, "I insist you call me Tina," and a very large limo driver. As Shields got into the vehicle, she hopped in the back seat with him.

"Mr. Shields, I understand you have been to the island before, but let me be your tour guide and point out the sights on our way to the hotel. I'll be quiet if you would rather rest."

"No, I'm not tired. Go ahead and talk. Is that an English accent?"

"It's South African, but the two can sound similar. Most people don't notice it at all. You're very observant."

Shields was uncomfortable with Tina in the back seat invading his space. She was an attractive woman, well built with long black hair rolled up in an old fashion bun. Her skirt was short and riding up. She was acting professional, but Shields suspected he was being set up by his host.

"On your left," Tina pointed, "is the house used in the James Bond movie 'Thunderball'." Shields remembered the film and Bond swimming in the pool filled with sharks.

Downtown Nassau was crowded with four cruise ships in port. With duty free trade in jewelry, liquor and electronics, the business district was a Caribbean mix of overcrowded nightclubs and expensive stores surrounded by island poverty.

Emerging on the other side of town, the limo took the bridge to the Atlantis Resort Island, entering a world of lavish opulence. Stopping at the grand entrance, busboys surrounded the vehicle. Tina jumped out and gave instructions to the Bell Captain.

"Mr. Shields, your luggage is being taken to your suite. The car is at your disposal if you would like to see more of the island nightlife this evening. I can recommend …"

"Nothing else tonight. I have some calls to make."

As they walked toward the lobby entrance, Shields looked over at the yacht basin. Being from Ohio, he didn't know much about seafaring vessels, but he knew about money. Some of those yachts cost more than his jet. They were certainly a hell of a lot bigger. *Great toys, but the game is always the same.*

The lobby had a towering dome ceiling, mural walls, and marble floors. It was big, gaudy, and a lot like Las Vegas.

"Your suite is ready in the East Wing, follow me."

Behind the lobby was an open area going down to the main restaurant. Looking straight back, Shields saw the moon rising through the large picture windows. It appeared that an ocean lagoon came right up to the hotel. The restaurant's back wall was a fifty yard long fish tank. Diners were sitting a few feet away from schools of brightly colored fish going up in size to a Manta Ray with an eleven foot wingspan slowly swimming back and forth in the tank. Large sharks looked down at the diners.

"In the West Wing is the casino, if you're feeling lucky tonight." Tina suggested with a smile.

"I only play when the odds are in my favor. I like to win," he replied smiling back at her. Shields wondered how long she was going to play this little game.

They walked past two night clubs, and he could hear a cabaret singer in one and steel drums in the other. Tina described everything in detail before taking the private elevator to the top floor, stopping in front of his suite.

The door opened. "Good evening Mr. Shields, I'm Louise, your personal secretary during your stay. Your luggage is in the master bedroom. You may wish to change into something more comfortable while I pour you a drink. Then you can relax while we go over tomorrow's itinerary."

Shields looked her over; she was younger and sensuous with a very innocent, teasing smile. He doubted she could take dictation. Louise wore a white blouse, top buttons open and short plaid skirt, the young schoolgirl look. With the two women standing together, he realized Tina was a tall hard body, Louise was short and well-rounded. Both were wearing high heels. Louise wore glasses, and had blond hair in a pony tail that made her look even younger.

Tina opened the sliding glass door and stepped onto the balcony. "Come and enjoy the beautiful view. Look at the sky so full of stars. Mr. Shields, what's your sign."

Louise wrapped herself in his arm, pressing against his leg. "Let's go out under the stars. That could be like so cool."

He had to make a decision and make it quick; there was a limit to how much titillation he could take. "Tina, give me the schedule for tomorrow?" he finally stated.

"We suggest you rest in tomorrow morning and have a leisurely breakfast. Then golf with Mr. Dumont. Next you will meet your hosts on their yacht for snorkeling on the reefs and dinner."

"I want a full breakfast served at 6:30 with tee off at 8:00 for 18 holes. Then we'll proceed with our snorkeling and business meetings. That's all, you're dismissed."

The women looked at each other before Tina spoke. "Very good, Mr. Shields, I'll make the arrangements. If you think of anything else you desire, here's my card. We'll be right below you if you need us." Louise looked rejected as they walked out.

Shields locked the door and walked to the bar for a nightcap. He opened a bottle of XO and poured a three finger shot in a brandy snifter. It was not the first time he had been tempted, but it was one of the better ones. He wouldn't be surprised if there were cameras in the bedroom. After all, he used them on his clients, but tonight he was here on business. He would stay focused and not give his opponents any advantage. His objective was simple— win at any costs.

Besides, Shields had a trophy wife that he was happy with. It was not worth the risks he took when he was younger. That risk was so much greater today with who knew what germs you could get. As newlyweds, both had been naïve and idealistic. But they had learned how the game was played. Shields slept well that night and felt confident of her support.

And he was right to feel that way. She liked her country club lifestyle and wanted to keep it for herself and her children. As the years went by, she came to understand there were people like her, and people that wanted to be like her.

In their gated, clubhouse community, many men were on their second or third younger wife. She spent hours in the gym making sure she stayed the perfect trophy wife who could handle the younger competition. A little silicone here and there didn't hurt either.

Everybody wanted more, but most people hadn't earned the right to be equal to her. It was not just her long family lineage. She set the community agenda by maintaining control over its social network.

She presided over the charity boards and their fundraising drives. Her operational control required hours of work. Sitting through town council meetings and country club board meetings to get what she wanted was torture. So, if she had an occasional one-nighter with her son's fraternity brothers, or her monthly encounter with the country club's tennis pro and his girlfriend— well, that was nobody's damn business.

****

Breakfast was served promptly at 6:30. The golf game was frustrating. Shields tied the score on the eighteenth hole, but was sure he'd been hustled. For a guy who claimed to be an amateur Sunday golfer, Dumont was a skilled athlete. Studying his swing, Shields noticed he was missing the tip of his trigger finger on his left hand.

They changed at the clubhouse by the bay and walked out on the pier to a waiting powerboat. Tina, wearing a revealing bikini under her bright blue windbreaker, sat waiting for them in the boat. The pilot extended his hand to help Shields as he stepped down from the pier. The hand was huge and completely rapped around Shields. The man was big, the same height, but carried another hundred pounds of muscle around a barrel chest.

Tina watched the encounter. As he sat down beside her, she turned to him. "Obviously," she said in the most nonchalant manner, "he's a bodyguard. Cuban born, American nationalized citizen, US Marine Sniper, wearing a bullet proof vest and packing heat."

From Shields's prospective, this was the equivalent of stepping into a twelve dimensional Universe. Tina remained sitting calm and relaxed, while this giant, carrying a gun, would be taking him somewhere out in the middle of the ocean.

He decided this fear tactic was another part of his adversary's negotiating strategy, like last night's temptations. Then, he concluded Tina was attracted to the bodyguard. *She likes the guy with big muscles and a big gun. Doesn't care about a big brain or a big wallet. Well, hell, screw you, bitch! I'll make you scream and beg for more.*

The craft went out three miles before turning parallel to the coast and traveling for another fifteen minutes. At the speed they were going, the wind and the roar of the engine made conversation almost impossible. Shields held on and tried to enjoy the ride as the sleek powerboat flew over the rolling blue waves. They were four miles past the point when they came to a lone yacht at anchor over the reefs.

Chapter 3

The yacht was enormous. Another large man helped them on board. Louise, wearing a pink bikini, was waiting for him with a cold, rum punch.

"Let me introduce our hosts," Dumont said as he led them up to the main deck.

Four men were sitting at the table playing cards. Looking like a character out of a 1940's Bogart movie, a very overweight man dressed in a white suit gave a small wave of his hand. Two of the players got up and walked away. The remaining man turned with a smile. "Welcome aboard my Lucky Lady, Mr. Shields. I'm Samuel Chen." He wore a bright Hawaiian shirt, swim trunks, baseball cap, and flip flops.

"Call me Chuck, nice meeting you... out here." He wasn't sure whether to call the vessel a boat or a ship.

"Call me Samuel, Chinese American, grew up in San Francisco. This is my associate Mr. Adakai. He's a skilled engineer, a senior partner, and technical advisor."

The engineer gave a nervous smile and moved in a jerky, high strung fashion. "It is my pleasure to meet you." The man responded in broken English.

Shields realized he was not getting a first name from the guy, but guessed him to be Pakistani or Indian.

Samuel spoke up during the lull in conversation, "You've had a busy morning. Let's grab a bite to eat, and then you can all go for a swim with the fishes."

What? Shields didn't know how to take that comment?

They stepped inside the cabin to the dining area with a table for twelve. Fresh lobster and shrimp on ice, along with several native Caribbean dishes, sat on the white linen tablecloth. The four men and two women relaxed while two crewmen acted as waiters. The conversation remained light, and Dumont reminded everybody not to eat too much as they would be swimming in a few minutes.

Tina escorted Shields to a stateroom to change into his bathing suit and was waiting when he came out. She studied him for a moment, then spoke in a firm tone he had not heard from her before. "I'll put sunscreen on you. Hold still." As she applied it to his face, she did not smile. "Now your back. Take off the shirt."

He did as requested without hesitation. She had a gentle touch and his mind started to drift. He wanted her.

"You're done," she said, then looked around to see if anyone was watching before she leaned in and whispered, "Don't swim too far from the boat and be careful." She looked at him a moment longer then turned and walked back up the steps letting him admire the view.

As he watched the motion of her athletic body, he noticed the scars on her back. Two were long thin lines in the small of her back running parallel to her spine. The third scar, high on the right shoulder, was round like a puncture wound.

His pleasure in seeing her beauty and confidence quickly turned to excitement, then to lust. He would get her back in his hotel. She was a woman he wanted, and she would look up to him, not that stupid bodyguard.

Returning topside, he got another surprise. Crewmen were throwing buckets of blood and leftover food overboard. Fish were swimming in for the feast.

"This is the best way to see nature, watching the food chain in action," Samuel declared with anticipation.

"Yes," Shields nodded. "But what about the big fish? I don't want to swim in their food chain."

"You have nothing to fear. I always make sure I'm the top predator. Look," Chen said, pointing to the top deck. "I've taken all the precautions necessary for my guests to have an enjoyable day."

Shields looked up to see the two large crewmen scanning the horizon with binoculars. Both were heavily armed. One was carrying a Navy SEAL 50 cal. sniper rifle. The other was holding an AK-47.

"If they see any sharks, they'll call us in with their bullhorn. And they're both excellent marksmen."

Dumont plunged in first without hesitation. Shields could see he was a powerful man and excellent swimmer. *I see why he has such a long drive on the links.*

Tina, Shields and Samuel followed. Louise, who was not a good swimmer, went in last wearing a flotation device. Adakai stayed on the boat.

The food thrown overboard had attracted schools of brightly colored fish moving through the water in a feeding frenzy. Any food missed on the surface was picked up by the bottom feeders.

Shields had snorkeled several times, but he had never seen so many fish. As he relaxed to enjoy the blue world, he realized the reef was dying. As a young man, he had been to these islands and the reefs were alive with color. The fish were still here, but the reef was a dull brown. In a few more years it would be dead. His grandchildren would never see this magical, colorful world.

It was twenty minutes before he heard the bullhorn and saw the bodyguards waving everyone in. For the first time in years, Shields felt a physical fear in his gut as he struggled to force more air through his snorkel.

He saw no danger, but imagined a giant fin cutting through the water. Shields made a beeline for the boat. Sprinting, he was out of breath when he got to the ship's stern. Dumont was already on board, and the crew was helping Samuel up the ladder.

The girls, where are they? He turned and saw them a few yards behind. Tina was helping Louise. Realizing all were accounted for, Chuck grabbed the step ladder and climbed on board. Then he saw the large dorsal fin slicing through the water and circling only a few yards away from the women. A second fin appeared, even larger, and moving straight for them.

He looked up at the riflemen with their guns at their side. "Shoot! Shoot them damn it!" He looked over and saw Samuel had pulled up the ladder with one hand while holding his other hand over his head signaling the riflemen to hold their fire.

"Tell me Mr. Shields," Samuel spoke calmly, "how many jokes have you heard comparing sharks to lawyers and bankers?"

Shields froze. "The women, help them," was all he could say.

"As you wish, but remember I am far more powerful than all the American sharks. You are in my waters now." He dropped his hand.

The sniper shouldered his rifle and fired two shots. Red blood flowed over the shark closest to the women. Samuel lowered the stepladder into the water, and they grabbed hold.

Shields felt his rage well up inside. He turned back to Samuel and was about to scream at him when he saw the short sword in Samuel's hand.

Monopoly Games

Chapter 4

Samuel threw the sword to the second gunman and shouted, "Go have your fun!" The man caught it and pulled the blade from its scabbard. Shields watched in amazement as the man leaped over the railing, landing on the deck below. He rushed past Shields and dove off the stern. Landing on the second shark's back, he drove the sword through it. The shark rolled. The man thrust the sword again into the soft underbelly, slicing open the flesh. Entrails spilled out and floated in the water.

The women had climbed on board as soon as the ladder hit the water. Tina looked furious but didn't speak. She clenched her fist, and Shields wondered if she was going to take a swing at Chen. *Why does she put up with this?* He wondered. Louise was shaking so badly that Tina had to take her below.

The crewman climbed out of the water, his white uniform now tinted red. He gave a small bow and presented the sword to Samuel. He took it, and holding it up to the sun, admired the blade. "Clean it, oil it, and return it to my weapons room." He tossed the sword back to the gunman.

"Well Chuck, I hope all this swimming has given you an appetite. My chef has prepared a wonderful meal, fresh fish of course. Before we change for dinner, I'd like you to try some wine. It's organic from a private vineyard in New Zealand. I think you'll like it."

As the ship gently swayed in the surf, Dumont, Samuel, Shields and Adakai sat on the deck, watching the sun sink into the blue horizon. Drinking wine, eating fresh shrimp and oysters, they watched a third shark devour the remains of the other two.

Samuel's voice interrupted the show. "Thomas, would you escort the ladies back to the hotel. They have to make arrangements for some new investors coming in tomorrow. Then return with the launch to pick up Mr. Shields.

"The women, they are beautiful. But now is the time to discuss business, and there is no place for a woman, only men who desire wealth and understand power."

A few minutes later, Shields saw the crew helping Dumont and the two women into the launch. Tina was complaining that she was supposed to stay onboard. They cast off and opened up the powerboat. The roar of the engine faded into the night.

"Don't worry Chuck," Samuel commented, "they will get home safely, and the launch will be back. So now let us eat and talk shop without distractions."

Shields remembered his instructions and didn't mention business while they were eating. The darkening night sky lit up with stars— more than he could ever see in Ohio. The food and wine were excellent, but he had lost his appetite. He ate only to keep up appearances, inside he was screaming. All he could think about was the sharks and Samuel's words, "you're in my water now."

Shields knew he was being intimidated, but he was determined to stand toe to toe with these pirates and show them who's the boss. He would take them up in his world, and see how they like it at 40,000 feet, executing a quick barrel roll, dive and barf time. *You come at me with a knife, I'll come at you with a shotgun.* Under the table, his foot was tapping the deck.

"Chuck, you seem to have drifted away in thought. Are you enjoying the wine?" Samuel asked.

"Very much, it's well balanced and a perfect complement to the seafood. I'll have to order a case for my wine cellar."

"Let me send you a case from my stock. This was a vintage year and no longer available on the market."

Smartass wine snob. I'll just order a more expensive bottle when I get home.

"Mr. Shields, you have something I want, and I believe you would sell it for the right price. My people have looked at your property and operations in Taiwan, and my organization is willing to pay you forty-six million American dollars for it."

Shields did not bat an eye. This was the part of the game he liked. He checked their body language while taking another sip of wine, savoring the taste and aroma of the moment. Samuel's people were good accountants. The number was the market value he placed on the land and assets. He felt they must want it badly to start the discussions at such a price.

"That's very kind of you to make such an offer, and that number would almost cover my assets." Shields could feel the adrenaline rush inside him as he stalked them for the kill. "But Samuel, being raised in America, you know what they say about ROI and profit. Why should I sell if I don't make any money on the deal? I can do better just by running the plant."

"Ah yes, profit, a concept discovered long before you Americans. We do want you to make a profit, why else would you continue to do business with us? We have looked carefully at your organization. It doesn't appear that you are making any profit from your Taiwan operation. So you are not fooling me, but let us think of a way to make this a win-win deal."

"Yes," added Adakai, his eyes nervously darting between the two men. "Win-win is what we all want."

Shields thought, if these two are supposed to be a negotiating team, they needed some practice.

"Let me put this on the table Mr. Shields…"

Shields had already realized that the importance of a statement depended on whether Samuel addressed him as Chuck or Shields.

"We will add twenty-two million cash wired directly to your numbered account here in the Bahamas. And you, Mr. Shields, can add the complete schematics, including all the cryptographic circuitry of your new military communications system."

Shields blinked. He was thrown back into the alternate Universe. *They're not business men, they're spies. Terrorist!* The wine came back up into his throat as he thought about the sharks.

"No pressure Mr. Shields," said Adakai "You can say no. It's not as if we're going to make you walk the plank." He laughed as his eyes continued to dart back and forth.

Shields put down his wine glass so they wouldn't see his hand shaking.

Samuel looked over at Adakai with a frown. "Now seriously, I do want to make you an offer you can't refuse. Right now you should be saying to yourself, if I sell the plans, they can build a radio, but they can't listen to or talk to the Americans because they don't have the codes and frequencies, and they both change every twenty-four hours. So we must sweeten the pot again.

"Let me make the offer an even-thirty million to your private account, and you throw in one set of the codes and frequencies, just twenty-four hours' worth. I don't know which one yet, but you get a thirty day supply every month. If all goes well, we would continue to buy more at five million bucks a pop."

Shields' head was spinning, all that money. Was there a danger of getting caught? It was a calculated risk: he had clearance, access, and he could do it. But should he do it? He didn't need this temptation.

"It's a seductive thought, but no, I must pass for now. First things first. Let's go back and just discuss the sale of the Taiwan location. One step at a time."

Samuel smiled then responded, "I'm sorry Chuck. The offer is a package deal. It's all or nothing. As they say, we don't want to break up a set." He laughed.

Shields was lost. "What on earth do you think you could do with it?"

"I have to tell you we don't know all the details. We're businessmen like you. We're an organization of facilitators, free-lance contractors who work for corporations and governments to provide services that resolve problems. Just brokers working on commission, but we run a disciplined, profitable enterprise. Believe me Chuck, you don't want to deal direct with our clients. Leave those people alone to play their silly power games, they're all crazy."

Shields looked at Chen. *Like you're not. You're a dangerous psychopath and a diabolical megalomaniac. I'm not at all like you.*

"Are you with the Russians?"

"No. We don't do business with them. They renege on their payments."

Samuel continued. "The land will be sold off and the plant moved to another country. They want their airplanes to talk to each other just like your U.S. military does.

"As for the codes, everybody wants those. America's allies like the Saudis, France and Israel will pay dearly just to listen in for a day like your government does to them. The Germans are still pissed at your NSA.

"People who don't like the United States will pay even more, but it's not the type of thing someone in the arms business needs to worry about.

Shields had never considered himself an arms dealer. He was in the communications business for the American military. He looked Samuel in the eye then quickly looked down and hugged himself. Something was wrong. He needed to stall for a moment to organize his thoughts. "There must be a non-compete clause. I don't want to be selling against the factory I used to own."

Samuel gave a puzzled look but responded politely, "Be assured nobody is interested in buying your factory for the development of a consumer model to sell in your markets. You can have your lawyers include any such verbiage in the contract if that makes you feel better."

"How do I do it?"

"It's simple. Burn a copy of the blueprints and we'll come by and pick it up. Or you fly it out here as part of your next weekend getaway. I've asked Thomas to be your contact if you have any questions. When you need to communicate with him, just buy a new cell phone.

"When we ask for the codes, it's just a string of numbers. You won't even need to fly out here, unless you just want to pay us and the girls a visit. I trust you can improvise on the details. We do want to work with a CEO who's got his act together."

"It's not that simple."

"Come on Chuck, it's your company. You're the boss, you own the place, and have the security clearance. Surely you can find a way, be creative. That's why we picked you, and why you make the big bucks. Right?"

"If it's too risky, the deal's off."

"Understood, we'll proceed with the real estate sale which can be wrapped up in a month. We've hired the firm of Gohmert, King, Cruz and Issa out of Washington to act as our agents. Are you familiar with them?"

"Only by reputation. I've heard they're a bunch of sharks." Shields smiled at his remark.

"Call Thomas if you have any problems with them. We'll sign when the radio blueprints are in our hands.

"I think those are reasonable terms for a win-win deal. If you can't meet the terms, then the deal is off, no multi-million tax free gift in your private account. You agree? Please tell us now. I hear the launch returning. Agreed?"

"Agreed." Shields didn't want to agree, but he had to agree. What else could he do? He just couldn't leave all that money on the table. Like a child, he had to have it now.

"Mr. Shields, to be crystal clear, it must be the newest version with all the bells and whistles for your latest upgrade. It's like cars, nobody wants to drive around in last year's model."

Mr. Adakai added, "Your model code name GL70, with the M2A6 upgrade for ground support of the weapon systems. It was approved by your government last December and in production at your facilities for at least three months. That should avoid any possible errors to our requirements."

As the launch pulled away with Shields, Adakai turned to Samuel, "Well, what do you think, is the American onboard?"

Samuel shrugged his shoulders. "Your unintended pun aside, I think he believes us. If he changes his mind, we apply a little pressure. I'm not going to let this deal get away. Too many countries have committed to our plan, and they will not be happy if we don't deliver."

He paused to reflect then added. "When all the dust settles, the maps will be redrawn. We'll be the most powerful organization in the world. Why steal a nuke from Russia when we can get the Americans to deliver one for us. With help from this stupid little shit, we'll get the information we need to communicate with America's Platform Strike Force and command the F-15's to drop the American nukes on our targets."

****

Shields' head was spinning when he got back to his hotel suite. Pouring a shot of XO, he sat down to reflect on what he had done. As he swirled the brandy sniffer, he realized he would have immense financial power, but the consequences were....

He saw Tina's card on the table where he'd left it the night before. The vision of her wearing the bikini overrode his concerns. Knocking back his brandy, he called the number. No one answered. He poured another drink and waited ten minutes before calling again. This time he left a message then paced around the room while watching the phone.

"Louise. You'll do," he blurted out. "They're one floor below. But which room?" He finished his drink and called it a night. He would be back to get them both.

Flying home the next morning, Shields sat in the pilot's seat and took the stick. It gave him control he needed.

Returning to the cabin, he sat along sipping his eighteen year old, single malt. He could think about the consequences of his action, or he could think about the money. He chose the money. Maybe his son would start acting his age and take an interest in the business. He could teach his son the ropes as his father had done. They would rule together.

With his superior intelligence, he would use those mentally deranged pirates to achieve his goals. *Other countries listening in for a day is not going to hurt America or my bottom line.*

The demand for secure communications was growing and the revenue opportunity for supplying a good product worldwide was enormous. Despite his manufacturing advantage, a multinational could push him out of business. He remembered the old Sony Betamax and did not want to get into a marketing battle.

He needed a marketing advantage, in addition to the patent's guarantee, to block the competition and insure a continued monopoly. To achieve his goal, it was critical that A3E adapt his system parameters as the new industry Standard.

It will be easy. No one could stop him. *What could go wrong?*

Chapter 5

As Welch ate breakfast, he watched the news to make sure the world didn't get blown up last night. Automatically going into the morning routine— shower, shave, *this shirt is good for one more day*. He finished up with a few drops of Rogaine, the Viagra for hair. After making a sandwich, he grabbed a yogurt, took all his vitamins, and hit the road.

He started his car with fingers crossed and placed his old 'Revolver' tape in the cassette. Taking a back road, he avoided I-287 which was a six lane, fifteen mile parking lot during rush hour. The term rush hour in New Jersey is really a misnomer. Atlanta, Georgia, had a rush hour; Kansas City had a rush minute.

New Jersey, the most densely populated state in the nation, had a rush morning, lunch hour traffic, and a rush afternoon. As Julius Caesar would have written, "All of Jersey is divided into three parts."

The Northern part commutes into The City, New York City. The Southern Part commutes into Philadelphia, or owns a farm, and is waiting to sell to the real-estate developers so they can move to Florida. The third part, where Welch lived, is the poorly defined, and little known Central Jersey. Most state residents question its existence.

A few miles from his congested commute were farms with acres of corn as high as an elephant's eye. It is the Garden State, even if developers are changing it to the Mall State. Central Jersey also had more horse farms than Kentucky. It's a nebulous, ill-defined section with Turnpike exits as imaginary borders. The Turnpike is so well known to Jerseyites, it's an acceptable address, as in "Where do you live?"

"Exit 8."

Despite the two terrible T's, traffic and taxes, Welch liked his adopted state. Parts of it were beautiful and the state could be compared to California—they had a similar shape.

Both states have four colorful seasons with sunbathing in the summer and snow skiing in the winter. New Jersey wins in the fall with forests of hardwood that turn red and gold in the autumn sunlight and flower in the spring. But California has a woman with gold in her hair. *There's always a woman.* Both states have ocean front. Californians call it a coast and Jerseyites call it 'down the Shore'. Both have mountains, well big hills in New Jersey's case.

But when people turned on their radio, nobody sang 'New Jersey Dreaming' and nobody wants to stay at the 'Hotel New Jersey.' Nobody is 'Going to Trenton wearing flowers in their Hair' and nobody 'Left their heart in Bayonne.' Well, maybe Jimmy Hoffa did.

The people of Jersey don't have the same narcissistic arrogance as say a person from Texas. In a quiet and self-assured way, they had developed their own attitude and swagger.

Welch liked to get to work early. Using his key card to enter the building, he headed for the Standards Department. Walking by Sharon's cubical to say hello, he saw she wasn't at her desk. *That's unusual, she's an early riser.*

He went to his office, which should be in the record books as the world's smallest office, but at least it wasn't a cubicle. Welch turned on his computer and entered his nine digit alpha (w/caps)-numeric-symbols password. Like most employees, he kept a copy of it in his unlocked desk drawer. Then he went to the cafeteria for coffee while the PC booted up. The morning was quiet time to spend on his projects before being overwhelmed with the day's events and everybody else's problems.

Returning to the department with his coffee, he stuck his head in Sharon's cube again.

"Oh shit."

Her pictures were gone. All her personal effects were gone. Sharon's existence has been deleted.

He thought back to Friday, she was here when he left. He walked to Karen's cubicle to get some answers, but she's wasn't in. Beginning to worry, he went back to his office and sipped his coffee. His ambition to work had dissolved as his mind slipped into a state of career anxiety. *Not again.*

Welch reflected on his prior life as a national sales manager. The money was good, and everybody thought they were going to be the next Bill Gates, or have an equity position in the next Google. He met with the owners, a pair of software system engineers enamored with their own technology. As he explained, the market didn't care if their software was twelve nanoseconds faster if it took ten minutes to turn the damn thing on.

A lot of ego was involved so he was gentle, he thought. He told them that if they didn't make a more user friendly app, they would be out of business in six months. Welch was canned the next day, and the company went under six months later. Two hundred rejection letters later, he landed at A3E.

His new job provided a real service with a real demand, which meant more job security— he thought. The job was intellectually stimulating, and he felt good going in. What he didn't expect was ending up in the most politically sensitive job of his life, and office politics was not his strong suit. *I stink at it.*

After wasting most of the morning, Welch walked to the HR Conference Room. The HR Director, wearing an expensive designer outfit and a rock the size of Gibraltar, was conducting the New Employee Orientation.

"Our next presenter," she continued, "is Mr. Greg Welch from the Standards Department, and as you see on your schedule, after his talk we'll take a break for lunch."

Greg stood before the group. "On a cold Sunday morning, February 2, 1904, the John Hurst Company in downtown Baltimore exploded. The ensuing fire lasted five days. Although it never gained the notoriety of the Chicago Fire, the Baltimore fire destroyed 1,526 buildings in a seventy block region.

"After the initial explosion, a call went out for help and fire companies as far south as Washington, D.C. drove their horse drawn, water pump wagons loaded with hoses and fire equipment to Baltimore. Companies as far north as New York also responded. America's oldest and best equipped department in the nation, the Philadelphia Fire Department, sent their best equipped wagons to help. In total, 57 wagons and over 1,200 volunteers traveled to Baltimore.

"Unfortunately, none of these water pumps or their hoses could be used, because they couldn't connect to Baltimore's water supply. In 1904, every city had its own fire hydrant design with its own hose connection. The wagons and desperately needed hoses were useless."

Greg smiled. *Good intro.* He continued, "In addition to the devastation, the fire produced two unusual consequences. First was the song "Baltimore Fire", as opposed to a poem about Miss O'Leary's cow.

"Second, the city fire departments involved requested help from the Society of Electrical Engineers in developing a standard size for all fire hydrants, hoses, and connections, so a hose in New

Jersey could connect to a hydrant in California. *Freudian slip.*

"The choice of an Electrical Engineer's society to standardize hoses and fire hydrants may seem strange today, but at the time, it was a logical choice. The society had already established a set of policies and procedures for developing 'standardization.'

"Using these procedures, the society had previously developed standards for the telegraph system that crisscrossed the United States and connected Europe and America by undersea cable. They had already standardized the basic components of the American electrical power grid. The society was also in the process of implementing standards for the new telephone services which were just starting in America.

"They accepted the request and developed the Hydrant and Hoses Standard which is still in effect today. Since then, the society has changed its name, and we're now called the Association for Electronic and Electrical Engineers.

"Abbreviated A3E, it has maintained its focus in two areas. The first, Electrical Engineering, includes power and energy. The second, Electronic Engineering, includes Information Technology.

"Today, power and energy could be battery, solar, wind and all other forms of power. Information technology includes computers and peripherals, all radio and wire communication, and new fields such

40

as nanotechnology, biomedical devices, and even electronic voting systems.

"The process is designed to be fair, honest, balanced and open. The resultant Standard is (He glanced at his notes.) a published document that sets requirements to insure consistent performance of services."

"A draft standard is published and interested parties are requested to vote on it and provide any corrections. The comments are rejected or incorporated by a review committee and the voting process repeated. This procedure is repeated until a consensus is reached or the draft is rejected.

"Years ago, the organization changed from balloting by mail to the latest technology for electronic distribution and internet balloting."

"Today, the latest update of the electronic process is about 80% complete. We always seem to be at 80% because it's an ongoing process as technology advances. The procedure gives the American Economy over a hundred standards a year. The published standard has met (reading from his notes) the requirements of interconnectivity and interoperability and assures the credibility of new products for domestic and international trade. Only products that meet this standard are used in the Military Industrial Complex, and most commercial and government markets." *Are thy still awake?* Thank you. *Now I get a free lunch for my services*

41

In reality, the process was complex with regulations to insure the balloting was fair. It was Welch's job to play cop, making sure everybody followed the rules. But when he said 'cop', the job description was more like a traffic cop, one step up from meter-maid, and not like detective.

The current upgrade was a more 'user-friendly' interface with apps to integrate balloting with a total management system for the digital world. Knowing the key to success was membership acceptance, he sent emails to the influential members asking for recommendations.

Of course, there were always skeptics who didn't believe him. Welch could empathize with their sentiment. After "the check is in the mail," the biggest lie in the business world is "I'm from headquarters, and I'm here to help you."

Chapter 6

"**M**r. Shields," Doris, his secretary, interrupted on the intercom, "I have Mr. Reisberg and Mr. Langstaff for your ten o'clock meeting."

"Tell them to come in and hold all my calls."

Doris escorted the two senior executives in. "Can I get you anything?"

"I'll have another cup of coffee, black, two sugars." Langstaff was a coffeeholic.

One side of the office had a large leather couch with three matching chairs around an oversize coffee table. The walls were covered with plaques, pictures of the Shields family with famous people, and three pieces of Post-Impressionist art. In the corner was a well-stocked wet bar. He motioned for the executives to join him around the coffee table.

When Shields gave a nod to Reisberg, EVP of Sales and Marketing, he proceeded. "I say A3E approval should be our priority. It proves our product has met the necessary performance requirements. Second, it guarantees our customers the interconnectivity they demand.

"A recognized A3E standard assures the credibility of our product. Setting the standard and promoting our military experience will give us brand recognition and perceived superiority in the market. With aviation, police, fire and government agencies accessing this new frequency spectrum, the buyers will be looking for standardization. A3E certification will seal the deal.

"In addition, our encryption gives the corporate world the security they need. Nobody wants their information posted on the Internet like a Paris Hilton video."

"Thanks Jason. What are your thoughts Bob as my top engineering guy?" Shields asked.

"Our GL70 radio optimizes performance in this frequency range and is the heart of the communications system. But making a standard only our technology can support still requires an 80% affirmative vote by the A3E's Radio Communications Committee, the RCC.

"So what's your point?"

"We patented the GL70 hardware, excluding the cryptographic systems, several years ago. All our competitors have engineers on the Committee. If they find out we're trying to make our patent into a performance standard, they're going to expose us. Most engineers don't pay that much attention to these things. But it only takes one whistle blower to kill the whole deal."

"Why?" Shields quietly enquired.

"It's against the rules. Our radio was actually designed by the military. We shouldn't have patented it to begin with. Our competitors will get the whole standard disqualified as an attempt to build a patent monopoly. We'll never be allowed to put it to vote. Our competitors will…"

"Let's stop the whining right here. Bottom line, its better technology, and we can sell it at a premium. I make a lot of money and if you can't find a way to this, then I'll find people that can.

"Now they don't know it's a patent, and we've never promoted it. And suppose we set up a license agreement with one of the big Japanese companies to get their people to vote with us. They would work with us for some overseas exclusivity. That and getting the neutral parties to support us should get us over that 80% mark before anybody knows what happened.

"These engineers have to realize we'll be hiring when we get this deal locked up. You know these people and could talk to them 'mono a mono' about employment opportunities. That should give us considerable leverage in winning their cooperation.

"Here's how I want us to proceed. Jason, you and Ed from Production work on the subcontractors that will be voting. I'll call on our friends in Japan. Bob, initiate the action at A3E to get that standard. Keep a low profile and doctor it up to hide our intent. We have to move this through under the radar.

"My Legal department is good at this. Work with the lawyers to craft language that gives us what we want, but looks harmless. Let someone from the ranks be our front in the A3E committee to keep it low profile.

"I'll visit the Association's Standards Department to get the lay of the land. Let me know who will front this, and he can go with me to start the ball rolling."

When the meeting ended, Langstaff walked back to his office. He knew it was the second biggest office on Executive Row. The need to pick a front man presented a problem.

John Gordon, his Senior Director should do the front work. He was a brilliant engineer, but he was arrogant and that made him a lousy people person. Gordon would throw a tantrum and be a pain for months if he wasn't selected. Langstaff didn't like personnel problems. He picked up the phone and dialed.

"John, are you free for lunch?"

Lunch was at the most expensive Italian restaurant in the area with white tablecloths and waiters in black ties. Langstaff tried to explain the big picture. "This will be a sensitive situation, and we can't ram it down peoples' throats. This is an opportunity to show us your skill to finesse and win people over. Do you understand what Mr. Shields and I expect of you?"

"Of course, I can do that, no problem."

Langstaff gave Gordon a worried look then laid out the strategy. "Let me emphasize, when you're at the A3E Standards Department, you need to keep it friendly and low key."

Chapter 7

Shields stepped out of his office and took the elevator down for an unscheduled visit to the Client Services Center. It used to be called the Sales Department. He liked to keep his people on their toes and wanted to get some unfiltered feedback on market reaction to his new product. Local government RFP's were coming in as reps promoted it. The corporate world was also showing strong interest in secure communications as hackers were constantly breaking into their networks.

Shields listened as Glen, the company's top salesman talked about the consulting firms in the Boston area. "A consulting engineer dies and goes to heaven where he meets Saint Peter at the Pearly Gates. 'Welcome old man, now you can rest in peace for eternity.'"

"There must be some mistake. I'm a single guy in the prime of my life. This place looks like an old folk's home, not heaven. I'm only forty two."

"Saint Peter smiled, "Well, we checked your billable hours and according to that, you're eighty four."

Shields laughed with the group, hiding his dislike for the salesman who had no allegiance to Shields Inc.

Glen had even hit on Shields's secretary. Shields knew this rep wouldn't last. He was a shooting star that would crash and burn. Management would give him the expensive perks he won until he went into rehab or overdosed.

The remainder of the day passed quickly, and at 6:30 Shields put away his budget projections, and he pulled out an unmarked folder. A phone number was penciled on the back of some old notes. It was time to buy insurance.

Locking his office, he took the private elevator to the executive parking lot under the building. Shields walked to his BMW 850Ci parked in his reserved space. He had liked his Mercedes SL600 Roadster better. It looked like a true sports car, it definitely made a statement. The gull wing doors were just cool. But it was too tight for an extra-tall basketball player, proving the old adage that money can't buy happiness. He returned the Roadster and leased the Beemer. Now he had a convertible, but never drove with the top down. Only his kids did when they borrowed the car, and they returned it with an empty gas tank, parking tickets, and a dented fender.

He didn't drive straight home; he pulled into the mall and parked in front of Best Buy. Inside, he paid cash for three burner cell phones. Back in his car, he struggled for five minutes to get the new phone out of its bubble pack. He dialed the number in his file cabinet from memory.

"Computer Security Services, please leave a message," came after the third ring.

"Hello, I would like to make an appointment with Mr. B.C. Smith this Saturday around noon. Thank you." Smith, not his real name, was the man he wanted to see. BC was Shields' identification and it told Smith who was calling.

Early Saturday morning, he drove to Chicago. In a rundown warehouse district a few miles from Midway Airport, his GPS found the address in a commercial strip mall. He noticed the bright yellow Cadillac convertible parked in the lot and was sure it belonged to his contact. Shields opened the office door and entered a closed off waiting area. He picked up the phone sitting on a small table and asked for B. C. Smith.

The door buzzed open and a middle aged, overweight man smoking a cigarette entered the waiting room. Wearing a suit appropriate for a Friday night seventies' disco party, his shirt was unbuttoned half way down exposing the gold chains around his neck.

"Mr. Shields, good to see you again. Welcome to my new facility." They walked through an open area with tables covered with security cameras and other electronic equipment. Two men sat in the back corner wearing headphones, watching several monitors.

Shields continued into a poorly lit, shabby office that smelled like three day old clamsauce. "Can I get you some coffee or perhaps something a little stronger? It's almost noon." Smith pointed toward the bar.

"Nothing for me thanks. You're an engineer and I want to know how the voting is going on a particular A3E standard and to make it go my way, since it's my standard. I need to know about the staff that administers the ballot process and see any relevant emails, and hear all their phone conversations."

"Which Standard?"

"It'll be submitted in a few days by my people on the Radio Communications Committee. Can you do it?"

Smith sat back in his chair. He looked up at the ceiling for a while then smiled. "You're a very good client Mr. Shields, and I want to keep you satisfied. For this project, I will require the usual retainer."

"No problem, the funds transfer will be made on Monday."

"Good, I will give you my answer in an hour. I always confirm my ability to deliver before I commit. Go have some lunch. There's a nice club three blocks down the street. The foods lousy, but the entertainments great."

Chuck looked at his watch, "I'll be back at 1:30." He drove until he found a casual dining restaurant. The place was almost empty, but he still had to wait for a hostess to seat him. She looked like a bored college coed but managed a pleasant smile. He ate a chicken something sandwich, read the paper and checked his email.

Sipping his coffee, he wondered whatever happened to the good old fashion diners. He remembered his college days at the diner with his fraternity brothers. Looking down at his meal he thought, *now everything is frozen, instant, prepackaged and tastes like salty sawdust.*

As soon as Shields returned, Smith started talking. "A3E does have a pretty good firewall, but not good enough. I can get you inside to see a person's email or the status on any voting. I can copy and steal any information you want, but I can't change or delete information or a vote without setting off an alarm.

"They wouldn't know who made the change, but the System Manager would know the data was altered. Their system is more secure than your Ohio state government electronic balloting. That was a piece of cake."

Shields frowned. "So, you're saying I have no way to find out who's voting against me or if the standard will even pass."

"Not at all, the A3E balloting is an open ballot process. With their electronic balloting, the results are posted on the website in real time. Everybody sees everybody's vote. A person votes and gets to see his ballot recorded. Any changes to a person's vote would most likely be noticed very quickly by the person who voted."

Chuck sat up. "Then, I'm not getting my money's worth. You can't change the election. What am I buying if all the results are posted for everyone to see anyway?"

Sensing the loss of a retainer, Smith spoke up. "I can still help you get what you want. The voting is an open process, but there's a lot of behind the scenes action going on. It's constant chatter between the members that are voting and A3E which acts as the policemen for the balloting. The A3E makes and interprets the rules and regulations, and there are a lot of rules. It's a complicated process that must be followed to the letter. Their phone and email communications are important. Let me show you something."

Smith worked the keyboard and turned the screen at an angle so Shields could see. "Check out this email by Greg Welch, the Manager for Standards balloting. He's like the paperwork cop on the scene. He's telling the Chairman of a Medical Devices Committee that some of the voters are ineligible. He's the gatekeeper to watch, that poor schmuck is responsible for blowing the whistle, and nobody likes a whistle blower? If there's a problem, this man will find it, and you have to deal with him. I can watch him for you."

Shields wanted a nice stuffing of the ballot box, but the open process would stop him from getting the clean win he wanted. "If I can't win one way, I'll win another way. I cannot afford to lose this one.

"Phone taps and email on the key people 24-7, Okay Smith, go for it. I want to know this guy Welch's every move, when he pisses and what color it is."

Chapter 8

John Gordon met Shields at the airport for the flight to New Jersey. Gordon had done his homework and had several ideas on how to circumvent the regulations. Langstaff had coached Gordon on working with the A3E staff, but Gordon was sure a little aggressive posturing was the way to go. It was his style and had worked well for him in the past.

Shields had done his homework too, learning about A3E's executives and key players. Their flight was uneventful, but not even Shields could file flight plans for a corporate jet to land at Newark Liberty International. They landed at Teterboro Airport with all the other executive jets ten miles further north.

Their limo was waiting to transport them through the New Jersey highway labyrinth. As they sat quietly reading their newspapers, the car took them down one of American Capitalisms' most spectacular drives. The limo pulled onto Route 17 south to Route 3 west to the 15W toll entrance leading onto the west wing of the New Jersey Turnpike going south.

Surrounded by zombie, New Jersey drivers weaving in and out of traffic, the limo passed the

Giant's and Jets' shared Football Stadium. "Are you a football fan," Gordon asked?

"Collage ball," he responded and went back to his paper.

The Turnpike traversed the Great Meadowlands Swamp next to the state's largest landfill on the right and the magnificent New York skyline on the left. Going under the Pulaski Skyway Bridge, the Turnpike west wing merged with the east wing to form 12 lanes of north south traffic. It linked eastern Canada and all of New England with Philadelphia, Baltimore, Washington DC and the South down to Miami. Over 800,000 vehicles a day used the Turnpike and a third of them are eighteen wheelers.

They rode past Newark Airport on the right, driving parallel with the main runways. Shields looked carefully to insure no private jets were on the field. On their left was the rail line and Port Newark, the second busiest seaport in the nation. Four large container ships were unloading; their massive cranes towering over the trucks below.

A few minutes later in Elizabeth, NJ, they passed the northern end of the largest pipeline in the US. For years it had been the largest pipeline in the world. The pipe started with Gulf of Mexico tankers unloading their oil into the line at Galveston Bay, Texas. It ended at the refinery in Elizabeth with a few hundred acres of storage tanks and a couple of electric cogeneration power plants. At Turnpike exit

10, they turned onto I-287 north and hit early lunch hour traffic.

Exiting the Interstate, they drove to a typical corporate park, and pulled into the visitors parking of a typical corporate office/warehouse building. They were greeted by the president's executive assistant, who escorted them to executive row and made the formal introductions. After meeting everyone, Shields and Gordon were taken on a tour of the facility by the Association President, Michael Ambrose.

Shields was fascinated with the collection of historic artifacts and pictures from the famous labs of Thomas Edison, Bell Labs, IBM, Livermore, and Einstein's Lab in Princeton. Shields imagined his picture alone side them.

During lunch, Gordon brought up the Standard Group, but Shields changed the subject keeping the lunch purely social by discussing golf. Shields agreed to call Michael next time he was in the area to get away for eighteen holes at a private club in the area.

Returning to the building, Michael escorted his guest to the Standards Department. It was the usual floor plan with offices along the windows and larger offices for senior managers at one end. Cubicles filled in the middle.

Michael introduced them to the Managing Director, Janet Winslow. Shields sized her up as professional, political and ambitious—qualities he could work with. She understood it was her job to keep her boss happy. As she walked them through the Department, Shields was struck by the number of women in the group. He knew there were thirty six people, but he saw only three men.

This was noteworthy because they supported an association that had an eighty five percent male membership. Dealing with engineers in his own company, he knew many treated their secretaries poorly. He filed the observation away to see if it was something he could leverage to his advantage. *She must ride her people hard to keep them in line.*

Welch sat in his office watching the visitors being escorted around the department. It was obvious they were VIP's with one very tall VIP. He wondered if Janet would introduce him, something she typically did not do, and went back to work.

Hearing a tap on his open door, Welch was surprised to see the group standing in front of his office. He stepped out to meet them as the idea of fitting four people comfortably into his little office was ridiculous.

Janet performed the introductions with her usual efficiency. Welch looked up at Shields. The guy was tall, extremely tall. A hundred thousand years of evolutionary biology overpowered Welch's thought process. Logic and all frontal-lobe critical thinking stopped. Jealousy, envy and physical intimidation flooded his brain.

He immediately disliked Shields. In competition for the Alpha Male position, Welch felt a distant second to the towering, and obviously wealthy stranger with perfect symmetrical features.

This was the senior executive and captain of the football team that got the Prom Queen in high school, college and everywhere else. Welch felt self-conscious and could not remember the name of the man he was just introduced too. He was looking at a man assertively smiling down at him with penetrating eye contact.

The imposing intruder had a full head of dark hair that fell perfectly into place. A little gray around the temples made him look even more regal. The man's skin and tan were perfect. His eyes and teeth were perfect. *This guy belongs on the cover of a fashion magazine.*

His business suit fit perfectly without a wrinkle. Welch was sure it was an expensive designer brand. The bright tie was a power tie. *Hell, all this guy's ties are power ties.*

Welch tried to regroup as they shook hands, each measuring the strength of the other. He looked up and stared wide-eyed at the towering figure. Welch blinked and looked away, breaking eye contact. His facial expression exposed his inner feelings.

The big guy won, establishing dominance in the corporate macho world. Shields knew what was going on in Welch's head.

"Gregory, this is John Gordon," Janet was speaking.

"Who?" *Did you call me Gregory? Why the hell did you do that?*

"John Gordon," Janet said again as she looked at Welch and frowned.

"Sorry, John Gordon, just call me Greg." He frowned back at Janet. She was no longer looking at him, but Shields saw it all.

Introductions were interrupted when Shields whipped out his iPhone. Welch reflected, *my cellphone is so old it has a rotary dial.*

They all stood in silence as Shields answered his phone, "I can't talk right now. I'm with some very important people and will call you back." Janet and Gordon were beaming with delight that they had been called 'very important people.' Welch thought, *what a great bullshit line. I'll have to remember to use it next time I need to kiss up to someone.*

Shields looked down at the group, "Greg, why don't you and John talk about Standards for a few minutes. Janet and I will be back in her office if you need anything from us."

"Good idea," Gordon responded and walked past Welch into his office. Welch eyed him as he went by, then walked in behind him.

As Shields walked away, he looked back over his shoulder to study the chemistry between the two men.

A sense of control returned as Welch slid in behind his desk. He realized he was reacting with anger to his feelings of intimidation. He took a deep breath and mentally prepared himself for his new visitor.

Gordon pulled a business card and casually flipped it onto the desk. On the card, Welch saw the logo. It looked familiar.

"John, do you guys have that logo on a corporate jet?"

"Yes, it's our jet. The president and I flew in on it this morning."

Welch wanted to know what it was like to fly in a private jet. He was impressed, but Gordon had scored his point and had no further interest in small talk.

"Greg," Gordon started talking without eye contact. "Shields Communications is submitting a Standard for balloting on the civilian radio spectrum. Because it's a new area with a new technology, we want to restrict the balloting to the engineers already up to speed. The minimum number of votes is ten, correct." He stated, Gordon was not asking.

Welch sat up realizing this guy was coming on fast. "Yes, ten is the minimum, but the ballot must be open to all members that want to vote. The whole idea is to make it available to all concerned. You know our association's policy, fair, balanced and open. That's my job." *And bla bla.*

Gordon's voice rose in volume as he responded. "Well if it's so open, then I'll bring in others from outside the committee. You don't know this business, I know you're not an engineer. I need to pick the right people, and some are in other committees. Some are not even in the A3E."

Welch's voice went up in pitch instead of volume as he tried to restrain himself. "If you want people from another committee, the procedure is to send an invitation to everyone in that committee. Whoever wants to vote can vote.

"As for outside experts not in A3E, as long as they're electrical engineers, and they pay the membership fee, and are approved by the committee chairman, not just you as the chairman for the ballot, they can participate.

"As for me not being an engineer, all I do is enforce the rules. You don't need to be an engineer to understand that, even us mortals can do that." Welch added with a smile, but then regretted his little display of arrogance.

Welch could see the guy was getting pissed, and he knew he was the one who could get in trouble. No A3E member ever got kicked out of the Association for pissing off an employee.

Welch tried to defuse the situation. "Look John, I don't make the rules. My job is to support you, so nobody files an objection to your standard. These rules were made by the executive board. I just administer them." *It's called passing the buck.*

Gordon was still grinding his teeth and avoiding eye contact.

"Tell you what John, email me the title of the proposed standard with a short description and copy your Radio Committee Chairman. I'll email you a sample ballot invitation which you approve. Then, I'll send it out to everybody you want. That starts the process and the whole procedure is laid out for you at our website. I'm here to support you every step of the way.

"I know the website," Gordon snarled. "You'll get your letter, and I want a response in twenty-four hours."

"As quick as we can." *You asshole,* "We're working with other committees too. We have about twenty ballots in process."

Welch tried to change the subject. "So how was your trip out here on the corporate jet? Like New Jersey? Follow baseball, how about those Mets?"

"New Jersey stinks."

"Literally, figuratively or both?" *He's no better at small talk than I am.*

Gordon continued grinding his teeth as they walked back to Janet's office. Welch heard her and Shields laughing. She motioned them in, and Gordon sat down next to Shields. Janet dismissed Welch.

Back in his office, Welch reviewed the situation. He reasoned that if this jerk would just read the rules and follow them, it would all be so simple. *Bad idea. It's a good thing these engineers are too busy to read all the rules. Their dysfunctionality keeps me employed. If it was so damn important, why didn't John just offer me a bribe? I wouldn't come cheap, maybe a Lamborghini.*

He played with the fantasy as he prepared a memo to file on the events and created a new electronic folder. He printed a copy to start a paper trail which he knew he would need shortly.

Sitting at his desk, Welch remembered watching two executives in a heated debate. The VP sat quietly listening to the other man rant about promised compensation. Then the VP simply said, "If I promised that, you and I would have documented it. Do you have it in writing?"

"No."

"If it's not in writing then it doesn't exist."

And that's why Welch put everything down on paper. He learned from the masters.

An hour after Shields left, Welch was called into his boss's office just as he expected. *Some things are so predictable.* He knew that Gordon was going to complain to Janet.

"How did it go with your guest today?" Caroline, his immediate boss, asked, letting Welch be the first to speak. He went over their conversation to prove his innocence, and that he had done nothing wrong to upset the engineer Gods. Gordon was the trouble maker, and Welch was just doing his job to protect the principles and purity of their sacred temple of wisdom, although he didn't word it exactly that way.

Caroline, a fair, no-nonsense boss came back at Welch with a line he would never forget. "It doesn't matter what you do here, it only matters if they like you."

When Welch got back in his office, he used his notes to send his boss a CYA email. It recapped his version of the meeting with Gordon, and his concern about him not following the procedures to push a standard through. Welch knew this was not going to be the end of it.

The air conditioner came on as he sat in his office contemplating the meaning of the universe, and why some people are assholes. He didn't understand why A3E's 400,000 engineers couldn't design an air conditioning system that didn't freeze his butt off. The system did balance things out by over-heating the building in the winter.

He walked over to Karen's cubical. Her walls were covered with crayon drawings and pictures of smiling toddlers. She was a computer whiz and had helped him out on more than one occasion. More important, she seemed to understand the politics that were going on in the building.

"Hi," he said, "got time for a walk today?" Once or twice a week they went for a walk after lunch. They say it's good for your digestion, and Welch knew it was good for his sanity.

"Yes," she replied, "just give me a minute to close this program out."

Stepping outside of the air-conditioned building, the heat almost felt good. "Excuse me a moment," she said and quickly sent a text message while Greg waited. "Sorry, I'm thinking of switching to a new service provider. Reception is not good in the center of the building. I have to walk to a window."

"Ya, I'm thinking of changing my provider too. My service is so old I'm on a party line."

They walked down the block to a bike trail lined with shade trees providing peace and solitude from the heat, noise and traffic.

Karen was married with two young kids. Welch even met her husband— *nice guy*. As attractive as she was, Welch wouldn't allow himself to make any advances toward her even though he wasn't sure she would refuse him— at least that was his fantasy. She was the kind of person he would never want to harm, and there's no way they could have an affair without someone getting hurt.

They engaged in small talk as they walked. She told him how her kids were doing in school, and about her weekend family get-together. Welch felt a little envious.

To change the subject, he asked, "What happened to Sharon?"

"She got fired last Friday."

"I figured that, but why? Nobody is talking."

"Supposedly, she threatened to kill someone. HR called the police and now there is a restraining order against her. Sharon can't come within 50 feet of our building."

"I don't believe it. She was a nice person, a little strange, well maybe very strange, but still definitely not the type to go postal. Who said she was going to kill them?"

"One of Janet's friends."

"That I could believe. Any chance you'd go fifty-fifty with me on getting her a gun?"

Karen smiled and continued, "Janet has a select in-crowd. Not even all women are equal, but Janet can be an equal opportunity fire-er. Like with the guys, it's all about loyalty."

"Seen it all before. Power corrupts. I really don't mind working for woman, but it's so disillusioning to learn that they can be as sleazy as men."

Chapter 9

Shields told Langstaff and Reisberg to work over the weekend and make a presentation to the executive group at the staff meeting, Monday, 7:00 am

The group was assembled with a war room mentality. Langstaff and Reisberg did their song and dance summing up their performance with research showing continued strong demand for wireless computing.

"The current 802 standard system operating in a different frequency spectrum offered a limited range. With our Shields System, we can provide a secure network and enable mobile laptop communication for people traveling all over the state."

"This could create a new opportunity. The average sales manager has ten to fifteen reps, and his biggest problem is making sure the reps are out pounding the pavement. Give the manager our system, and he can have live, real-time communications with all his reps. Add a GPS navigation module and the manager now has total control of his team.

"He can curb conference with the reps, and the reps can't fake it because the manager knows their location. It's like our communications in an air force squadron with everybody talking to home base. This is a multi-million dollar opportunity in Business To Business sales".

"What about competition?" Shields asked.

"We have to move quickly and be first to market." Reisberg responded. "We are getting the law changed before anybody knows what's going on. This is a competitive industry that loves standards. People have to feel confident to drop their old system and buy a new one."

After everyone was assigned their next step actions, Shields returned to his office. He sat alone separating anger from logic after seeing Welch's email about Gordon pushing the rules. Shields could see their meeting had become a pissing contest. The situation was not likely to change.

The petty bickering would eventually expose his plan. 'People didn't change' was Shields' experience. Shields figured Welch would be on guard to continue the contest. Immediate action was required.

From his conversation with Janet, he knew Welch was not part of her inner circle. He was expendable and Janet would be relieved if he were gone. She knew her climb up the corporate ladder was based on keeping the members happy.

Welch had taken a paper intensive operation and integrated it into the electronic system. This was no small feat and Shields was impressed. But only Welch was running the operation, and he had just started writing the new Policies and Procedures Manual. In a profit-driven company, his unique knowledge would be good job security. But Janet didn't think that way. And without Welch as a watchdog, just about anything could sail through the Standards Department.

The new standard was ready to submit. Shields made a business decision based on time frame and the bottom line. He dialed his Director of Security. "Cory, I'll be down in ten minutes." Shields had his hands full dealing with pirates. He would have to delegate this responsibility, and he knew he had the right man for the job.

Shields took the elevator to the basement then walked to the back of the building. The steel door with a large sign printed in red letters read 'Security, Authorized Personnel Only.' He used his pass key to open the door and enter the cage. He looked at the mirror and spoke, "Cory is expecting me," and was buzzed in.

Off to the right was the locker room for the guards complete with showers, a weapons room and a well-equipped weight room. The security for the front doors and parking lot was rent-a-cop, but they were not allowed in this area.

The guards here were armed, full time employees, often ex-military, guarding the secure areas as per military contract requirements. Behind the next door was the control room where they monitored the security camera system. The first door on the left was a small office for the Sergeant of the

Guard who ran the day-to-day operations. In the corner office was Richard Cory.

Shields had met Cory, a business major on a football scholarship, pledging at Ohio State. Cory was Richard Cory Junior, and he came from old money, or what was left of it. His dad was the president of the town's largest bank. He owned half the town with all the connections to spread his wealth around.

It was the good life for junior with nannies and private schools. He had been a big overweight boy and in America that meant football. Playing the game, he learned he could hurt people and get rewarded for it. The son's good life came to an end when the Senior Richard Cory went home one night and put a bullet in his head. It was the only time Junior ever cried and the last time he let anybody call him Junior.

At the frat house, Cory was a useful friend. One could go anywhere on campus or in town with someone that big. To keep up with his wealthier brothers, Cory became the unofficial supplier of booze, drugs, IDs and women for the frat house. He used these activities to supplement his diminished inheritance and enjoy activities with his more privileged brothers.

As Pledge Master, Cory got prostitutes for the pledges, but he also put two in the hospital. As a BMOC football star, he was able to force cheerleaders to stay the night at the frat house. He managed to graduate and joined the army where he went Airborne, but couldn't cut it in Ranger training.

Young men join the military for many reasons: to get out of small towns or something in their past. Some just want to see the world. A few join out of genuine patriotism or to be like their father. Others, like Cory, joined because they were angry and wanted to kill people.

Returning to civilian life, he contacted his frat brothers to help him enter the job market. Shields was looking for a Security Manager that could handle special assignments. Cory took good care of Shields' customers, and Shields had the photographs to prove it. Cory could still bench four hundred pounds, but his stomach was now bigger than his chest.

Shields walked into Cory's office and shut the door behind him. The basement office was big for a director, but the furniture was catalog prefab. Football trophies and sports memorabilia decorated the office. On one wall were the mounted heads of a wolf and a bear.

Shields sat down. "I have another project, a very sensitive one for your personal attention." He pulled a 5X7 photo from a folder. "This guy, Greg Welch, he's a trouble maker. I don't think he's the type to be bribed or blackmailed, so he must be eliminated."

"Eliminated?" Cory said with surprise as a smile crossed his face.

Shields paused, a little shocked as he realized the implications of his own words. "Eliminated, removed. I don't care as long as he doesn't show up at work.

"This file gives you the information you need, his emails along with a picture of him. Here is our contact that's monitoring his office communications. It's critical this looks like an accident that can't be traced back to his job. Can you handle it?"

Cory smiled with enthusiasm, but wanted to appear professional. He nodded yes. "An accident, away from his office, got it. Time frame and budget?"

"The sooner the better. Read his emails. He'll be traveling to Chicago this week on business, then taking time off with some bimbo. That could be your opportunity. Don't worry about the cost. Expediency and a clean disposal is what I want. Destroy the file when you finish."

Shields suddenly felt cold and wanted some fresh air. "I'm delegating this responsibility to you. You don't need to keep me advised unless there's a problem, and there better not be a problem." He got up and left.

As Shields drove home that night, he started to think about the elimination he had ordered. He told himself it was no big deal, because he would have to be as ruthless as those pirates to have the things he deserved. *It's the kings and emperors that made fortunes. It's as true today in the global economy as it was in ancient times. The leaders of great civilizations were men of power, and they never let some little person interfere with their destiny.*

When Shields got home that night, he changed into his tux and went to the children's charity benefit with his wife. It was a lavish affair. With a little help from the champagne, he knew he had made the right decision; this was where he belonged.

The elimination of Welch fit nicely into his moral compass. His 'True North' was the natural law that great men fulfilled their own destiny. Like all the great men, he had moral and intellectual superiority over inferior people.

After Shields left, Cory went to the weight room. The exercise gave him an adrenaline rush and a flood of endorphins. Going on an elimination mission and the victory he would achieve flooded his brain with dopamine. It made him higher than any drug ever could.

He did want to kill somebody, but he was not a psychopath. Just because his father was abusive and his mother drank too much, it didn't make him a monster. He still respected them as much as he loved football.

As a child, he had learned that if he played dirty and hurt the other person, he could win. When he won, he was a hero, and everybody loved him. Military training reinforced his view of defeating an opponent as the patriotic American way of life.

The idea of killing a woman or child was repulsive to him. He was already stronger than they were. Even big game hunting held little excitement. Cory had killed his first buck when he was twelve, but with a good rifle, even a woman could kill an elephant. Big game hunting really wasn't even a sport, and the kill meant nothing if it wasn't a worthy and evil opponent.

The dilemma was determining who was evil, and Cory let Shields make the decision for him. A twisted view of American Exceptionalism was the 'True North' in his compass; and he found it in his country's corporate wealth.

By following orders and killing Welch, he was the protector of the American way of life. He could get his thrills killing evil men, and good American citizens would love him. Using this logic, Cory could justify what he wanted to do in the first place.

That night, Welch exercised at his gym. His moral compass had long since lost the idealistic 'True North' of his youth, and he never found a new one. He was worried the meeting with Gordon had set off a chain of events he could not control. He felt depressed because he did not know what the right thing to do was. While performing a heavy lift, he strained his back and had to take ibuprofen for the next three days.

Chapter 10

Its three miles of back road from the corporate park where Welch worked to his apartment. He thanked God for small favors because even a short commute can feel like a day's journey in Jersey traffic. He lived in a large garden apartment complex, but had never found a garden. The address was never considered a home, it was more like a safe house. He parked the car and walked to his apartment.

He'd overdone it at the gym, but that was not what bothered him. Last week was the incident with John Gordon. Today was his first annual review at A3E and it didn't go well. Despite accomplishing all his mission objectives, he got failing marks in cooperation, coordination and communication. Welch had not been a team player.

He had butted heads with the other managers. Welch felt it was unfair to be given a hard deadline then criticized for making it. He felt frustrated with the good job, bad review, and worried that he could be the next person to disappear.

It was the best of times.
It was the worst of times.
But mostly, it was the worst of times.

Using quotes from the masters, Welch could eloquently express in words the thoughts he did not want to feel.

He opened the apartment door and was hit with a blast of hot air. He looked at the silent air-conditioner, thought about his electric bill, and began to open the windows. Sitting on his green couch in front of the old fat-screen TV, he went through his mail, only bills.

He checked his land line for messages: no calls for job interviews, no old girlfriends, no new girlfriends, no damsels in distress. This was not Jim Rockford's phone. He flipped the remote to the evening news, emptied his gym bag, and made a large protein shake in the blender.

Dinner was fruit with yogurt, and a Lean Cuisine served with a side of veggies. Healthy, but boring. To wash it down, a shot of vodka, or two, with whatever juice was in the fridge. For dessert, it was two Hershey's chocolate nuggets.

Last, a glass of skim milk washed down two ibuprofens and a pack of vitamins. Welch feared he was so full of antioxidants that one day, while walking down the street, he would collide with an oxidant and be annihilated in a giant implosion.

His motivation for eating healthy and hours at the gym was the same as with most guys. As a small kid, he got bullied by big kids. Being a Yankee from New York growing up in a small southern town in Texas didn't help.

Attending college in New Jersey, Welch sprouted to a lean six feet and studied the martial arts with great motivation. After three years firing long range artillery in the army, he returned home with broader shoulders. Life had put gravel in his gut and given him a strong working knowledge of the Tenacity Principle. It enabled Welch to earn a couple of black belts in Okinawan Karate. Too many years later, he was working out to keep his six-pack abs from growing into a baby keg.

Whether a fighting style is called karate, tae kwon do, or kung fu, they're all fundamentally the same— an Asian fighting art. Only a few become true masters of their art. Welch wasn't one of them, but he had perfected a few good moves, like his wicked front kick. For him, karate was the art of who hit harder and hit first. Being able to do that took years of intense training.

In boxing, the heavier one will win. That posed a serious problem since he had never been bullied by someone smaller. They were always bigger, stronger, and now, younger.

Legend has it the martial arts were started by Buddhist monks who were not allowed to carry weapons. To a monk, the discipline to learn the art had a value beyond this practical aspect. Only when the body was disciplined to live at peace, could the mind be free to meditate on higher spiritual goals, like being one with the universe or hearing the sound of one hand clapping.

Welch never found that peace, but one insight he did gain was that a person had to be a little paranoid to become a black belt. Why else would they spend so much time learning to defend themselves if they weren't afraid someone was out to get them?

Unfortunately, Welch couldn't use karate to solve problems in the corporate world. The boss may be a sadistic, incompetent idiot, but an employee can't break his arm when given something stupid to do. Karate, a game Welch was good at, was a talent for other arenas. For career advancement, he would have been better off if he had spent all that effort on the golf course, or a Dale Carnegie course.

Dinner over, Welch worked on his reports with the TV running in the background, then called it a night. The open windows provided little cross ventilation while letting in dust, noise and light. But no matter what the conditions, he would sleep poorly and wake up around four in the morning.

This time, a dream woke him. He was traveling to meet Linda at a business convention, but was lost in a housing project. He had to walk from an empty house to a large building under construction. Stepping onto an open field of tall grass, it suddenly became dark. He was alone, but could see the lights of his destination in the distance.

As he continued walking, two great lions appeared. The large beasts had broken free from their chains. One lion charged him, and he knew he could not outrun it. He defiantly stood his ground as the great beast ran through him. Welch was afraid part of the beast was still in him.

Monopoly Games

Chapter 11

Having assigned Cory the cleanup detail at A3E, Shields flew to Washington DC to take care of step three. His limo driver was a well-built black man wearing a dark suit and black tie. "Good morning sir. I'm Ken your driver, at your service." He slid behind the wheel, confirmed the destination then asked, "Sir, would you like the divider up or down?"

"You can close it."

"Yes, sir." The divider went up, separating the two worlds.

Shields had no interest in listening to a driver talk about cars, or complain about traffic and weather. He would stay focused on his plan.

As he sat reading his email, the limo negotiated the airport ramps and merged into highway traffic. Shields never noticed a black Ford Crown Victoria pulling onto the road and following two cars behind.

Driving the Crown Vic was FBI Special Agent Carl Segal, wearing his aviator shades. He was known in the Washington DC area as the best wheel man in law enforcement. A '68 green 427 Mustang GT sat in his garage.

For important assignments, Carl got pulled off his desk job to be the designated driver. He'd been the driver/bodyguard for many a politician, diplomat or corporate executive needing extra protection while in town. As the transporter, he had moved high profile prisoners and witnesses in protective custody between the jails, the court houses and the safe houses. Today's mission required the finesse to move in and out of DC traffic tailing a car without losing it and without being seen.

Riding shotgun was agent Joan Moore, nicknamed Dirty Joan, a female field agent in a not too friendly, male-dominated, government bureaucracy. An attractive woman with short blonde hair, she followed the FBI dress code to hide her tattoos.

"He's making a right turn."

"Got it."

"You're getting kind of close."

"Backseat driver."

"I'm not in the backseat."

Women.

Recruited right out of law school, Joan had proven her worth by stopping four heavily armed bank robbers belonging to a Minnesota paramilitary group. Apparently, they needed more money to defend themselves against the Socialist Fascist Homosexual non-Aryan government that was coming to take away their guns. Joan earned the respect of her peers in a violent shootout by taking a bullet while putting two robbers in the hospital and one in the morgue.

"Children, be nice," came a golden baritone voice from the backseat.

Montgomery Kirk, the senior gentleman in the back, who had handpicked the other two, was the Special Agent in Charge. He had earned the nickname Captain Kirk over the years with his sometimes eloquent, but often overly dramatic speeches.

He was known for his ability to finesse his way around the procedural red tape that could hinder an investigation or lose a case in court. He came across as a persuasive witness on the stand or in front of the TV camera, and this case would require both to win. Kirk viewed all the world a stage— or at least a series of television sound bites.

The Captain and his superiors, all the way up to the Director, did not want to lose this case. This was not robbery, arson, kidnapping or even murder. It was far more important to the Bureau— bribery and extortion 'by' a congressman. With all the crap the Bureau had to put up with from Congress, this was its chance for payback. Kirk would employ all his organization's resources, and exploit every legal loophole to get his congressman.

A circuitous course of events brought the three agents to this point. The investigation had started when a Florida builder complained to the FBI that he'd been kicked off a government contract for not making a political contribution. Without enough evidence to prosecute, but enough to get a wiretap, it led to a payoff by the state's second largest bank. It involved a complicated financial deal with the congressman, a multinational corporation, and international banks, making it very difficult to prosecute.

To strengthen their case, the FBI asked the NSA to help with wiretapping as they gathered evidence. In an unrelated incident, the name Shields came up as someone with funny financial transactions linked to the congressman's family.

Riding in the Ford, there was little conversation as the three agents concentrated on their assignment. While each struggled to maintain their own sense of individuality, they all worked hard to play the character that fit the organization's profile.

In the limo ahead, Shields passed near Arlington National Cemetery before turning onto the Potomac River Bridge. Across the river, a hazy dome of smog covered the Nation's Capital. Halfway over the river, the limo came to a complete stop in rush hour traffic.

As Shields sat reading the newspaper, he listened to a departing jet pass directly overhead. He remembered being in Washington during that winter storm when an airliner crashed on the middle of the bridge. Looking down into the water where the plane had hit, he felt a chill. There was something tragically ironic about surviving an airline crash, only to drown in the frozen river.

The feelings of anxiety were closed off by remembering the accident was called pilot error. As an experienced pilot, Shields knew the other flyer didn't have the right stuff.

The limo crawled along for the next quarter mile before reaching the District. Snaking through downtown traffic, it pulled up in front of the Sam Rayburn Congressional Office Building. Shields called to let Congressmen Mills know he would be in the lobby. The distinguished congressmen was the senior Democratic member of the House Armed Services Committee. He was also a powerful member of the Broadcast and Communications Committee, which pretty much told the FCC what to do.

The outside of the Sam Rayburn Building was an impressive architectural design befitting the power and prestige of its occupants. The inspiring marble columns at the front entrance funneled visitors into a cramped lobby filled with guards, security equipment and a long line of complaining people not accustomed to waiting.

A congressional aide met Shields in the lobby. They negotiated security and took the elevator. After entering Mills' office, the aide pointed out that he was a few minutes early (he knew that), that he should sit in the lounge until the congressman would see him (he expected that), and that Congressman Mills was a very busy man (which meant he was going to make him wait). The aide offered coffee, tea or fresh Florida Orange Juice. Shields said no thanks, sat down, and checked his iPhone.

Damn Democrats, he thought and smiled to himself. *Republicans know it's their patriotic duty to support the American CEO. Sure I give them fat political donations, but everybody wins. Democrats have a different agenda, and it always involved taxing me to help those other people. This guy Mills, he's old school. Thinks he's at war with the business world. Won't take a campaign donation from me, but sure will take a bribe—guess he doesn't like paying taxes either.* He rolled his eyes and went back to his iPhone.

Fifteen minutes later, the aide escorted Shields to a windowless conference room with pictures of Florida and an American flag on the wall. The door was metallic, and Chuck figured the room was soundproof.

The congressman wore an expensive, but off the rack, chalk-striped suit to cover his overweight frame. Mills had a white monogrammed shirt, blue power tie, bright red suspenders and a large American Flag lapel pin. His full head of snow white hair was in sharp contrast to his Florida tanned face.

Mills always wore the smile of a good old Southern Boy, but his eyes showed a disdain for his guest. He rose from his large leather chair at the end of the mahogany conference table.

"Good morning Chuck," Mills said with his slow Southern drawl. He extended his arm and gave a firm handshake as the two sized each other up.

"Thank you, congressman, it's nice to be back in Washington."

"Yep, it's an exciting little town these days, but it's 'bout as far north as I'd wanta go. It does keep me hopping, so let's you and me just get on down to business. You can talk freely in here," he said as he looked around to reassure himself, they were alone in the soundproof room.

"Congressman, I've met twice with Mr. James Cabot, your associate, and he's made it clear how you wish to proceed." Shields knew the congressman's first name, but Mills did not give it to him so he would continue to call him by the title the man so loved to hear.

"Trust me on this one, Chuck. James is a very prestigious lobbyist on the Hill for the communications industry. I'm glad you took my advice and put him on retainer. He's been a friend of the family for years, has a nice house on the beach just north of Ft. Lauderdale, and lets me use it on special occasions for fundraisers. He's even got one of them big old power boats. I always think it's better doing business with people we know."

"I agree he's good, but expensive for a guy like me who isn't familiar with the ways of Washington." Chuck slid that point in to let Mills know he was not a money pit for the Congressman's political organization.

"Don't bullshit me Shields." The accent disappeared. "You know this town, and lobbyists are part of the cost of doing business," Mills snapped, then grinned ear to ear to defuse his little burst of hostility. He opened a folder lying on the table and glanced at its contents. "I like to know all about the people I work with. Seems your family is well acquainted with the ways of our little town.

"I see in your dossier that we even have some family history working together. Your little business was started by Grandpa Shields back in 1940. During World War II, you folks turned out thousands of radios for the defense of democracy and capitalism.

"After the war, your daddy took over and incorporated. Met him my freshman year regarding some Air Force appropriations, so I know how your family works.

"Your mammy, the nanny and the best private schools in Ohio raised you." He glanced down at his folder. "A talented athlete, you went to Ohio State to play basketball, and get a liberal arts education. After graduation and a holiday in Europe, you came home to learn the family business from the bottom up."

"As the owner's son, I started at the bottom of the VP pile." Chuck responded, trying not to smirk, he knew where the conversation was going.

"Your dad was diagnosed with cancer, but the old man held on for five more years. God bless his soul. Guess daddy taught you well, cause your company has been awarded several lucrative military contracts."

"He taught me well, and I will honor his legacy. *And I'm determined to out-do him.* I became President with the resolve and a plan to expand the corporate business. I'm adding a new commercial line using declassified technology for police, fire, and rescue.

"That's where you come in. I need Congress to take a specific radio frequency range reserved for military communications, Cabot has all the details, then allocate it to the civilian sector for public use." *Said the spider to the fly. The financial implications of this simple government giveaway will be enormous.*

Shields smiled politely, then stared down at Mills. "I do know this town, and I have done my homework too. Your Lobbyist, Mr. Cabot, and your niece are announcing their engagement next week so don't expect me to pay for their wedding. Now getting back to the subject at hand, do you have a pencil and paper? I have the numbers you want." He recited the Bahamas bank numbered account from memory.

Mills jotted it down and replied, "It will take a few weeks to deliver the legislation you want. Cabot will write it as a defense appropriations rider, but Congress rushes for no man." Mills looked up smiling at his gem of wisdom.

"As soon as it passes both Houses, I expect the remainder of our agreement wired to the account. I expect the President will sign your Communications Act, but that's not part of the deal. So think that concludes our business today. Maybe next time you're in town we can talk about additional tax breaks for corporate jet maintenance. Hear you may have an interest in that." He smiled again as he rose from his seat.

Mills opened the door and stepped into the hallway, busy with young aides rushing about. The young men were preppy and handsome. The young women were preppy and hot. It was a testosterone powder keg waiting to go off, and every few years it did. Mills turned, speaking just loud enough for all to hear, "This has been a very productive meeting, and I look forward to seeing y'all again real soon. Let me get Susan to show you the way out."

Going down in the elevator, Shields watched Susan admire herself in the mirror since she could see all the men in the elevator were admiring her. Chuck mentally recapped his meeting. *Soundproof room, big chair. Who does this guy think he is, M in James Bond? Why do people have to boost their ego by making life a dramatic game? He's a little man with visions of grandeur.* Shields walked past security and out the front of the building.

****

Ken, being a retired cop, had been able to park the limo in front of the building. Three cars behind the limo in his Ford, the Captain saw his opportunity while waiting for Shields. Joan hopped out of the Ford, undid the top two buttons of her blouse, then leaned over to ask Ken for directions as he sat in the parked limo. Their conversation took just long enough for the Captain to slip a tracking device under the rear bumper.

He didn't have a warrant, but decided it was a prudent step since the bug could be retrieved and no courtroom would ever know about it. Monitoring any conversation in the Congressman's office would have been technically difficult and politically impossible. He knew he had a better chance of getting a recording from the Pope's Confessionals entered into evidence than a Congressman's conversation in his own office.

****

Seeing Shields in the side view mirror, Ken got out then opened the car door. They would pick up Shields' Congressman and a few friends for a day at the nearby country club and eighteen holes of golf. The conversation would be about FEMA, Katrina, and Sandy. Emergency Communications had failed on a national and local level. Shields had the product to fix the problem. The contracts would be huge.

First, an unannounced stop, "Ken, we need to make a little detour before my next appointment. Please drive over to the 400 block of K Street."

"Yes sir," he replied with a little surprise in his voice. Although the location was only a few blocks away, Ken noted he was not given an exact street address or business name. He knew that area was expensive stores and office buildings filled with high-priced lobbying firms.

"We're almost there sir, it's the next block."

"After this light, pull over to the curb. I'll be ten or fifteen minutes and traffic is heavy here so don't double park. Drive around the block a few times." Shields got out and started walking west as the limo pulled out into traffic heading south.

As soon as the limo was out of sight, he crossed the street and walked down the block. Ducking into the side entrance of a large office building to take a shortcut, he walked through the lobby and exited the front door on the other side of the building.

Agent Segal saw his mark exit the limo, but he was a block away and stopped at a red light. Pulling over to the curb, Joan and the Captain jumped out of the car and rushed into the office building. Segal continued to follow the limo.

The building lobby had security guards and a large contingent of Japanese businessmen taking pictures while patiently waiting in line to go through the electronic metal detectors. A quick search and the agents knew their man had given them the slip.

Shields was a block away walking in front of a nondescript glass office building next to a trendy Vietnamese restaurant. He continued around the corner, entering the building through a small metal door with a pair of security cameras and the letters BGB in bronze over the entrance. It stood for Bank of the Grand Bahamans. Inside the small lobby, two strategically placed armed guards and two attractive women sat behind a high marble reception counter.

He walked up to the desk and gave the woman his ID code. She entered the information and his profile appeared on her screen. "Right this way sir" as she hit the buzzer, escorting him through a large ornate bronze door. They walked down the narrow hallway and stopped in front of the third office. "This is Mr. Walker, he'll assist you. May I get you anything to drink or something to eat?"

"No thanks, I'll only be a few minutes."

As she closed the door behind her, Walker started talking. He already had Shields's file on the computer screen. All Shields required today was a funds transfer into the numbered account he had set up for Mills' next payoff. The bank was experienced at this type of service and the whole process took less than five minutes.

Back outside, Shields looked down K Street for his limo. Not seeing it, he crossed the street and walked back two blocks to the point where he had been dropped off. The limo came around the corner a minute later and he flagged it down. "Okay Ken, back on schedule. You know who to pick up and where the club is?"

"Yes sir." Ken was perplexed. The unscheduled stop was too short for a sexual encounter. There was no briefcase or bulges in his jacket to hide money or drugs. The man was not even carrying a gun. His suit fit too well. No longer a cop, Ken knew he was only paid to be a driver. Still, old habits die hard, and he made a mental note of the event.

Agent Segal saw Shields get back in the limo, and called his partners. They rushed back to their car, and Segal resumed his tail. The Captain was furious, his professional pride had been hurt, and he took it personal. In a Shakespearian soliloquy, the frustrated Captain befuddled his proclamation.

"There is something rotten in Washington. A CEO does not come to our city to do one's bidding by one's self, without company of entourage. Mind you, a military defense contractor who pretends to be, but a businessman doesn't give me the slip, and disappear without reason. I want the truth! This man has spots of dirt on his hand, and I shall place him under electronic surveillance twenty-four -seven, and this shall be the thing to catch our congressman."

The country club in Virginia was impressive with classic plantation architecture and exceptional dining. Shields enjoyed the Lobster Thermidor with a watercress salad for lunch while discussing business. The golf course was in perfect condition with the greens cut at a height of .125 inches. But playing in a suburban area near a busy highway and hearing trucks go by was an unpleasant distraction to the beauty of the game. *My grandfather never would have put up with this.* It wasn't natural and players like him shouldn't be subjected to it.

He shot par on the first hole, and the other players did better than expected. Shields was glad because he didn't want anybody to slow him down. He had never thrown a game, but he would be less competitive playing with Congressmen who pouted whenever they didn't win. On the fourth tee, he shot a hole in one and decided this was a sign of good things to come and tomorrow would be a great day.

Chapter 12

After a light lunch in his office, Shields grabbed his briefcase and took the elevator down to the main floor. He walked to the secure building where the military radios were built. As with any top secret, military installation, two armed guards stood inside the electrical fence that surrounded the building. Signing in, one guard opened and inspected his briefcase while the second eyed him suspiciously. They were surprised when he showed them his clearance and security keycard to open the building's textured metal door, designed to block any electronic eavesdropping.

As the door closed behind him, the obvious fact jumped out. The space had no windows, making it feel both expansive and confining. Most of the floor space was used for inventory and the production lines. In the rear corner was a windowless room situated three feet from the outside walls. The space helped prevent any outside electronic listening devices from picking up sound in the room.

The room was filled with testing equipment and computers. In the center was a shaft carrying an antenna 100 feet above the roof. In an emergency, the radio equipment could communicate with the military anywhere in the world via satellite after the proper codes were authenticated. Under normal conditions, one secure frequency was in a standby mode so the military could contact them on technical issues.

Three senior engineers working in the room acknowledged his presence and went about their business. The schematics Shields wanted were in the computers and he could just download a copy as long as nobody was looking. Sitting at a terminal, he was trying to remember the password when he realized Ted, a new engineer in the company was watching him.

"Can I help you sir?" Ted asked?

"Ted, I appreciate your help, but I better get going." Shields got up and headed toward the door.

"Sir, you forgot your briefcase."

"Thanks Ted." As Shields walked to the door, he realized he would have to do his homework. He would go over the Clearance and Operation Procedures Manual, but a quick download of the blue prints seemed doable.

The codes presented more of a problem. His people only used test codes for diagnostic authentication of new radios before shipping. The real, field codes being used by the military were kept in the secure room safe. His facility was not part of the military network, and he did not have electronic access to the codes.

Shields Inc. kept a month's supply of the military codes to provide maintenance support around the world. It was a rarely used contingency that had not been required since the second gulf war. Nonetheless, Shields' support group was required to be available 24/7 and it was a profitable service he was happy to bill the government for.

The codes were delivered in a box monthly by military courier. Every twenty-four hours had its own set of codes— twelve two digit numbers to set the crypto equipment. It was the same principle used for coding since World War II. Today, each number set a series of interconnected micro circuits programmed with algorithms giving billions of variations.

To access the codes, one had to open the safe and retrieve the folder with the needed twenty-four hour period. But inside the folder was a plastic envelope which had to be broken open to read the codes and couldn't be re-sealed. Anyone checking the folder would see the plastic was broken and the time period had been compromised.

But who looked? At the end of the month when the new box was put in the safe, the old box was dropped in a secure trash incinerator referred to as the crematory. As long as nobody looked, nobody would know a seal had been broken. As long as Samuel's clients were just listening in, the military would never know a code was compromised.

Chapter 13

Wednesday night after work, Welch hopped the shuttle to Chicago without an upgrade. On Thursday, he would make a presentation to thirty A3E members from the Micro Processing Committee at their quarterly meeting. From the airport, he took a shuttle bus to the Palmer House Hotel. The building, a rich part of Chicago's history, was constructed in the city's golden age, and was home and hotel to the rich and powerful.

What struck Welch was the two story lobby with its giant, classical murals on the walls and ceiling. Over a hundred years old, it had the elegance of an Italian castle. He imagined it was like walking through the Sistine Chapel and decided to steal a hotel towel as a souvenir.

He unpacked and went downstairs for dinner. Welch avoided sitting alone at a restaurant table by sitting at the bar. He saw some engineers still wearing their nametags at the other end of the bar, but avoided them. Back in his hotel room for the night, he flipped the TV channels for a while. Lying in bed, he felt the excitement of anticipation. *No need to rent an adult movie tonight. Tomorrow night I'll make my own.*

He pulled out the paperback thriller he bought for the trip and found the story was set in San Francisco. It was a great city to visit, but it was twenty five hundred miles from New Jersey. He hadn't planned on getting involved with a woman who lived there and wondered if the relationship would have taken off if she lived in North Dakota. The wine tasting in Napa, rock climbing in Yosemite, dining and jazz by the bay, they had done so much together.

He remembered the first time he saw her, sitting in the hotel lobby; her long athletic legs sweeping across the couch gave her a physical grace that could catch any man's eye. Her smile was warm and inviting.

Her Irish ancestry gave her light blond hair and lightly freckled skin. It also gave her bright blue eyes that were windows to a beautiful spirit. She was a happy person, at peace with herself, which was wonderful to be with.

Opposites attract; lucky me.

Welch sat across from her and four other women but couldn't remember what the other four women even looked like. Linda's conversation was intelligent and most important, friendly. She made the small talk easy, asking questions and looking interested in what Welch had to say no matter how inept his responses. She had no ax to grind, no lectures to give, no anger to vent.

Welch tried to come on to her. He didn't get too far, but scored enough points to get a second chance.

I have no clue why. His own desire blocked the empathy to comprehend that the corporate world could leave a tall, attractive, intelligent woman lonely and bored.

****

The next morning as the Committee meeting started, Welch sat smiling his best business smile in his best business suit in the conference room. The meeting involved the next generation of microprocessors, so security was air tight. A private LAN network was set up in the conference room for secure file sharing. Computer engineers were using Q.R. codes, 'write-on screen' technology and PC facial recognition security software. Everything was state of the art from cutting edge to bleeding edge. These were the engineers that design chips and computers.

The first hour and a half was administrative committee bureaucracy. Welch kept his head up and tried not to yawn. Next was a fifteen minute break to gulp down hot coffee and eat oversize donuts while shaking hands and passing out business cards.

Break over, Welch was called up to the podium and looked out over his audience. He didn't imagine them naked. That trick, depending on the audience, could be very distracting or disgusting. He could see some of his audience had partied hard last night. Many had dark circles under their eyes, and a few had nodded off already. *That usually doesn't happen until after I start speaking.*

Like any group, eighty percent of the engineers were nice guys who did their job. Fifteen percent were real leaders, smart people who were a pleasure to work with. Then, there was that last five percent who were bastards that make life miserable.

Welch had learned a few good tricks from his old friend and mentor Andy, the master of the deal, on working with very difficult people. As Andy would say, "We can work together and do this deal or I can leave right now, because at the end of day, I'm going home to play with my kids and the kids' mother. Whether or not we do this deal is really not important in the grand scheme of life."

Welch had never seen anybody get up and leave. Andy would also tell them, "I will do everything I can for you, but we have to work together as partners, which means you treat my people with respect. They don't get paid enough to take abuse from you." Most people came around and Andy held up his end of the bargain.

At A3E, the members had to come around because they had no place else to go, except to complain to Welch's boss. So to survive, a successful manager must know what the boss wants. In Welch's case, the boss wanted him to kiss their ass. The boss may not be right, but they're the boss. Unfortunately, he could only give this gem of wisdom from his plethora of extensive and painful hindsight.

Welch's presentation to the Committee was essentially a PR plug to improve relations between his department and the membership. Most of Welch's fellow department managers were married women who wanted to get home and be with their kids, so they had no interest in business travel.

Since Welch was not married, or female, or popular in the office, he was frequently volunteered for travel. To him this was a good thing because it got him out of the office and earned him frequent flyer miles. Most important, he got to be with the love of his life.

His 'stump' presentation went well. He reviewed the electronic ballot system the Committee was already using and got a few questions and complaints. *You can't please everybody.* Welch reminded them he would be around all day to answer questions or take abuse. The next speaker was from IBM and talked about their new micro-processor. The group adjourned for lunch at noon.

Sitting at the table with six engineers during lunch, Welch asked questions about the current electronic process and how he could improve it. They were glad somebody from headquarters had an interest in their opinions. He hoped word would get back to his boss. From a business standpoint, this informal lunch meeting made the whole trip worthwhile. From a personal standpoint, his excitement was building, and it would all be worthwhile in about five hours. *I've been told I have a one track mind.*

The group returned in the afternoon for an educational seminar on the latest advancements in parallel architecture with functional diversity. The concept is to build a computer that functions more like the human brain. Welch wondered if that was really a good idea.

He looked like he was enjoying the lecture, and he would have enjoyed it if his mind wasn't so far away, thinking of their first night together. They met in her hotel room. After a little wine and some small talk, he kissed her neck, and she closed her eyes. Welch lifted her up and carried her to the bed. He tried to gently put her down, but they both fell on the bed. She laughed.

And when she was good, she was very good.
And when she was bad, she was fantastic.

She lived in San Francisco, and the idea of a long distance relationship didn't appeal to Welch. He had just finalized his divorce and wanted to play the field. *But from that first, friendly conversation, that woman cast a spell on me. Each time we meet, I fall deeper and deeper.* It started with coordinating business trips and tradeshows, now it was all his vacation time, and most of his money.

She was six feet tall according to her driver's license, and a member of the National Tall Club. They had gone to several San Francisco Chapter parties. As far as he was concerned, the woman he wanted was there with him. It didn't matter how tall the other guys were, at least he hoped it didn't matter.

The last order of Committee business was working on a new standard for the super-high capacity WORM (write once read many) chip. A3E procedure required all negative votes be addressed and responded to before another ballot can be conducted. This process can be done on the internet or in a meeting.

Most of the negatives were for clarification. Two negative votes were cast because they found an error in the calculations. The correction did not change the statistical significance of the equation. Other negatives were things that only engineers could argue about.

Data storage is critical in any industry. Once data is written (stored), it must be there when you need it. A storage device must work within a wide range of temperatures, humidity, deceleration (being dropped), dust and other conditions. A negative vote was cast because the Standard verbiage stated the chip must hold its stored data after being submerged in boiling water with a temperature of 212 degrees Fahrenheit (or 100 Centigrade) for twenty seconds.

Dr. Yarbrough, EE, PhD who cast the negative vote, stood to explain the problem. The discussion went something like this. "Water boils in Denver, Colorado at a different temperature than at sea level. If the intent of the Standard is to have a chip that works in boiling water, we cannot use a set temperature because water boils at different temperatures depending on atmospheric pressure. The correct wording must be simply boiling water without stating a temperature."

An engineer from the manufacturer rose to explain. "The information may not survive in rapidly boiling water with violent turbulence for twenty seconds. The standard is that the chip will store information without degradation at a low boil, a simmer."

"Objection! A boil is not a simmer. Simmer is at or below boiling." stated another engineer as everyone opened their electronic dictionary and PC thesaurus.

"Steam?" another suggested.

"No, steam is defined as the vapor phase of water. Steam can be over a 1,000 degrees." The group spent the next ten minutes on the semantics of energized water: a slow boil, a non-rapid boil, a tepid boil, a low boil, a 212 degree boil at sea level, the temperature at which a body of water will boil, etc. Hopelessly deadlocked and unable to reach a decision, a committee of three engineers was selected, voted on, and approved to research and recommend the proper wording for the Standard.

Work for the day concluded with the chairman warning the group about last night's incident in the hotel bar. A little after midnight, a large man stumbled in. The big drunk grabbed a metal barstool, walked over to a table with two engineers, and smashed their computers while yelling, "All engineers are assholes."

Dragging the metal barstool behind him, he walked over to the next table and looked at the four men sitting with their drinks. Again he repeated, "All engineers are assholes."

A little guy sitting by himself at the bar picked up his drink and walked over to the big man. "Excuse me sir, I'm not sure I heard what you said?"

"I said all engineers are assholes!" He yelled at the top of his lungs as he raised the barstool over the little man's head.

"Well I want you to know that I resent that remark."

"Are you an engineer?"

"No, I'm an asshole."

****

Despite popular belief, there is no Murder Inc. (dba, Murder Depot, Murder Are Us). Marketing would always be a problem, and local competition would be undercutting the advertised price. However, having a Valentine's Day Sale would be an interesting event.

Cory had maintained contact with his school connections for drugs and prostitution. He was good at networking in these circles, and after Cory confirmed his target was in Chicago, he sprang into action.

Taking his military issue Colt 45, a childhood grift from his father, he drove to Chicago and parked at O'Hare International where he rented a car. After an hour's drive, he checked into the Sleep EZ Motel on the south side of Chicago. Cory was in his room for less than two hours when seven members of the Chicago chapter of the MR-13 gang showed up.

It took less than twenty minutes to negotiate a price for the murder contract. An upfront deposit was given with the remainder on delivery. Cory thought his plan was brilliant in meeting the non-work related requirement his boss had imposed on him.

Chapter 14

The meeting was scheduled to end at 5:00 but went until 6:00. No surprise there. Welch had taken off Friday, so he was looking forward to three days and nights of heaven. The anticipation was driving him wild.

Tonight's the night. He rushed back to his room. The message was on the hotel phone. She was in her room waiting for him. A thousand wonderful feelings rushed through his head and body. He checked himself in the mirror, flexed his muscles, took a deep breath and headed for her room.

"Come in." She opened the door.

He rushed in, grabbed her and gave her a sweep-her-off-her-feet kiss.

They held each other for a long time, he couldn't let go. "Okay, you want to do a quickie, don't you?" she whispered in his ear. He nodded then kissed her again. She was still in her business suit, but their clothing quickly landed on the floor as they jumped into bed.

Twenty minutes later, he got out of bed and opened the California chardonnay chilling in the ice bucket. She even remembered to bring a corkscrew. *She thinks of everything.*

He poured the wine and handed her a glass, thinking how lucky he was to be with her. "You're beautiful." The world was beautiful— a happy, peaceful, beautiful place. "It's good to hold you again,"

She smiled. "How was your big presentation?"

"Good, it went well. Damn, you look so beautiful," now annoyed for repeating himself. Just being with her made his mind buzz. "How'd your day go?"

"Thank you for asking," as she took a sip of wine. "Really well, the new people in the Chicago office are smart. I like them, and I think they're team players." The office was Wells Fargo and she was Linda Flanagan, Senior Librarian and Manager in the Legal Department working out of the home office in San Francisco.

They'd first met shortly after her father passed away. As an only child, she took care of her ailing mother. While her mother was alive, Linda could live with a long distance romantic relationship because her primary responsibility was to her surviving parent. Last year her mother passed away.

Welch wondered if he should just move out west. He had an invitation to move in, but then the practical side of life i.e. money came into play. Finding a good job with his resume would be difficult. A lousy job wouldn't pay the rent.

He was sure being a freeloader was not a long term solution. *Maybe I'm just afraid to take that chance.*

He suspected she wouldn't move to New Jersey for similar reasons. In affairs of the heart, neither was acting young and reckless. He loved her, but because of his indecision, she could slip away.

****

Welch had lived with the nagging fear of losing her since the tradeshow in New Orleans six months ago. Dinner for two at the Commander's Palace was followed by an evening riverboat ride on the mighty Mississippi, dancing to the Dukes of Dixieland Band. They walked up and down Bourbon Street with a stop at Preservation Hall. He put twenty bucks in the tin so she could hear 'When the Saints Come Marching In'.

They stopped at the Oyster Bar on their way back to the hotel. The place wasn't much to look at as they sat in front of the oyster shuckers. They shared two dozen oysters, heavy on the horseradish. She ate a few, but he figured he needed them more than she did. They added two bowls of gumbo with Jack Daniels shots and draft Jax chasers to wash it all down.

Next morning they rode the streetcars, couldn't find Desire, and toured the historic part of town with its old southern homes surrounded by the sweet smell of large magnolia trees. There was another couple in the streetcar, and the women started a conversation, as women always do.

A true southern couple, he was Henry Lee and she was Barbara Lou. He was a builder from Atlanta there for a long weekend with family and friends. In conversation they learned they were all going to the same jazz club that evening. The women told each other, "We'll see you there." Linda and Welch spent the remainder of the afternoon at the city aquarium, which Welch had always found peaceful.

That night they found Henry and Barbara at the club with three other couples: a cousin, a friend, and a business partner so they could write it off. The place had a blues trio that was part of the 'Brother Where Art Thou' album. The show was great, and Henry was buying drinks for everyone. He asked Welch if he would like to join them for some club hopping.

Sure, you're buying, why not? "We'll grab a cab and follow you."

"Oh no, we've got room, ya'll come ride with us."

Seems old Henry had gotten lucky at the black jack tables that afternoon and was up ten big ones. Parked out front for Henry and his entourage was a stretch limo, now only partially stocked with Champagne. They all piled in and headed for the next club. After two more jazz shows, they ended up at the Bombay Club just off Bourbon Street for drinks and food. It was the "in place" of the day.

As the sun came up, they all piled back in the limo and rode around looking for a place to have breakfast. Henry Lee, feeling no pain, said, "Well we all can go get breakfast or we can head on back to the hotel and all get naked and make love in the pool."

Barbara Lou, Southern Belle and patient wife of twenty years looked up, rolled her eyes and responded, "I'd rather have eggs."

Later that morning Linda and Welch were back in their hotel room alone. She suddenly started talking about the difficulty of their long distance affair. Welch interpreted her frustration as a need for a commitment. He panicked. "I think you should date other men."

Dead silence.

He started to back pedal—damage control. Words flew out to cover the void. "One of two things will happen. Either you will meet someone, fall in love, marry and live okay ever after, or you'll find out I'm the right man for you. Maybe the only man that can handle a strong woman like you."

She started to cry, but only replied, "You're a good man." She did not say the word 'love'.

Men know being told you're 'a good man' is the kiss of death.

****

As they sat in their Chicago hotel room, Welch wished he could take back those words, but that was six months ago. He decided, again, not to bring it up. So tonight, they drank the wine. They enjoyed their time together catching up on recent events then dressed for dinner. She reappeared in a little black dress, and wore the dangling earrings he had given her for her birthday. The high heels were high enough to flatter her athletic legs, but not high enough to make her taller than him.

She loved Greek food, so they grabbed a cab for the old Greek neighborhood. It was a short ride, crossing another bridge, they saw the row of restaurants. "I can't read the names, they're all Greek to me." He joked and saw a slight smile as she ignored the remark. They selected one that looked authentic and smelled delightful.

They ordered four appetizers, including octopus, then salad and dinner. Their only disagreement occurred when Welch asked the waiter to hold the olives on his meal.

"If you dislike olives so much," she wanted to know, "why are you dipping your bread in olive oil?"

"Dah?"

He had no problem deferring to her expertise ordering the wine. It was not something to experiment with in a Greek restaurant. She found a Chardonnay that was surprisingly dry and crisp, high acidity. "You'll like this," she explained. "Most American west coast wines, because they have so much sugar, are bold and can overpower your food. This East Coast vineyard is in the European tradition, their wine is designed to complement the food."

Another advantage to dating a librarian was intelligent conversation; the dumb blond jokes didn't apply. While enjoying the octopus, Welch complained about the obnoxious jerk submitting a standard for the new frequency allocations.

"I'm sure they're trying to rig the system to pass something illegal, but I don't know what or have any proof to stop them."

"As they say in the Accounting Department, follow the money."

"But the big money comes after it passes, and they create a monopoly."

In Legal, we look for proof of criminality."

"This gets technical fast. I'm in over my head."

"Then go for expert testimony."

"I like that idea. You're good. They must be hiding the truth from somebody who would stand up and say this is wrong."

She took a bite of her salad, "You said it was frequency allocation. What do you mean?"

He labored to explain. "Visible light is one kind of electromagnetic energy. The complete electromagnetic spectrum is the range of radiation energy from its lowest to highest frequency. At the lowest frequency are radio waves with the greatest usable range. We use radio to communicate with satellites over a billion miles away in deep space. After radio waves, come microwaves, then infrared waves followed by visible light waves.

She tilted her head, took a sip of the wine and asked. "So what makes one wave different from another?"

"The dualistic character of a light wave is a fundamental law of nature that not even Albert Einstein could fully explain. Waves are created at different quantum energy levels and propagated with different wavelengths. After visible light comes ultraviolet light, X-rays and Gamma-rays with the highest energy, highest frequency and shortest wavelength.

"Within these broad categories, we use different frequencies to perform different applications. This is where standards come into play. Radio waves are a large segment of the spectrum which is further divided into TV, FM, AM and shortwave radio. The lowest frequency in the radio wave spectrum is used by aircraft and ships where the need for extended range is critical. This makes the frequency range very valuable for military and commercial use.

"The U.S. airways are further segmented to facilitate communications without interference and to give priority to those who used it for the national interest. Large parts of the spectrum are reserved for the military and no civilian can broadcast in that range.

"Other smaller segments are reserved for civil defense, fire, and police with the remainder going to civilian use, including cellular and PC wireless. The law was suddenly changed so a small slice of the spectrum that was reserved for military use got reassigned to the non-military domain. Now, engineers want to standardize the transmitting equipment."

She smiled as she sat back in her chair, crossing her legs, letting one shoe dangle. He refilled the wine glasses and continued talking as he maintained an adoring eye contact. Anyone watching could imagine they were planning a romantic getaway.

The conversation changed subjects with the serving of the main course. They still had room for dessert and coffee. She ordered a Greek Espresso and politely mentioned in genteel conversation that the coffee was a little mild.

Back on the street and enjoying a walk through the neighborhood, they heard good old rock 'n' roll music coming from the roof of a two story restaurant. They headed upstairs and found a band, a bar and a hundred fifty people in party mode.

A full moon treated them to a beautiful view of the Chicago skyline. The band was hot as they danced fast and slow. They were a good fit, and knew how to get down and have fun on the dance floor. Around midnight during a slow dance in the cool night air, he felt the warmth of her body. He was lost in her splendor as he looked into her moonlit eyes. Pulling her closer, he softly kissed her ear and smelled her perfume. She snuggled against him, welcoming his affection. They stopped dancing and embraced in a deep kiss.

"Check please."

Chapter 15

They raced back to the hotel, his body going crazy with anticipation in ways it had never responded with any other woman. He could not think of any other time, or place, or woman. Time and space collapsed into a singularity as his mind moved completely in their desire. He started gently, kissing her lips and then her neck as he ran his hand through her hair. She breathed deeply and took off her earrings while he unbuttoned her dress. As they kissed, she moaned softly.

They helped each other undress and got under the covers. As their warm bodies came together, his mind started flashing with powerful waves that moved faster and faster. Raw masculine biology drove him. It was power and aggression, uninhibited and domineering. He was the Alpha Male. He was on top, holding her down, pinning her arms above her head, gripping her neck. He felt incredible power and freedom being with her.

A wave of playful emotions washed over them. Laughing like teenagers, they were in adult-Disneyland trying twelve different positions— on the bed, on the table, in the tub, swinging on the chandelier, on the hotel balcony. Bubbling over with excitement, they immersed themselves in joy.

A great wave was building. He was in love with her, holding her tenderly, gently kissing her, doing whatever she wanted, whatever she wished, living only for her every need and desire. His mind was a strobe light, flashing from one wave to the next. His reality exploded as they came together as one. He connected to her. Yes! He was connected to the universe and no longer alone.

Of these powerful waves, he knew love was the key; and the longer he stayed with her the more important it became. From her, he found the love that set him free and gave him peace. With her, he touched the human condition that starts the day we are born. It's that connection that took him outside of himself and made life worthwhile. It was the gift from another person that we hold and carry with us; and it does not die, it lives forever.

The only trouble was, Greg, like many guys, really sucked at it. He tried, and he desperately wanted to love and to share with her. But the ways of his past didn't work, and learning a new way to be, to love a woman proved to be difficult to learn. Old habits were hard to break when they only met every few months. And when they were together it felt like they were living in a dreamland and not the real world.

Putting her on a pedestal was not a strong foundation for developing a healthy relationship. He couldn't tell her all his feelings or fears if he had to impress her. Even with money, he couldn't just say that she made more money than him did, so he couldn't afford this or that. But those thoughts were not with him now.

Yes. He held her, pinning down her arms as she lay passively under his control. He sensed her desire. Intuitively, they rolled together as one, and she was on top, in control, possessing him. They sensed each other's needs. He laid back and enjoyed it. She had her way with him.

He kissed every inch of her body, listening to her moans to guide him. She returned the favor. She seemed to know everything he wanted. His mind flashed as the waves rolled on. In a blissful state of happiness, they were together as one.

Resting in bed, her feet rubbed against his, massaging him. Her hands ran over his chest and followed the contour of his physique. He flexed his chest muscles and she laughed. Her hand went lower and rubbed his stomach. Welch was so relaxed he started to doze off, but she was the Alpha female teasing him while he was trying to sleep. Her hand went lower, and he woke up. She kissed his chest and moved down on him. He tried to sleep, but his mind started flashing as the process repeated itself again. Linda felt his strength and power as well as the tenderness and caring of his love for her.

They snuggled up together, and he felt her breathing next to him as he closed his eyes. Falling into restful sleep, Welch knew she would be by his side when he awoke in the morning. In deep sleep he dreamed of eagles soaring and it was the best night ever.

He woke up holding her in his arms and kissed her. Linda opened her eyes, smiled and kissed him. She was so beautiful in the morning light. He ran his hand over the contour of her body admiring the beautiful curve in the small of her back. She gave out a little sigh, and he felt aggressive, the waves rolled in. It was the only way to start the day. Yes!

They showered together and he washed her hair. As they dressed, he listened to her singing as she added a touch of makeup. Both had a big breakfast and drank lots of coffee. She liked Starbucks; he was a Dunkin Donuts kind of guy.

From the lobby, they exited the back door of the hotel, walking toward the lake for five blocks to the Chicago Art Museum. Never had a woman taken him to a museum until he met Linda. Now, every city they met in, the art museum was on top of their 'To Do in Daylight' list.

Chicago's Impressionists Exhibit had all the names even he recognized. Large rooms with Degas, Monet, Renoir and more. Linda found it amusing that he would read the little sign by the paintings as he desperately tried to understand why a painting appealed to him or how a Van Gogh touched him. "So Linda, help me out here. Why is this called art and worth a hundred million bucks?"

The Picasso exhibit was her highlight of the day. Welch wondered, "Was the artist able to see the world on a different emotional level and paint those feelings so they could affect others. Or was he really just dyslexic and people read into it whatever they wanted?"

In the afternoon sunlight, they walked through the park and took pictures of the old fountain and the Cloud Gate. He told her the photos wouldn't be good shooting into the sun. She laughed and said, "Everything will be alright."

They walked back to the Palmer House and had coffee in the lobby. She took snapshots of all the murals. Back in their room, they freshened up and had a glass of Sauvignon Blanc. Linda had been given the name of a new Japanese Sushi place by her friends at the bank.

They caught a cab and rode north past the lakefront apartments, marinas and playgrounds then exited going west past the university campus. A mile later, the cab pulled in front of the packed restaurant. They sat at the sushi bar and tried a little of everything while drinking hot sake, cold beer and plum wine. Everybody was having a good time as they chatted with the couples sitting on both sides.

They showed off their talent for eating with chopsticks; she was better at it. Welch added. "I remember the time at a Japanese steak house, when I was struggling to use the chopsticks to impress my date. It was late and the restaurant staff, all Japanese, started eating at the next table, all using silverware."

It was dark and Welch was full when they stepped into the cool night. Passing a homemade ice cream parlor, they went in for cones with hot fudge sauce. She got sprinkles. They strolled a few blocks before hailing a cab back to the hotel then stopped for cocktails in the lobby.

Welch talked about his job, and she discussed the artist she liked. But mostly, they sat quietly together admiring the murals. She took one more picture before going back to the room. They made love, and he thought it was the best night ever. He believed she was awake when he whispered, "I love you."

They slept late Saturday morning. After breakfast, they slipped out the side door toward Michigan Avenue. Walking to the river, they looked at the stores and the architecture of Chicago. Protruding from the Wrigley Building's brick is a collection of stone from every famous castle and monument from the Great Wall to the Berlin Wall. He had to touch each one. Linda laughed as she walked along beside him. "Get down from there, you can't rock climb on the building."

"But nobody's watching."

"The policeman over there is."

"Ops, I'm down."

There was a craft fair in the park, and they spent the afternoon enjoying the art and indulging in

Chicago Deep Dish Pizza. It was after dark when they returned to the hotel. He bought another bottle of wine for the evening. It was the best night ever. As they drifted off to sleep, she snuggled close to him and he told her, "I love you."

Sunday was their last day together. They made love in the morning. She was still playful, but he told her he was tapped out. Once again, she proved him wrong. They showered together, then he lay on the bed listening to her sing as she got ready.

At breakfast, a change could be detected in their moods. They were beginning to disconnect. In a few hours they would be flying in different directions and would not see each other for some time. They didn't talk about their feelings that morning, instead, discussing things to do before they departed. She wanted to walk over to the Picasso sculpture in the City Hall Plaza.

Monopoly Games

Chapter 16

Cory staked out the front entrance to the Palmer Hotel early Saturday morning, but did not see his target all day. He had Welch's picture, but was smart enough not to give it to his two shooters. He would paint the target to make sure there were no screwups, but he was not a happy camper babysitting two punk gang members. No way could he let them go in the hotel, security would be all over them in a minute. Like a good military marksman, he would be patience and wait for the shot.

Sunday morning he saw his target leaving the hotel front entrance with a woman by his side. The streets were deserted in the soft morning light and Cory worried if anybody would be around to witness a mugging by two gang members.

The witnesses were required so police would have a robbery motive. Doing the deed himself would have been more sporting, but he knew his boss wanted a good cover story on the killing.

Tank was the gang name of the banger that would pull the trigger, this was his initiation into the local chapter. Though only sixteen, he was obese. Kicker, the backup shooter, was a senior member of the gang at twenty one. He was sitting in the car with them, because Cory had insisted on an experienced killer being present. It was his company's money, and he didn't want any screw-ups. Cory was forced to spend the day with the two pill popping junkies sitting in his car with 9mm Glocks.

The plan was simple. The shooters would take out the target, grab his wallet and phone, then run around the corner, out of sight, where Cory would be waiting in the rented car.

Cory drove a block past the target, let out the two shooters, and then continued driving around the corner. Kicker placed himself between two parked SUVs. Tank walked another fifty feet and leaned against the building. The trap was set.

When the target was about fifty feet from Kicker, Tank would start walking and they would all converge at one point. The woman would have to be killed. It was a bonus for Tank, but Kicker would demand more money.

Linda and Welch were walking hand in hand. He remembered a gentleman was supposed to walk on the street side of his lady. He was about to step to the other side of her when he saw the large figure walking directly at him. The big guy was staring at Welch with a crazy look in his eye. Something was wrong, but not knowing what, Welch stared back.

If Tank was smart, he wouldn't be there in the first place. If he was a little smarter, he would use the gun to his advantage and shot his target in the back from five feet away—he wasn't that smart.

Tank continued walking toward his target as he reached across his fat gut with his right hand and pulled the Glock from his low hanging jeans. All he had to do was place the gun in the Welch's face then pull the trigger. Nobody had stopped walking, and they were within arm's reach.

Welch could read aloud month drunk who thought he was Superman. But he was caught flat footed looking into the eyes of a deprived juvenile ready to kill two people. Suddenly a large arm with something black in its massive hand was swinging toward his face.

In a reflex action, Welch thrust up both arms in a block to protect Linda as he stepped in and braced for impact with the large attacker. Tank's arm was blocked while in step, knocking him off balance.

Kicker, standing to the side, saw that Tank had lost his advantage and pulled his weapon. Tank's arm was out straight with the gun pointed toward the street less than a foot from Linda's face. Her self-preservation reflexes were strong as she ducked and threw her handbag at Kicker.

Welch saw Linda being attacked. His counter was aikido 101, which he had practiced a hundred times in the dojo against a rubber knife.

While sliding his hands down Tank's arm, Welch grabbed the wrist to control the weapon. Holding the wrist for balance, Welch executed a side thrust kick into Kicker, knocking him away from Linda.

Tank, struggling to regain his balance, tightened all his muscles and firing his gun over Linda's head, hitting Kicker in the shoulder.

Linda screamed as the blast rang in her ears and power burns marked the sleeves of her blouse.

Welch stepped behind Tank swinging the gun arm over and behind Tank's head while twisting his wrist. The momentum carried Tank's center of gravity behind his feet. The fat body fell backwards crashing into the sidewalk.

Out of position from the kick and filled with adrenalin, Welch overreacted and pushed his opponent too far. Struggling to keep his grip on the weapon, Welch fell on top of Tank driving the weapon into the kid's chest.

The gun fired again. Tank was dead with a bullet through the heart. Welch jumped to his feet holding the weapon and looking for the second attacker, but he had already fled.

Linda stopped screaming and quickly regained her composure before the police arrived. She was the calm one that told the police what happened.

Welch was still pumped up and shaken when the cops interviewed him. He was not dealing well with the conflict between self-preservation and killing a person. He knew it was self-defense, but he had killed somebody's kid. A fat, baby-faced child, some stupid kid that was given a gun.

When the cops looked at the clothing and tattoos on the dead body, they called the police gang squad into the investigation. They said it was unusual in this part of town, but concluded it was a robbery gone bad or a gang initiation hit. Either way, there was no reason or evidence to suspect anything other than a random act of opportunity.

Welch and Linda spent the rest of the day at the police station answering questions, looking at mug shots, and preparing statements. A witness, who was out walking her dog, corroborated their stories. Compliments of a city councilman, they were given a free ride in a police cruiser to the airport, insuring they didn't talk to any reporters. A police captain even reminded them that Chicago was a friendly city for tourists.

Sitting in the back of the cruiser, Linda broke her silence. "Something's wrong here. It doesn't add up. There are no coincidences in life, things happen for a reason."

"What do you mean?"

"Like the police said, this is not a gang neighborhood. It's the middle of the damn city, a few blocks from town hall. And it's Sunday morning for Christ sake."

"You think they should be in church?"

"There's more to this. Did you see the look on their faces?"

"I was busy keeping us alive. Look, you're the most perceptive person I've ever met, and I value your opinion, but what more could there be? I'm not so important that someone wants me dead. Well, maybe a few old girlfriends. What about you? Have any stalkers you're not telling me about?

It was difficult to believe her theory, but he filed it in his obsessive worry basket where it would fester.

The rush to the airport left them with only enough time for a quick kiss goodbye before boarding their flights. Welch wanted to say more but was hesitant to express his feelings while rushing through a busy airport. In the brief encounter, they played their part then flew off in opposite directions.

Later that day, police found another dead banger in a vacant lot a few blocks away from the crime scene. The body had a bullet in the shoulder. A second bullet to the back of the head fired from a large caliber gun blew off half his face.

****

"Amateurs. Stupid, unprofessional punks." Never again, Cory told himself, would he recruit an amateur when he needed a pro. The lesson had cost him over two grand, but he did get to kill a bad person. It was a super rush killing Kicker, and it tied up any lose ends, but Cory's mission had not been accomplished.

He wasn't going to tell Shields about the mess he had to clean up. Cory needed to come up with another plan quickly and a second shooting would raise a red flag. He would have to think of something else.

After a few drinks at an airport bar, Cory had calmed down and was relaxed. *I have a worthy opponent, but I can take him down that loser. I'll win.*

I have to come up with a new plan, an offensive operation with professionals. After guns, how do most people get killed in New Jersey?

Chapter 17

Welch didn't want to worry about flying, guns, or separation anxiety on the flight home. He laid out twenty five bucks and had three Jack Daniels, but he still played out the events. Linda's warning turned over and over in his head. *"There are no coincidences in life."*

The winning was exciting. Death, the killing was disturbing. This high level of violence was all new to him, and he didn't like the feeling.

The plane landed but he was still flying and drove home in record time. Welch remembered getting his thrills driving as a teenager on the open roads of the Red River Bayou. It was pretty stupid then and pretty stupid now as he thought about it.

It wasn't until he crawled into bed that it hit him. He was alone again. Long after the grip of violence and death had faded from memory, he would be thinking of her. Tonight, he wouldn't hear her breathing, or the beating of her heart. There were no curves on a soft body to touch.

He wouldn't feel the warmth of her arm resting on his chest. He had the whole bed to himself and would not have to worry about somebody taking all the covers. There would be no one to cuddle with. He would sleep alone and wake up alone in the morning.

He wanted to tell her how isolated he felt and considered calling her, but didn't. He wished that his time with her wasn't just a crazy wild vacation, and he wished some stupid dead kid hadn't distracted him from what was important. The joy of being with her was more than just the best night ever.

Drifting off to sleep, he wanted to be with her to protect her. From now on, he would always walk beside her and never in front of her. He wished that she knew who he was and how he felt. Welch didn't sleep well, and although he was sure he had dreamed, he could not remember them when he woke up alone.

He fired off a quick email before leaving for work.

Dear Linda,

Thank you for the great weekend. Part of it wasn't what we were expecting, and definitely not boring.

I had a wonderful time and miss you already very much. Liked the walks and seeing the sights and just talking with you. Want to continue our discussions on so many subjects and hear your views.

Sorry about the violence. Remember what I said.

Love,
Greg

At the office, Welch didn't talk about his feelings or his relationship with Linda, but he did talk about the shooting incident and it was not a cathartic release.

The women in the office kept asking him, "Did you have to hurt him?"

"Were you in the wrong neighborhood?"

"What did you do to provoke him?"

This line of questioning was not making Welch feel any better about killing the kid. He was back in New Jersey without a scratch on him. No scars to wear like medals, no bruises to show his bravery and sacrifice. Who was really going to believe he killed a man, a kid, in self-defense anyway?

There was a big difference between practicing in a dojo and taking a human life. Welch needed to know he had done the right thing and have someone to celebrate a victory with. He wanted to, needed to brag and feel good about it. *Who ya gonna call? My old karate instructors.*

Also, deep in the recesses of his mind, Linda's warning, there are no coincidences still bothered him. These karate practitioners were men that knew violence. Perhaps they could shed some light on the nagging question. *Why would those kids want to kill me?*

He had two teachers, but he hadn't seen them in years. Both were high ranking belts, although their philosophies on the art, and life, were very different.

Phil Setford drove a big red Cadillac convertible, was a private detective, and owned a karate school where Welch had met him as a student. The high belt students and Welch had many a beer listening to Setford's colorful exploits as a private detective, since most of his business was divorce cases. As he would say, "When I started my business, ninety-five percent of my clients were women getting proof of a cheating husband. Today, ninety-five percent of the business is husbands after a cheating wife."

In the dressing room in back of the dojo was a bed which he used frequently for private lessons before he met and married Edna. She was a nurse that could have married any doctor she wanted and been a trophy wife staying home in a big house. But Edna was a smart nurse that wanted to become a doctor, and Setford supported her through med school. She became a prominent and successful neurologist.

Guys want to marry doctors too. Setford upgraded to a Mercedes sports coupe and makes reservations at all the finest restaurants. When the maître d' called out "Table for Doctor Setford," he would say, "Here I am." Edna would quietly laugh and follow along behind him.

Welch arrived at Setford's house at 8:00. It was clearly not an invitation to dinner. Welch told his story of self-defense with all the drama of Homer telling the tales of 'Ulysses' while Setford listened and laughed. They joked, drank a beer, and went over the karate movement Welch had used. It was Setford who had taught him the technique that saved his life and reminded him of it a dozen times.

Welch mentioned his ambivalence about the killing, but Setford just said, "I'm glad you took out the punk." They spent the evening going over all the old war stories.

Around 10:00, Phil put down his drink. "Time to go to work."

"What are you talking about?"

"Come on, I may need some back up. They're staying at his brother's house."

"Who?"

"The runaway husband. I know the store the guy works at, so I called the manager and identified myself as the state police investigating a hit and run to get a home address where the guy is hiding."

Driving to the residence, Setford locked his revolver in the glove compartment. "This guy doesn't carry."

"This is still all fun and games for you, not anything dangerous."

The front door was unlocked so they walked in the house and were face to face with the wayward husband, his brother and some "nineteen year-old pregnant blond babe". Phil took out his camera and started taking pictures. The boyfriend grabbed a glass ashtray, broke it on the floor and picked up a large sliver of glass. Setford grabbed a chair.

"Let's not get carried away. You put down the glass and I'll put down the chair."

They both dropped their weapons. The guy rushed Phil who blocked the charge while throwing the camera to Welch.

"Hold this for me."

Welch caught the camera and looked up to see the brother walking towards him.

"Stop! This is their fight. Can't we just watch, and nobody gets hurt?"

Setford uncoiled his right hand into the husband's gut while his left pulled back into a high position. He followed up with a karate chop to the side of the neck and finished the guy off with a wheel kick.

Just another fun day for a PI.

****

Still looking for answers and not even sure what the questions were, Welch tried to contact his other instructor, Roger. He was one of the magic ones. A quiet little Irishman, he had studied in Japan under master sensei Hanoie, a 10th degree black belt and one of the karate gods. Hanoie, using an Okinawan style, had killed more than a dozen people. Several of the bodies were buried in his backyard.

On the wooden floor in Hanoie's dojo was a large nick that must not be sanded when students cleaned and purified the surface. The chip was from a legendary Japanese master that had given a demonstration to the senior belts.

The old master called up Roger, already a 2nd degree black belt, and gave him a live samurai sword. The young black belt was told to strike the old man. Roger raised the blade then attacked with full force. He stopped the blade less than an inch from the old man's head when he realized the master was not moving. The old master told the student he was weak and pointed his finger right into the young American's face.

Finger pointing is a great insult. The only way the young black belt could regain his honor was by killing the old man or live in shame. This was the way of the samurai.

Roger raised the sword high over his head and brought it down full force on the old man. The sword came down with such speed the blade stuck in the wooden floor, but the old man was now standing behind the student and smiling.

Force equals mass times acceleration and the acceleration of Roger's hands was beyond comprehension. Welch had seen that force shatter bricks.

While Roger's eyes stared right through you, his peripheral vision could tell you the sex of a fly that landed on the wall ten feet to his right. The old expression that when you look in his eyes you see no fear only tells you what wasn't there. *When Roger focused his stare on you, what you did see was death.*

That gaze always seemed a contradiction, because he was a soft spoken man that taught Zen

Meditation. Welch didn't think the guy's heart rate ever went over sixty two beats per minute. Even the time he was in an eight against one knife fight and required over two hundred stiches, he laid them all out without killing anybody or breathing hard.

At the tavern after practice, students were treated to some good war stories. Like that night a troublemaker wearing a black belt showed up at the school looking for a fight.

"I watched him smack around my low belts." Roger reminisced in a relaxed voice as he downed a shot then sipped his beer. "I knew he would get to me soon enough, so I just waited. Before long, he came strutting up and challenged me to a fight."

"We squared off and the guy rushed in with a wheel kick. He was sloppy so I parried it, spinning him around. He was just standing there, disoriented, so I threw a punch to the guy's kidney stopping just short of penetration."

"He looks at me and goes, 'Is that all ya got?'".

"Big mistake cause it kinda annoyed me. I threw a front thrust kick through the guy's guard breaking his arm. The ball of my foot thrust into a floating rib and cracked it. Made sure my kick stopped short of driving the rib into the lung."

"Before the guy could fall, without putting my right foot down, I spun around in the air and hit him with a left foot wheel kick to the side of his head. I hit him pretty hard. He woke up the next morning in the hospital."

Roger finished his beer. "Who's buying the next round?"

Welch asked Roger why he broke so many floating ribs.

"I don't want to hurt anyone," was the answer.

Welch was sure his teacher could make sense of this whole episode and explain his ambivalent feelings about killing. But Sensei Roger had disappeared. The last anybody heard, he had moved out west. Welch knew he was not going to see his friend again. He could only wish him well.

School was out. There would be no more lessons.

Monopoly Games

Chapter 18

Welch called one more old friend to tell his heroic tale. They agreed to meet for a drink after work at an old college hangout, The Shepherd and the Knucklehead Pub. The bar was located on Belmont Avenue, a rundown area about a mile down the hill from William Paterson University.

Hopping on I-287 to the NJ Turnpike north to the Parkway, he took a back road shortcut through Clifton to I-80 west. After passing Lambert Castle, perched high on the side of Garrett Mountain, he took the exit for downtown Paterson.

After flying down the interstate highway, he looped around a cloverleaf exit ramp a hundred feet off the ground and came to a halt at a stoplight. Like stepping out of a time machine, a different world surrounded him. The old narrow streets of Paterson were built for horse drawn wagons to take cotton bails to the textile mills.

Waiting for the light to change, he locked the doors and closed the windows. An old panhandler approached the waiting line of cars. Greg looked straight ahead as the old man passed. *There but for the grace of God go I.*

Traveling two blocks, he passed the Lou Costello (partner of Abbott of <u>Who's on First</u> fame) Memorial Park. Next to a swing set was a large statue of Christopher Columbus, showing that this Spanish neighborhood was once Italian. In another generation, it will be Arab. The great American melting pot was at work, even though it occasionally boiled over.

He passed the Paterson Great Falls. A towering seventy seven foot waterfall on the Passaic River, one of the largest in the United States. In 1790, Alexander Hamilton selected the site for "harnessing the eternal flow of nature" to drive the cotton spinning mills and power a young nation. Paterson became the textile capital of the United States.

By 1814, the falls powered continuous roll papermills. The giant water wheels were converted to generate hydroelectric power, making it one of the first commercial power plants in America.

Once upon a time, Paterson made everything from men's underwear to railroad locomotives, and Colt revolvers in factories all along the river bank. The J-5 Whirlwind engine that powered Lindbergh's Sprit of St. Louis was built here in 1926. The J-5 was also used by Admiral Byrd on his flights over the North and South Poles. Curtis Wright Aviation Corporation manufactured the R1820 Cyclone series a mile from the Falls. The engine was used in the Douglas DC-3 and later improved for the Air Force

B-17. A more advanced supercharged model was used to power the B-29.

Things have changed since Alexander Hamilton was here and industry had thrived along the river. Now abandoned buildings sit in various stages of deterioration, or for a few, restoration. Their rebirth came as museums, office buildings and loft apartments. The Falls was designated a National Park in 2009. The changes have not been rapid or glorious history, but it is American History.

Welch drove on between the Salvation Army Drug Rehabilitation Center with its busy Thrift Shop and the county courthouse. He continued past a high rise apartment complex struggling to maintain its working class existence. Another two miles down the road he came to the pub in an old two story building sharing the ground floor with a tropical fish store.

At first glance, it looked like most old bars with a collection of license plates and memorabilia nailed to the wall. There were a few pictures of Mickey and The Babe, but this was no sports bar. There were no TV sets blaring. This bar was a shrine to Jack Kerouac, the writer-poet who started the Beat Movement. Jack begot the Beat Generation, which begot the Beatniks, which begot the Hippies, which begot the Yuppies.

Jack Kerouac was born in Lowell, Massachusetts but traveled to Paterson— only God knows why. There he met Allen Ginsburg and William Carlos Williams, both born and raised in

Paterson. They continued their story in San Francisco.

Fred, the pub's owner, bartender and writer, said the pub was a place where all patrons could "self-publish, even if only in conversation." It was, as he describes it, a microbrewery club with draft brands from all over the US on tap, so patrons can travel the country as Kerouac did in his book 'On the Road.' *The place has the world's greatest jukebox filled with old-time rock and roll.* Greg grabbed a seat at the bar and ordered a Brooklyn dark draft beer while he waited for his friend. Just as the bartender served him, he got a tap on the shoulder.

"Hey buddy. That's my seat," came a loud voice.

Welch turned around to see a group of young men behind him. He paused for a moment to consider his response then said with a smile, "Sorry, no problem." He grabbed his beer and slid down to the end of the bar. *There's nothing like a real draft beer* he thought and quickly forgot the incident.

His friend Ralph Bender got there fifteen minutes later. Bender, a successful lawyer in auto insurance subrogation, spent a week or two at his Jersey office then flew off for the rest of the month to his country club home on the golf course at Hilton Head with his second wife.

Welch and Bender had been good friends since that day in college when Welch said, "Road Trip."

Bender had responded, "When do we leave?" He didn't ask, "Where are we going," which was good because Welch had no idea anyway.

They flipped a coin and started driving north, reaching Montreal, Canada for a week in what one would think was scripted by the writers of "Animal House." But that was another story involving lots of beer, several women, the police and waking up in strange places.

That was so long ago, but the friendship remained. It was good to have a beer and laugh with an old buddy. Welch told his Chicago war story with passion, but with more humor and less enthusiasm for the violence.

Bender told Welch all his new jokes and there were many.

"You should do stand up," Welch suggested.

"I already do, I'm a lawyer."

"Hey Bender, you know a lot of lawyer jokes, know any jokes about engineers?"

"I know a joke and a song about Casey Jones. He was an engineer, drove his engine to a ...."

"No, not railroad engineers, electrical engineers."

Ralph paused to think. "The only joke about engineers is that there are no jokes about engineers. Just take some golf jokes and say calculators instead of clubs. They'll never know the difference."

Welch told him about his girlfriend in California. He listened perceptively as a good friend and lawyer should then asked, "So why the hell are you still here in New Jersey?"

Welch paused to ponder the question before responding with his best answer, "I got nothing."

They spent the next two hours complaining about work and politics, and laughing at stories from their good old 'Glory Days'.

Welch asked, "You still jogging?"

"No, whenever I go over my target weight, I stop eating the olives in my martinis."

"Yea, I use diet coke with my Rum."

Welch noticed it was late, and the bar was getting crowded as more young people came in. He scanned the room then turned to his friend. "Remember when we first came here? We were the young, wise-ass know-it-alls. But now, ever get the feeling your life is disconnected as your past doesn't fit with your present conditions?"

Welch belched, took another drink, then continued. "The different parts of my life, the different friends and people I know don't fit together into one continuum that's me. It's like books from different sections of a library all placed on one shelf. And now this killing. I keep looking for the common theme or purpose that ties me all together in the meaning of life, but I don't see one. Am I asking for too much? I hope it's not a forest for the trees thing."

"Okay Nietzsche, it's time to get you home and sleep it off."

As they stumbled out, a group of young men were stumbling in, and Bender got bumped into the wall. Welch stepped in between his friend and the group.

Bender quickly placed his hand on Welch's shoulder. "I'm alright, it was an accident."

In the dim light, Welch could see they were young and laughing, then he smelled the marijuana. They didn't look old enough to be in a bar and probably weren't.

"Sorry Pops," the big kid said, laughing as they paraded past him into the tavern, followed by several attractive coeds.

Welch turned to his friend, "I think he just called us old."

"No, he just called you old."

"Thanks for that clarification. Are those coeds? They look too young. Guess it's been a long time. Hell."

"Well, it beats the alternative."

Driving home Welch knew he was driving too fast for someone with a couple of beers in him. After all, one of the best ways to die in New Jersey is in a car wreck.

Chapter 19

Next morning, Welch reviewed the progress of the Radio Communications Committee (RCC) proposed standard. John Gordon, as chairman of the now titled Radio Frequency Standardization Ballot Initiative, approved Welch's email announcing the ballot. It was emailed to all members of the committee, and Gordon provided another thirty seven names to be contacted.

A hundred twenty people signed up immediately. Gordon sent Welch an email in his usual blunt tone stating the invitation should be closed as the people knowledgeable on the subject had all responded. Welch replied in a polite, politically correct rebuttal, "The invitation was required by A3E procedural rules to remain open for ten days to give everyone a chance to respond."

Welch's staff verified that all participants were active dues-paying members and had paid an additional twenty dollars for the 'privilege' of voting. *This has got to be the most unpopular fee since the colonies were taxed on tea, and I'm not going to win any popularity contest trying to collect it.*

Gordon added twelve names not currently A3E members and submitted their annual membership fee. *I think he's stacking the deck.* Previous members would simply be reinstated. If they had never been a member, their schools would be contacted to verify college accreditation and a degree in Electrical Engineering. Welch lamented, *God forbid a mere mortal non-engineer was ever allowed to infiltrate the A3E Standards Ballot process.*

Gordon had FedExed a check to cover the dues for those not currently A3E members. Since this was unusual, Welch sent an email to Thomas Howard, Chairman of the RCC as an FYI. Howard, as chairman, seldom got involved, but Welch hoped he would share his concerns about events so far out of the ordinary.

John emailed an electronic copy of the proposed Standard. Welch forwarded it to IT for posting on the A3E website. The address, password and voting instructions were emailed to all individuals approved to ballot.

Whether it was a game, a challenge or just a super annoyance, Welch was not sure. He instructed Kathy, his staff supervisor, "to watch this one carefully, and let me sign-off on each step." She asked what he was looking for, and he told her he didn't know. "That's why I want you to watch it."

Since A3E passed about a hundred new standards a year, there were other problems to deal with, some more complicated, but none as irritating. He put aside his suspicions of Gordon and focused on the other issues of the day. The Antenna

Propagation ballot was stuck in committee. The Electrical Power Switches Committee wanted to conduct its ballot by mail. *No wonder we still have regional blackouts.*

Returning to his desk, he had a voice mail from Professor Howard. After two hours of phone tag, they connected. Welch was leery of someone who referred to himself with a title, but Howard turned out to be a down to earth guy. Still, Welch couldn't resist having a little fun.

"Professor Howard, Mr. Welch."

"Mr. Welch, thank you for returning my call."

Professor Howard, you're welcome."

"Mr. Welch..."

"Yes Professor Howard?"

"Have you read the new Radio Frequency Standardization initiative yet?"

"No Professor Howard... Not all of it." *I know what the next question is.*

"Are you an engineer?"

"No Professor Howard, my department conducts balloting procedures for almost two hundred committees on things from power lines to diodes and no one person, engineer or not, is going to be technically proficient in all of them. That's why we have a ballot. My job is to help manage the process and support the membership as you vote on a new standard, Professor." *I'm a great bureaucrat. Do I have this bullshit down or what?*

"You don't have to call me Professor. You should read it. It's an interesting read when you know the background. In this innocuous little document, the Shields Company is setting up a monopoly standard. They'll be toasting with champagne if it passes. "

Bingo! No gloating. Welch jumped up and closed the door to his office.

"Monopoly is a powerful word. I do have similar concerns based on the procedures they have attempted to circumvent in the balloting. Does anybody else agree with your assessment?"

"I don't know who else has read it. I'm sure those who work for Shields will vote for it. Their competitors, if they read it carefully and study the fine print, will go crazy when they figure out what this does. It's well written and you have to read between the lines, but here's the key. The performance requirements restrict your design options in this frequency range.

What the fuck does that mean?

"Most important, no company can patent what they are producing for the military. Shields obtained a patent on the closest thing to it that's not classified Top Secret. Anybody who tries to build this to meet the performance specs is going to bump into their patent."

"How do you know?" Welch was furiously jotting down notes he hoped he would be able to read later.

"I helped develop this radio system for the military while doing postgraduate work at Stanford."

Welch hid his excitement. "Look Howard, you, as chairman, need to get this in writing to the A3E Executive Board and cc me." He wanted a copy to show his boss he was right.

"No problem, I'm leaving town for a few days, but I'll put something together next week as soon as I'm back."

"But Professor Howard, this is going out for a vote. I would like to get this in the open before the ballot goes out. A3E won't want this broadcast to the world when it all hits the fan."

"I see what you mean, but my flight is leaving in a few hours. I'll do it first thing when I get back. If it goes out to vote, there's still plenty of time to stop it."

He was right, but Welch wanted instant gratification, and he feared Murphy's Law. "I understand, but is there anything I can do to help you?"

"No, I'll be out of town."

"Taking a little vacation?"

"Not sure you could call it a vacation, I'm climbing Mt. Rainier."

"Great! Cool, I've climbed in Colorado and California, and that mountain is high on my bucket list. Wish I could join you. It's the third highest peak in the continental United States." *And don't fall and kill yourself, I need your ass to come back and write that letter for me.* "Be careful."

"I will. Say, why don't you join us if you really want to climb it? We can discuss the Shields initiative, then I can write the travel off as a business expense. That would help me."

"I'd love to, but my boss would never let me get away with that, especially on such short notice." *This guy is awfully free with the A3E's money.*

"Don't worry. I'll talk to your people there in Jersey, and tell them it's important that I meet with you to discuss the RCC before we move forward on some balloting. You hop a jet to Seattle and give me a call when you land."

"Are you sure about this?" Welch wanted to climb that peak, but was not sure he was in condition for altitude or had the proper equipment to make the top. "What route will you take to the summit? I'm not an experienced technical climber, and I've never climbed on ice."

"Not much technical climbing. We're not taking the milk run, but it's not a difficult route except for one pitch. If you need to stop, you just wait. We'll link back up on the way down. Murphy, my partner, is an excellent technical climber and ice man. Very strong and experienced with the best equipment. You'll be safe."

Didn't they say that about the Titanic? Wait. His name is Murphy?

Fifteen minutes later, Welch's boss stuck her head in his office. "I don't know what the hell you're up to, but you have permission to fly to Seattle." He ran upstairs to the travel department and got a flight out of Newark.

I don't have the equipment for this type of climb. Why is Howard so anxious to get me on the mountain? Is this some sort of Eiger Sanction? It would be an easy place to get rid of a pesky manager interfering with a million dollar swindle.

As Welch waited for boarding, he watched two men arguing over the last available first class upgrade. He had seen grown men come to blows over the prize. He hoped they would start a fight, and both get kicked off, but it was not to be. He spent five hours in the middle seat near the rear of a packed plane.

He tried to relax and read his paperback, but worried about the problems he was creating for himself. *My boss has one more reason to be mad. But I do want that summit. Doing it on the company dime is a nice perk. It's a dangerous climb, and who's going to be on the other end of the rope?*

Chapter 20

Shields had a good news, bad news morning.

The Civilian Communications Rider sailed through Congress with little fanfare. He was always amazed at how fast the government could get something done when you paid them. But Shields went ballistic when he heard the recorded conversation between Welch and Professor Howard. Jumping up, he paced around the room taking deep breaths to control his rage. "Doris," he yelled, "Get Bob Langstaff in here right now."

She called back, "He's down in Engineering, he'll be right up." That Langstaff was away from his office gave Shields a few minutes to calm down. Closing his eyes to concentrate, he mentally inventoried his resources and applied them to a list of possible solution scenarios. He smiled, looked up, and thanked heaven he was given a few days to resolve this dilemma before Howard could put anything in writing. He had dodged a bullet. The Gods had smiled on him as well they should.

He hit his intercom. "Doris, have Gladys in the library build a dossier on Thomas Howard, doctor as in PhD from Stanford. Google him, credit reports, market profiles, military service. I want everything and I want it now."

"Yes sir, Bob is here."

"Send him in."

Langstaff walked in with a nervous grin; his mind was racing. *What have I done now?*

Shields motioned for him to sit. "Do you remember Tom Howard, the professor?"

"No. Should I."

"Yes damn it. You should. Think back when we got the contract for the F16 Falcon. You and I flew out to Bakersfield, home of the right stuff test pilots. We met with some military brass and a civilian from Stanford University."

"Oh yeah. That was when we got the government contract to produce the RU234-A1 system, predecessor to our GL70-A1."

Shields thought, *He remembers numbers, but not names. Engineers do think differently.*

"The civilian on the project from Stanford was Thomas Howard. He was the guy with the red sports car, ordered the damn bottle of expensive French Champagne when we took him out to dinner. Now, he's the Chairman of the RCC. You and John should have known that. It seems he has read our ballot initiative and has figured out our little plan."

"Shit." Looking at the floor, Bob felt like he should be committing hara-kari. "We're screwed."

"Stay with me Bob. Now, you should have anticipated this from him. You messed up, but you have got to learn to find the positive in life, like I do. Now, Bill Moss, the new engineer in your department, he's a mountain climber, isn't he?"

"Yes, maybe. Why?"

"Bob, you should know these things about your people, born in Arkansas, Colorado State graduate, comes across as a good old boy, but smart, right."

"Yes he's a popular fellow, very laid back."

"Is he loyal? That's important to me?" was Shields' next question.

"To the company, very."

"Bob, will he be loyal to me? We need him on our ballot initiative. Can you make sure he works with us on this project?"

Bob considered the question carefully before hedging, "Well, yes and no. He will commit to the company, but not to our strategic plan for the standard.

He's not the type that will make that kind of commitment yet. He's young, idealistic. He's one of those Libertarians. Believes everything will turn out good because nobody will find a way to cheat."

"All right, so we know how far he'll go. I'm counting on you as his boss to insure his compliance with what we tell him to do. Get him. Both of you run home and pack during lunch. Meet me here in my office at 5:00."

"What about John Gordon?"

"Forget him."

"What are we packing for?"

"Mountain climbing."

Shields called Cory and told him to get ready. The primary mission was to get to Howard, but if Welch was on the mountain, this could be the perfect place for Cory to arrange an accident.

He dialed his pilot. "I know this is short notice, but I must fly to Seattle this afternoon."

"Sir, she's down for scheduled engine maintenance, FAA regulations. I can tell the service crew to work overtime, but parts are all over the floor. We're talking about 10:00 tonight."

"What's the point in buying a multimillion dollar aircraft if I can't use it? Put a rush on it. We'll be arriving at the airport around 6:30 and I want to leave as soon as possible. Do it." Shields hung up.

He made a call to BC Smith on a burner phone. "My targets are on the move. I need you to monitor their phone conversations so I can keep track of them?"

"Can I put a bug in it? If not, I'll have to hack it. No guarantees, only the Feds can do that. I'll put a rush on it and contact you with whatever I get."

For what Shields thought was his last call, he phoned his wife to tell her he would not be home for a few days. After she hung up on him, he made his last call to the florist and ordered three dozen red roses.

****

Welch's flight touched down in Seattle around 9:00 pm, but he had to wait for his luggage. The airline didn't allow people to put their ice axes in the overhead compartment. *Another expense to submit that the boss would question.*

He drove to the edge of the park and checked into a cheap motel to catch a few hours' sleep, but he just laid in bed thinking about the challenge. He reminded himself he was good at this and drove into the park just before sunrise.

He knew there was a problem. In New Jersey, Welch had been working out near sea level. Since he didn't get to the mountains until the morning of the climb, he had no time to acclimate to the higher altitude.

After climbing Long's Peak, Colorado, he had done his research and recounted what he had learned. The recommended rate of acclimation is 1,000 feet of altitude gain per day after 7,000 feet. If a person slept at 7,000 feet, he can climb as high as he wants the next day, but he should sleep no higher than 8,000 feet. At night the body would repair itself by producing additional red blood cells to recuperate. Continuing the climb next day, there was minimal danger from altitude sickness, which can kill.

The practice is apparent on Mt. Everest where climbers will repeat the acclimation process several times on their way to the summit. On the South Slope, climbers will go up to 20,000 feet one night only to return to camp the next day below 15,000 feet to rest for two days as they continue their acclimation. At around 14,000 feet for the average person or up to 23,000 feet for a professional climber, the body's inability to repair itself becomes a slow and painful suffocation.

As dawn broke, Welch drove the narrow road winding through a primal forest of giant fir trees. Driving into the ancient forest was a spiritual journey. He slowed down as the trees seemed to engulf him. He could feel the forest beckon and knew nature was with him. The earth was at peace with him.

The road began to climb, winding back and forth while bridging small streams of rushing water. Looking through the green canopy, he saw the white, snow-capped monolith. It excited him, and worried him that he would attempt to reach its summit.

At 5,000 feet, the road ended at the base camp. Already breathing hard with excitement, he had to remind himself to stay calm in the thin mountain air. *God, I want to do this.*

He called Howard. The signal was weak, but he could make out Howard's words. "We didn't know what time you would get here so we already started. You should meet us at the climber's shelter at 11,000 feet, we'll spend the night there."

You couldn't wait for me. We're supposed to be a team. "I see the shelter on the map. I'll be a few hours behind you." Welch stopped at the rental shop, but they were out of adjustable crampons, so he had to rent the older model. They didn't fit properly on his hiking boots, forcing him to rent the heavier expedition boots. He also bought a few energy bars and stuffed them in his pocket.

Stepping off the sidewalk onto the green earth, he started trekking up a steep, grass slope. He could smell the soil and see yellow and blue flowers along the trail. Noise from the road quickly faded away. In the distance, a herd of bighorn mountain sheep grazed in the open field near a rock outcropping.

He watched young bucks practicing the behavior traits evolution had given them. Rising up on their rear legs, Welch could hear the crash as they charged into each other, banging heads with enough force to put down an all-pro lineman. The larger bucks would mount the smaller to show their dominance. As the females grazed quietly, the kids played together in a nursery, jumping from rock to rock as all children do.

Standing on the high ground, the large alpha male with his head held high surveyed his domain. Perhaps watching to see which buck would be the next to challenge him for control of the herd and all its privileges.

Moving at a steady pace, Welch stepped on the snow field at 6,000 feet. High above him, great condors glided in and out of the clouds. The sun was strong, but he felt a chill in the air, and knew he was not equipped for cold weather climbing. Wearing a ski jacket, he carried a ten pound army sleeping bag, extra clothes, two day's food, and water in his old army pack.

Looking up the mountain, he saw the sky had turned cloudy and the summit was overcast. There wouldn't be a grand view from the summit this afternoon. Anybody on the peak was in a dangerous whiteout. It's easy to get lost when your visibility is less than thirty feet, and it's disorienting when up and down are the same color.

The bottom section of the climb was miles of steep uphill trekking. The air was getting thinner, his pack was getting heavier, and all Welch could do was focus on putting one foot in front of the other. Step, breathe, rest. Step, breathe, rest. But as he relaxed with the earth, each step seemed to take him further away from his anxiety.

Step.

Breathe.

Rest.

His concerns, worries and all of his plans disappeared. His brain only thought about inhaling and the next step in the here and now. *Where have I felt this way before?* The pack became lighter, and there were no distractions as he focused on his respiration. Soon there was no effort, only the awareness of stepping, breathing, and peace.

When he reached the shelter, he saw it was a large stone hut with a raised plywood floor for sleeping bags. Next to it was an old solar outhouse. Blackbirds hopped around the building begging campers for food. Welch saw a group of three long haired teenagers and felt envious of their youth and lifestyle. Young people doing every weekend what for him was a once in a lifetime opportunity.

He met a young couple from Utah. The woman was attractive and very athletic. They looked happy together. She told him two men were staying at the shelter, but had gone hiking on the glacier. Welch took his gear inside the hut to reserve his bunk space. The altitude was 11,200, and he desperately needed to sit and rest. A small rodent ran across his lap, but he didn't care. He was dozing off when two men entered the hut.

"Are you Greg from A3E? I'm Howard. It's good to finally meet you."

Howard reached out with a big smile and they shook hands. He was a short man with an iced-over goatee who came across as a likable guy. Welch was sizing Howard up for the difficult climb ahead, and noticed Howard's clothes and gear were the best that money can buy. Welch turned his attention to the second man as he stepped in.

"Are you Murphy?" He asked looking at the other person. He was a younger guy, lean, very tan and looked like he should be a model for outdoor apparel or underwear.

"Yes, I'm Tim Murphy. Is this your gear? It looks pretty old. It's cold at the top and the climb is difficult. Are you sure you're equipped for this?"

"Yes, I'm ready."

It was a fair question. Blunt, but fair. If they were going to be roped in together, Tim, as the team leader, needed to know if he could depend on Welch. After going this far, Welch was not going to admit any doubt. He felt he was being attacked and answered defensively. "I've climbed a few hills with this gear, you can trust me. My old aluminum ice axe will keep up with your fancy titanium axe. Me, or my gear aren't going to put our team in danger." *Did I say that right?*

"You look tired. Sure you're up for this?"

"I flew in late last night. It's just a little jet lag. I'll be fine with a good night's sleep."

"We're starting our run tomorrow at 2:30 in the morning. Not much time to rest up."

"I'm good. You lead, and I'll keep up." *Enough of this crap.*

"Tim, Greg," Howard broke in, "this is supposed to be a fun adventure. The sky is clearing and it's going to be a beautiful sunset. Let's enjoy the view and eat before it gets dark and turns cold."

Murphy took a gas stove out of his pack and proceeded to cook a three course dinner with hot chocolate drinks for the two of them. Welch ate two cold tins of sardines, a bag of mixed nuts and two energy bars. The altitude was giving him a headache, so he drank a liter of water and started taking aspirin.

He thanked God there was only a light wind as he crawled into his sleeping bag on the plywood platform. It was going to be an uncomfortable night, but tomorrow was the big day. Welch was nervous but confident of his ability to make it to the top. *But can I trust these guys? Who are they working for?*

Exhaustion and sleep ended his conversation.

Chapter 21

Welch and Howard were at the stone hut when Shields and his entourage arrived at the mountain's base camp by limo. Moss took Cory to the rental shop for an equipment fitting. Cory insisted he was up for the mission, but Moss knew he would never reach the climber's shelter, much less the summit. By nine thousand feet, the big man was done in by the altitude. Moss was afraid he would have to call for a medical evac.

Moss contacted the boss with his hand-held radio. "I'm bringing Cory down. He could die if he doesn't get to a lower altitude immediately."

Shields responded. "If he can walk, he can come down on his own. I still need you to do your job and make contact with Howard."

"No, I won't leave a climber alone on the mountain. He's in trouble, and it's the Christian thing to do. We're coming down to the base camp parking lot. The limo can take him down to a lower altitude to recover."

Cory's ego was bruised, and he seethed with anger. Not only had he been beaten by his competition, but Shields and the other men had seen him lose. He swore he would get Welch for this and make him pay. The limo driver drove Cory down while Moss, Langstaff and Shields waited at the lodge for Howard to return.

****

Welch's alarm went off at 2:00 am. He dressed in his sleeping bag, ate two more granola bars, some nuts and drank his orange juice. He took all his vitamins and some more aspirin. Outside the hut, the air was dead still and a million stars filled a black sky. A crescent moon hung low in the sky. He tried to relax and enjoy the view as the Milky Way glowed above him. Looking up, he filed the spectacular image of light deep in his brain so he could forever contemplate its beauty.

He struggled in the dark with the flashlight between his knees to securely strap the crampons to his boots. It was the first time he had ever worn them, and he worried about his footing on the icy slope. The three men put on their day packs and roped in. It was three in the morning when Welch picked up his ice axe and Murphy gave the command, "Let's go."

They stepped onto the hard glacier ice. The trio started early to reduce the risk of avalanche. Most snow and ice movement is in the afternoon, when the warmer temperature weakened the interstice ice layers.

The crampons worked well, and he found his footing was secure. *Wow, this is not so bad.* The first section was easy, and Howard took the lead. Murphy was roped in the middle and Welch brought up the rear. Howard and Murphy were wearing climbing helmets for protection against falling rocks. Attached to the helmets, they wore powerful diode lanterns.

Welch wore his old wool ski cap. He had the rope in one hand and struggled to see where he was stepping with his ice axe and flashlight in the other hand. They ascended the glacier for several hours negotiating yawning crevasses ten feet wide and hundreds of feet deep.

When the soft glow of sunlight broke the horizon, they stopped for a rest. Murphy gave Welch a funny look. "Your crampons are on backwards."

"That's so I can get down fast without having to turn around."

On break, Welch fixed the crampons, adjusted his pack, drank lots of water and took more aspirin. Before starting up again, he sucked down a chocolate granola bar. It had no taste but satisfied his craving for sugar.

The rest of the route was steep and treacherous, so Murphy took the lead. Welch stayed in the rear, which was okay with him, because he was breathing hard and getting a headache, but he was not going to let Murphy know.

They scrambled hand over foot up a steep rock section to traverse another lobe of the glacier.

Looking ahead, Welch saw an ice covered rock cliff rising above him. If the climb was a marathon, this would be the twenty mile mark where the runner 'hits the wall'. Only this wall was a lot more dangerous.

Even with polarized sunglasses, the sky was too bright in the thin air. The ice was glaring, the rock was gray and the snow flat white. Nature's cold, harsh landscape was giving them a final warning.

Welch asked the athlete's question, "Can I go on? Should I stop to rest? Why am I doing this? Why do I care?" He had no answers, but he would not stop. The slope got steeper as they continued working their way up a narrow ledge to the base of the icy cliff.

In the morning sunlight, the ice was wet and slippery, making the climb more difficult. After scrambling over a section of rock, they came to the vertical pitch of the climb. The route followed a sixty foot crack in the rock, two to five inches wide, good for climbing if you know what you're doing.

Howard went first, belayed by Tim. As he struggled upward, Welch could see some good hand holds, but worried because Howard was not placing many anchors in the rock.

If a climber is eight feet above an anchor and falls, he would fall eight feet to the anchor plus another eight feet before the slack in the line tightened. Falling sixteen feet is a long way, and the jar can hurt. Being injured while slamming into a rock and dangling on the end of a rope at fourteen thousand feet is not fun. Welch didn't allow himself to think about it, but his brain did think about trusting Howard.

Climbing, like religion, has a leap of blind faith. After all the training and preparation, you have to trust in your partner. If you want to reach nirvana, fear and doubt must be abandoned. You must commit; either you go, or you don't.

Welch stepped up to the rock. With Howard belaying from above, he climbed cautiously making sure he always had three points in secure contact with the mountain. Focusing on one move at a time, he was excited but maintained control. It felt good.

Half way up, while standing on a small ledge, Welch turned and looked down, allowing himself to admire the view. Silver lakes on green rolling mountains against a soft blue sky created a rich panoramic vision, and he thought how beautiful the world could be

After another few minutes of climbing, he joined Howard who was sitting on a large ledge. Welch turned to him. "What a thrill. I love this shit." He knew he had the right stuff to make the summit.

Howard was in good position with his legs braced on a rock outcropping and the climbing rope wrapped around his waist in a hip belay. He also had a short line securing himself to the rock wall behind him, which would catch him if he was pulled off the ledge by a falling climber. Welch rested a little easier seeing that Howard was practicing safe climbing, and it looked like he knew what he was doing if Welch got into trouble.

Then Welch saw the problem. "What the fuck!" Howard had not secured the end of the belay rope to the rock or anything. If Welch had fallen, Howard would be safely secured to the mountain. But if Howard let go of the rope, it would fall two thousand feet down the mountain with Welch attached to it. Before Welch could say anything, Murphy popped up and joined them on the ridge.

Welch was upset, but decided to let it go for now. Starting a fight with a person you are tied to was probably not a good idea.

Continuing their climb up a narrow gorge, he could hear the wind howling and saw the summit through the blowing snow. They were only a few hundred yards from the third highest peak in the continental US. Stepping out of the gorge onto the exposed slope, they were pounded by a cutting wind. Any water on their clothing froze immediately.

All three ducked back in the gorge to zip up their parkas. Welch could see Murphy was tired, and Howard looked exhausted. It was fifteen degrees below freezing, and the wind gusts were in their face at forty five mph.

They hiked to the summit leaning into the wind. Yesterday was a whiteout. Today, they were blessed with an endless horizon of clear sky with distant peaks breaching the skyline.

"I'm on top of the world."

His energy returned as he looked into the quarter mile wide crater of the extinct volcano. Knowing it was millions of years old gave Welch's sense of time a new perspective. He imagined dinosaurs roaming below in the primal forest.

"Here, take my picture."

The three men took pictures, shook hands, and congratulated themselves. Murphy climbed around on the summit, then descended fifty feet to the floor of the frozen crater. Howard and Welch sat behind a large boulder for protection from the elements. Despite the fierce wind, Welch felt a sense of inner peace.

"We made it." He breathed deeply as he took it all in.

While feeding his senses as much joy as possible, he could not help but wondered what chain of events got him here. Shields, Howard, and his wish for adventure got him to the top. But he still had to get down alive, and more people die climbing down than climbing up.

The couple from Utah and a group from the climbing school that took the milk run joined them on the summit. Thirty minutes later, the three climbers took their last look around and started their descent.

They quickly negotiated the gorge going down the same route they came up. Water runoff on the summit had created a small stream flowing down the gorge. Welch checked to make sure Murphy had safely anchored himself and the rope before starting the belay.

Going down as fast as possible, bits of ice pelted Welch from above. A small fragment hit him in the face, almost knocking off his sunglasses. A large block of ice missed his head by inches.

Welch's legs were fatigued as they walked onto the glacier and spread out on the rope. The wet ice was slippery from the afternoon sunlight. He knew this was not the time to relax. Howard took the lead and moved toward some rocks protruding through the ice. Murphy was in the middle.

Welch was about to tell Murphy he wanted to take the lead when he felt the earth move under his feet. It was not what Carole King had in mind. It started with a loud crack, and the rumble of a moving glacier. It was the sound the ice cubes make in your glass when you pour in the gin, only a hundred thousand times louder.

"Oops," he uttered the ultimate understatement as his brain felt the ice giving way beneath him. Howard was already on the rocks and Murphy was running for them. Roped together, Welch started to follow.

Murphy made it to the edge of the rocks when the ice opened between them. If he kept running, he would pull Welch over the widening crevasse, a bottomless death pit already ten feet wide and growing.

"Stop!" Welch yelled and braced himself.

The rope went tight, and Murphy was yanked backwards on his ass. The pit was growing as it moved toward Welch. Unhooking from the rope was the wrong option. He dropped flat on the ice and braced himself for the fall.

Murphy jumped up and saw what was happening. With all his strength, he thrust his ice axe between two large rocks then looped the rope around it. When Welch fell in the abyss, the axe would be an anchor, stopping Welch's fall. Welch peered down into the dark void as the ice fell away in front of him.

Abruptly, the collapse stopped less than two feet away. He lay still on the ice and waited. Murphy yelled, "You okay?"

Welch gave a quick thumbs up, then cautiously walked uphill around the great pit. Murphy sat braced against a boulder holding the rope around his ice axe until Welch made it to the rocks. Welch nodded a thank you, and Murphy nodded back. With nothing more to say, they continued their descent.

The three rested at the shelter, their bodies appreciating the thicker air. They ate and loaded up the camp gear in their heavy packs for the trip down to base camp.

They heard what sounded like at 155 mm artillery shell going off. All three froze in their tracks, looking in the direction of the explosion. Somewhere on the mountain was an avalanche. He felt relieved he was not under it.

As they sat in the warmth of the sun, he turned to Howard. "Just for the record, we need to talk a little business."

"Right Greg. For the record, you can put on your report that we discussed the electronic balloting, and I completely support your effort and any recommendations you have for its improvement."

"What about Shields?" Welch asked.

"I'm too tired to think so just tell your people I'm reviewing the initiative with other documentation and will respond with a detailed report shortly. That should keep them happy until I get back to the office. We better start walking. If we sit too long our legs are going to cramp up."

"I'll quote you in my report." *That's it. I flew 2,500 miles for that.*

A bright sun was reflecting off the snow as they walked down, and Welch's face was getting sunburned. At base camp, he had to hit the road to catch his plane. Howard and Murphy said they had a room at the lodge to relax for a few days and do some sightseeing before heading home. *Lucky you.*

Welch took his last look at the summit from the parking lot. *I wasn't the best equipped or most fashionable climber, but the mountain really doesn't care. Only a few make it to the top, and not all get to walk away. But for a brief moment in time, I stood on the summit. The mountain let me pass; I didn't conquer the mountain, but today I conquered my fear.*

He realized that nature had energized his soul but exhausted his body. The climb had pushed him to the limit. It would be months before he had any desire to scale another peak— but the hunger would return.

The scenic drive back to Seattle was interrupted by the clear-cut lumbering. It cast a devastating scar on the land. The destruction was so massive he had to pull over. His mind went blank as he tried to justify it.

The flight path out of Seattle flew passed the great mountain: so large he was flying under the summit. Around the park, he saw the clear-cut scars in the earth's ancient forest.

****

Two days after returning to the east coast, Welch's big toenails turned black. The trek from the summit down to the car was 9,200 vertical feet. His mind was too preoccupied to even notice the minor discomfort of his rented footwear. With every step down, his foot slid a fraction of an inch, bumping his big toes into the front of his boots over 18,400 times on each foot. A week later, his toenails fell off, and it would take months to grow them back.

Chapter 22

Welch hadn't heard from Howard for three days and tried to call him. He got no answer and assumed they were in a dead zone in the mountains. He thought about the forest and how beautiful the world was when you don't live in a Standard Metropolitan Area.

Welch's boss brought him back to the here and now when she stuck her head in his office to remind him it was time for the department staff meeting. The hour and a half meeting was little more than a weekly show and tell. Welch gave his status report on the movement of initiatives through the pipeline. He considered talking about Howard and the RRC, but bringing up problems is the last thing anybody wants to hear in a staff meeting. Besides, what could he have said? They were following the procedures.

The meeting ended and Welch grabbed his lunch from the refrigerator in the coffee room. He ate his cold turkey sandwich and plain yogurt alone in his office. He remembered the three tech companies he had worked for in the past ten years and felt sorry for himself. They all went belly-up. One had even given him a large signing bonus. Welch had gone into his boss's office, an Ivy League MBA grad who had worked as a Bain Consultant. *A consultant is someone who looks at your watch, tells you what time it is, and then breaks it. If someone tells you they can fix everything, they're a liar and a consultant—but that's redundant.*

Welch had told his VP boss that unless they made significant changes in their strategy, they would be out of business in six months. Bosses really don't want to hear bad news. Next day same old same old *Deja' vu* all over again, fired. But Welch was wrong, it took nine months. He mused. *So why can't I predict lottery numbers? Being right is a nice consolation prize, but you can't take it to the bank. I don't believe in Hell, I believe in unemployment.*

The phone rang, snapping him out of his depression. It was time to get back to work. The call was from Barbra Lockhart, looking for a copy of the old Wireless Standard, 802.12. She had a deep sexy voice, and Welch tried to picture what she looked like. He explained what he was going to do, then put her on hold and forwarded the call to Jill down the hall. Providing copies of existing standards was Jill's job.

Getting back on his PC, he checked the system status report and saw the CCR initiative had gone out to ballot. "What the heck?"

Welch ran down the hall to his staff's cubical and stood in front of Kathy's desk. She reported to him and supervised the two other clerks. "What happened?" he demanded. "Why did the CCR initiative go out?"

"It was approved to go. John Gordon sent me an email authorizing the go-ahead on the ballot."

"I told you to keep me posted on this. I wanted to monitor every step. Isn't that what I said?"

"I'm sorry," she responded in a despondent tone. "I was trying to be helpful. Mr. Gordon and the Committee Chairman, Doctor Howard, were on a speaker phone with me while you were in the staff meeting and asked that I send it out right away."

Greg stood there with his mouth open. "You spoke to them together on the same call?"

"Yes, they sounded together."

What in the hell was going on? The frustration paralyzed him. The only thing he could think to do was lash out in anger. "I told you to keep me posted on this. I wanted to check everything before it moved to the next step. Isn't that what I said?"

"I'm sorry. You weren't here and John was insistent that I send out the ballots immediately. He was very pushy."

"I'll bet he was. If this goes bad, you're in trouble. You should have told me about this right away, and not let me find out about it four hours later." When all else fails, shoot the messenger.

"I'm sorry."

"Please stop saying you're sorry, it doesn't help anything."

"I'm sorry."

"Oh, hell.... don't worry about it, what's done is done. Please, next time tell them you're not allowed to act until you check with me. Blame it on me. I'll take the heat if they complain. But if I tell you to put something on hold, it's for a reason, even if I don't know what the reason is." *And please stop getting passive aggressive on me.*

Back in his office, Welch closed the door and sulked. He called Howard's cell again but there was still no answer, so he called his office at the University. The school's Engineering Department admin assistant, who sounded like an intern, picked up. Welch asked to speak with Howard.

"I'm sorry he's not in. May I take a message? The professor will be calling in."

"Has the guy returned from the climbing trip? He told me they would only be gone a few days. I've tried to reach him on his cellphone, and he's not picking up."

"You mean his climbing trip to Seattle. That's all done, but he called to say the trip was being extended because of a new consulting contract."

"What's he consulting on, altitude sickness?" Welch heard his voice heat up and tried to calm his words. "Does the professor have another number I can use to reach him?"

"I can't give out his cell number. The extension you called is for his consulting business. He is working and does call in. Can I take a message?"

"He already gave me his cellphone. This is Greg Welch at A3E. I'm the Standards Manager." Welch tried to make it sound like business and a matter of life and death. "This is important, and we must contact him. Can you give me the number where he's staying?"

"You're with A3E." Her voice suddenly sounded excited. "I'm a student member of the association. I'll be graduating next year with my EE degree. Do you think I should stay in school full time and go for my PhD, or should I get a job and get some experience first?"

How the hell should I know? "It depends on your goals and money. Do you have enough money to support yourself in school? The job market is not very good right now."

"My parents are paying for it all."

"If they're rich, stay in school, party and drink as much as you can. You're going to be working the rest of your life, so why rush into it?"

She didn't know how to respond, so she changed the subject. "I suppose I could give you a number. Hold on, here it is, try this number, 234/555-2000. That's where he's consulting."

Welch thanked her, then he apologized and hung up. He knew he wasn't handling things very well today. Negotiating the ice on a glacier was much simpler than dealing with the bureaucracy of a corporation. He vowed again not to let the small stuff get to him.

He dialed the number and waited as the phone rang.

Murphy's Law is well known and true to its own premise. The law is being misquoted when one hears

"Anything that can go wrong will go wrong." Although the meaning is technically the same, the emphasis is different in his actual quote, "Everything that can go wrong will go wrong."

"Shields Communications, good afternoon, how may I direct your call?"

Welch put down the phone. "Son of bitch, he's been bought off."

****

Shields had left Seattle two days ago in his private jet with his new consultant, Professor Howard. They had met at the basecamp lodge. Shields would be consultant heavy for a few months with all his promises to hire. But with all the new business he would get after setting the standard, there would be enough work to go around. For now, the added headcount was a drain on his resources. Time was becoming a critical factor, and he could ill afford any delays. If those foreign pirates saw any weakness in his position, if they smelled blood, he was sure they would lower their financial offer immediately.

Shields understood why congressmen complained about the cost of winning an election, and they only had to get 50% of the vote; he needed 80%. Thanks to B. C. Smith, Shields could see that he already had a 75% affirmative vote. He could get to 80 on the first ballot as long as nobody blew the lid off his monopoly scam.

Welch was still an unresolved problem that could not be allowed to change the game. Shields yielded to the temptation and placed a quick call to Cory.

"I'm checking to see how your new project is going. I expected you to have that wrapped up by now.

"Nothing to worry about. It's under control," Cory quickly responded. "Some new travel plans have been developed and the details are falling into place. The package will be delivered, and you will find everything in order. I know it's important that this be done the right way."

"Cory, spare me your babble. I've given you a business assignment and you know what you have to do. No excuses. When I delegate to you, I expect you to make me look good. Do you understand?"

"Yes sir, I've got it. I can handle this mission." Cory stood up as he responded.

"Is this job too difficult for you?"

"No sir."

"Then get to it." Shields hung up. He did not like these messy little details when he needed results. People like Welch and Cory needed to understand that there are more important things in the world. His company required that they do their part.

Shields went back to the list of balloters. He needed to get some more converts. *Maybe my congressman will lend me his campaign manager until this ballot initiative is over.*

Howard had provided him with several recommendations. *Considering the size of his consulting fee, he better have some useful suggestions.* The man had negotiated a four year deal that a major league baseball player would be proud of.

The first recommendation was on changes to the initiative's verbiage that would better conceal its intent. Legal was working on it. Second, he knew three voters who could be persuaded to come over to their side without demanding any financial favors in return. He also provided a list of names not to contact. These people were boy scouts that could derail his standard and must be closely monitored.

Doris interrupted his thoughts, "Sir, you have a meeting scheduled with Legal. There're ready for you now."

The first draft of the contract was ready to go to Thomas's legal team of sharks. Versions of the contract could go back and forth for weeks as lawyers argued over each word. Accounting was involved to get every tax advantage possible out of the deal. The meeting went on until Shields broke it up around nine o'clock that evening.

It was time for him to make another trip to the military secure area. By dropping in more often, people weren't so surprised when he showed up. He studied the shift schedules for the guards and staff to make sure he was seen by different people. He went in once during the graveyard shift, but the technicians were so shocked to have anybody visit them they just stood and watched him the whole time.

The second shift, Mona and Steven around 10:00 pm, seemed like the best opportunity. She was a single mother going to school three nights a week, exhausted and probably sleeping when no one else was there. Shields was impressed with her commitment; he would promote her when she graduated. Steven played video games and never looked up; Shields would 'promote' him to the graveyard shift when this was all over.

****

Cory left his office to catch a plane to Philadelphia and meet his contact. Together they would drive unnoticed into New Jersey (like anybody would notice another car in New Jersey). Sitting in the Boeing 737 waiting for takeoff, he thought about his airborne training and wished he could parachute into his objective. It was good to be in the hunt. The kill was what he lived for, and his opportunity was coming soon.

Chapter 23

Welch was in shock that someone in the building, maybe even in his own department was working for John, or was it his imagination? *Do I have trouble making decisions? Well yes and no? Could it really be just a coincidence John and Professor Howard called to start the balloting when I was in a staff meeting? How did they know I would be unavailable?*

Was it Janet? That wouldn't surprise me, but she could just walk into my office and tell me to send it out, unless she didn't want me to suspect she was in on it. Was it somebody on my own staff who betrayed me? It could have been any engineer working in the building.

Welch wanted to tell someone with authority that bad things were happening. Unable to sit still, he got up to go for a walk. Stepping out of the air-conditioned building, he was hit by a humid blanket of stale air baking on the asphalt parking lot. After five minutes, he realized how miserable it was outside and turned around.

To the west, thunderheads were starting to form in the hazy summer sky. The long day's heat would generate an afternoon downpour. Returning to his desk, there was a phone message. "Now what?" He picked up to listen.

"Good afternoon Mr. Welch, this is Doctor Wilson." A woman's voice spoke softly. "I'm in the building over in the International Relations Department. If you have a few minutes, I would like to stop by and introduce myself. Again, it's Doctor Wilson and I look forward to meeting you."

What the heck was that all about? He wanted to dismiss the call and get back to work, or better yet, daydreaming, but he wondered why someone from International was coming by to chat. The last phone call didn't work out too well. Welch looked up just as a woman passed by his window and walked into Janet's office. Professionally dressed, she was tall, slender, and appeared to be Asian.

A minute later, she was walking toward his office. Now he could see her appearance was striking. She had that exotic look that could drive a guy wild. She was a standout, what an American Alpha Male would find haunting—and a doctor.

"Good afternoon, I'm Doctor Wilson. I left a message on your machine. Mind if I come in?" She was standing at his door.

"That was you? Come in, please," he stood to greet her.

She extended her hand and gave a warm enchanting smile as they touched. "Thank you," she said closing the door behind her before sitting down. "You must be wondering why I wanted to meet you."

Well yah. Who are you? And why did you close my office door?

"The reason is I work as a consultant, and many of my clients are either US or Indian firms. Their concern is…"

"Excuse me. PhD or MD?

"Engineering, PhD."

"You're a consultant? Who do you represent, Bain, one of the big firms, or are you independent? " The word consultant left a bad taste. He remembered dealing with the gangsters in pinstripes in previous employment. They would trample any manager who got in their way, and Welch was stupid enough to try.

She could see by his facial expression that the word 'consultant' was a problem. "It's my company, we're not one of those large corporations. I have seven fulltime employees. Here's my card. Maybe you should just consider me a marketing engineer, more like an advisor in public relations.

"Please give me a minute to explain. In today's global economy, standardization is more important than ever. Here's the simple sample example I like to use. America is not on the metric system and uses 110 volts while the rest of the world is on 220. Or, the engineering and safety standards are different for a Boeing aircraft than for an Airbus. The list goes on and on. I work with companies to resolve engineering differences in the international markets, and wanted to meet you as I'm trying to take a more proactive approach to these standardization issues."

"Okay." Welch recognized a good elevator speech but was still a little leery. "What does all that mean, and do you represent any governments?"

"Very good questions. I have dual citizenship, US and Indian. I work for companies in both countries and my current client list also has a company headquartered in England, but they're relatives and don't pay very well."

Welch smiled, but realized that she was not answering his questions. Still, her evasion was mesmerizing. "So where do you call home?" *And why don't you have an accent? Your English is perfect.*

"I was born in northern India, but graduated from MIT and now reside in the US, so I call Virginia home."

That explains the accent. But he was still uncomfortable and gave her an inquisitive look.

"Greg, let me be blunt with you. India has Russia to its north, Pakistan on one border, and China on the other. And they all have nuclear weapons. I'm very happy to have America as an ally and friend to India. My interest is cooperation between the countries as well as improved business and engineering relationships."

Welch relaxed a bit and leaned back in his chair. He was no longer frowning, and realized he was looking her over.

She continued, "I love this country. You do love your country, don't you?"

"Yes I do. It's the planet's best chance." He responded with conviction, but wasn't sure where she was going with it.

"Why, if you don't mine me asking."

For 8,000 years of civilization, humans were ruled by the Divine Right of Kings. About 250 years ago, we decided to try democracy. It provided better government than King George, and was able to defeat Hitler and Stalin. But we killed millions of Native American Indians and keep a lot of slaves. Now, we're 2 and 2, and in the tie breaker. Can we survive our own arrogance and greed?" He stopped talking as he suddenly got the feeling that she was checking him out.

Time to change the subject. "Wilson doesn't sound very Indian." Greg asked, attempting a more playful tone.

"A generation or two back on my father's side, Sir Wilson from the British Empire was one of the last Robber Barons to plunder India before its independence. He married a native Indian and thus begot my father. My mother is half Tibetan and half Thai but that's another story."

"Don't tell me, they met in Brazil."

"No, UCLA Berkeley."

"My second guess. You're a real Heinz 57." He saw the puzzled look on her face. "It means you're a beautiful mix."

She smiled and looked down, then changed the subject, "I heard you were mountain climbing. Isn't it dangerous?"

"Yes, but I get to conquer my fear even if I don't make the summit. The mountain doesn't judge. When I stand on the edge, I have incredible control. I once asked a skydiver with over a hundred jumps that same question about danger. He said, 'Why would you just keep doing something over and over again if you had no fear of it?'"

"Is it your hobby?"

"I wish, but don't get many chances around here. You said India, have you climbed in the Himalayas? That must be a true Zen experience."

"I've trekked in the valleys along the glaciers, and yes, it's a Zen experience. Humans need the horizon to maintain their sense of balance. In the Himalayas, with up and down, you move in a third spatial boundary with an unclear horizon.

"If the mountain you see is green, you may be looking at agriculture that's been there since the dawn of civilization. If you see rock, it was formed under the ocean millions of years ago and is now ten thousand feet above sea level. Yes, it does make you look at time and space in a different way."

She glanced at her watch, "I got carried away and lost track of time. I have to run and catch a plane, but let me ask you. The International Standards meeting in Europe this Fall, will you be going?"

"I wish. That trip is a perk reserved for senior people. It's the one trip everybody wants to take."

"Too bad. I'm surprised. Your experience in getting consensus could be helpful."

"Helpful, in building consensus? Are you sure you have the right Welch?"

"Yes, I'm sure." She smiled, "I think we should get together for lunch next time I'm in town and continue our discussion on international standards, and Zen. Who knows, you may get to go to the International Meeting after all. Besides, I want to try a new Indian restaurant not far from here."

"How about Italian or French or something?" *Anything but Indian food.*

Welch escorted her to the front door and watched her as she walked to her car. She knew he was watching. He noted the high-heels she was wearing, and her shapely legs as she walked away. The skirt of her well-tailored business suit swayed from side to side. *How does she do that?* She was exotic, and something didn't add up and… "How did she know that I went mountain climbing?"

After work, he headed for the gym and did three miles on the treadmill. The workout made his head feel better, but his left knee was sore again, but he could medicate that with vodka and lime.

The alarm woke him from a restless sleep. Welch had dreamed he was back in the army, getting ready to go into combat. A severe weather pattern was approaching, but he couldn't find his gear and had to clean the latrine. It was going to be a bad storm.

Chapter 24

Cory's flight circled for half an hour before landing at Philadelphia International. It took another forty minutes to retrieve his suitcase. But even with the delays, his ride had not shown up. He was about to make a call when he saw the tall, lean man wearing a red NASCAR jacket, cowboy boots, and a Stetson. The man was Clifton Bonner, but he liked the nickname Cowboy— a little odd since Mississippi didn't have many cattle ranches.

The man waved at Cory and walked directly to him. Cory would have preferred something inconspicuous like a head nod or brush of the nose. The Cowboy gave him a good old boy, possum-eaten grin, and grabbed his hand for an oil pumping hand shake. Cory went stiff and pushed Cowboy away, afraid he was going to hug him.

"You're late," Cory said.

"Yea, I couldn't find the place."

"You mean the luggage area?"

"Nah, the airport. Lot of road construction going on, so I missed the turn and took forever to get back."

"Are you sure you weren't being followed?"

"Na, no car in Mississippi can keep up with me."

It was Etta Lou Erwin that Cory could thank for this professional wheelman. At the age of twenty-one, after five years of marriage and four kids, Etta decided it was time to make some changes in her life. She started by shooting her husband Earl. Fortunately for her and him, she only winged him, twice.

Shooting your husband was frowned upon in Mississippi, but when Etta told the Sheriff what was hidden in the tool shed, she was home free. Too bad her husband wasn't smart enough to rent storage space. He was keeping his two bails of weed, three kilos of coke, twelve TV sets and other assorted stolen goods in the tool shed.

After four kids, Etta no longer had the proper asset allocation to make the big bucks at the topless bars like she did when she was single and underage. Instead, she got a job at the new Shields plant that opened just a hoot and holler down the road. She was good with her hands, and even though she was only making minimum wage, it was better than having four kids hanging on her all day. Her dedication was rewarded with a supervisory position giving her the clout to select cousins and other relatives for job openings.

Clifton was her second cousin and had no interest in working a production line. He was going to be a NASCAR driver. He had the mechanical ability, raw nerve, and driving skill to be successful, but he lacked the business smarts, charm, and TV good looks to get a sponsor. Undaunted, Cliff took on jobs to get money to pay for his racing car and pit crew of cousins. He had several wins on the small tracks and was sure that another sponsor could get him into the big time.

If his face held him back in the TV image department, looking mean and ugly was an asset for a security guard. He broke up a gang of five guys who were stealing company equipment and put a cafeteria worker in the hospital for stealing hams. It was these incidents that had brought him to Cory's attention.

They walked to the parking garage, but Cowboy didn't remember where he had parked the car. "Gosh, I've never been in a four story parking lot in my whole life."

Cory was beginning to understand why this guy liked driving on an oval track. He couldn't get lost.

"There it is, right over there where I left it."

You could see why the car might be hard to notice. At first glance, it was a very nondescript late model Chevy, either dark blue or black under a coat of dust. There were no bumper stickers, rebel flags or insignias touting a high performance racing machine.

The Cowboy used his car for business, and he understood the value of being inconspicuous on the interstate. If you did look carefully, you would notice the over-sized tires and a closer inspection would show a beefed-up suspension. But nothing indicated a big block, supercharged, high-performance V8 under the hood. The car was a sleeper.

Cowboy unlocked the trunk and Cory started to throw in his suitcase but stopped.

"Holy shit, what the hell." Lying between an old suitcase and a new toolbox was a sawed off pump, twelve gage next to an aluminum baseball bat.

"Thought we ought to have a little backup firepower just in case, or we could go squirrel hunting if we got some free time."

"This is not Mississippi. Do you have any idea what would happen if we get caught with that in the car? Where are the hand guns? Let me guess, in the toolbox or in the tire well?"

"Na, mine's under the driver's seat where I always keep it, and your 45 is in the glove compartment. I got a hidden compartment under the dash. We can put the handguns there if that will make you feel better."

"Are there any more weapons?"

"Na, no more guns, but I got my little hunting knife in my boot."

"Great, just keep it there."

The two men got in the car and Cory started to pull the seatbelt across his huge midsection. Looking over, he saw the Cowboy wasn't even bothering to buckle up.

"You're a professional driver, don't you use your seat belts?"

"Only when I need them. I've got me this here racing harness, and I'll strap it on when the action starts."

"Think it's the law here. Better buckle up now."

Cowboy locked the waist strap of his harness and turned on the ignition. Cory braced himself, expecting the engine to roar, but the sound was a pleasant surprise. The car did not shake, and the noise was a deep soft rumble. Looking down, he saw Cowboy reach for the Hurst Linkage on the floor shift.

"Four on the floor," Cory commented with a smile. "I always drove an automatic."

"Nope. Six."

They backed out of the parking space and Cowboy put the car in first.

Cory caught the gleam in Cowboy's eye and a smile on his face when he hit the gas. Tires screamed.

Cory was thrown back in his seat. The engine roared as they accelerated though the parking lot until Cowboy slammed on the brakes at the end of the row. "Just wanted ya'll to know that you ain't got nothin' to worry about. You ridin' with the fastest and the best."

It took Cory a few seconds to regain his composure. The car's burst of speed had jarred him, and the noise had disoriented him. He turned to his driver. "Look at me Cliff Cowboy. I'm only going to say this once. Stop the car, put it in park and look at me."

Cowboy realized this was probably not the right time to explain that a stick shift didn't have a park.

"Now," Cory spoke, trying to be cool but commanding like a good drill sergeant. "I'm only going to say this once. You will not speed, and you will obey every law on the books for whatever state we're in. You will only do what I say. If you do not, I will take that shotgun and stick it up your ass and blow your head off. Are we completely clear on who's in charge here?"

"Yes sir. You da man." He replied calmly as he kept right on smiling.

"Good, we understand each other. Let's go." They headed for the exit. "Maps in the glove compartment? You do have maps?"

"Nope, never use'm."

"Pull back around to the airport again, and I'll run into the car rental and get some." *Damn amateurs again, thought he was a pro.*

"How bout we use this?" and he pulled a GPS, out of his glove compartment."

They finally got out of the airport and drove past the Eagles stadium heading for New Jersey. They passed the old Navy shipyard but missed the turnoff for the Walt Whitman Bridge to cross the Delaware River. Doubling back, they got on the bridge, but with all the traffic and construction on I-676, plus the confusion of the intersection, they got on I-295 south instead of north— even with the GPS. Cory was beginning to worry if his plan was such a great idea after all.

"Hey Cowboy, have you ever driven up here before?" Cory asked his new partner. "I need to understand your ability to carry out your part of my plan and follow my orders."

The Cowboy thought he was nobody's fool. "Well, I likes to play my cards close to the vest and not give too much away. But yea, I road shotgun or drove with cousin Red a while back when we was bringing hand guns and ammo all the way up to New York City to sell. So yea, I've been north of the Mason-Dixon Line couple times. The road signs are all still the same. Just less road kill and more cars up in these parts. Been out west to Texas and El Paso, that's one big state, and down into Mexico.

"You won't believe how long it takes to drive cross Texas. Drove out there with Duane and his cousin Hightower. He's a little strange sometimes. Made over $4,000 selling guns and blasting caps the first trip. Now I hear they get'n automatic weapons from Arizona, and don't need transporters to move them down from South Carolina. Used what was left of my share of the money to buy a new set of racing tires and took second at the Birmingham track."

Cory found the Jersey highway system confusing and crowded, especially the circles and jug-handle turns. It seemed they were either bouncing in pot holes or sitting in construction zone traffic. They slowly followed I-295 north. "Your exit is coming up."

"Yep. That's what Hal is tell'en me.

"Who the hell is Hal?

"My GPS. I named him HAL. After the computer in that old movie, '2001, A Space Odyssey'. Remember, that computer that tried to take over the spaceship. Hay, we're get'en on the Turnpike real soon. It's a toll road. You got some cash, right?"

"Yes, I got it."

"Oh, about Texas, you know, once, on the way back from Mexico, we all stopped off at their State Fair just outside of Big D. That's what they calls Dallas down there. That's where Duane lost his ear and couple of fingers in a knife fight with some big ole Mexican hombre. That old wetback was one tough dude. Man that night was like forty miles of bad road.

"Did I ever tell you about the pretty little gal I met in Dallas after we dropped Duane off at the emergency room? We was in this honkey tonk road house outside city limits, and this sweet little blond gal was pole dancing by the piano …"

"Pull into this rest stop coming up. I'm going to run in and get some maps and information"

Back on the road, they drove forty-five miles before getting off at Exit 10 for I-287 where they sat in afternoon rush traffic.

After checking into a hotel in South Plainfield a few miles from the A3E office, the two men carried their belongings up to the room. Cory inspected his new handgun, another Colt 45 semi-automatic. While Cowboy was checking out movies on the TV, Cory studied the GPS and New Jersey maps he had purchased at the rest stop, then he opened Goggle maps. When he found what he wanted, he went to Night Clubs in the Yellow pages.

It was time to go to work.

Chapter 25

It was Friday and Welch had to present his e-ballot system upgrade to the department managers. He had planned to go over the presentation with his boss Caroline that morning to make sure she was on his side, but she was too busy to see him. Now she was sitting in the conference room with Janet and six other managers waiting for his presentation.

As soon as the meeting started, one of Janet's friends brought up some urgent questions about her work, and the meeting was sidetracked for half an hour. When it was Welch's turn to present, Janet interrupted, "could you keep your presentation under twenty minutes, since we're running late."

Throwing his formal presentation out the window, he gave a brief overview, then covered the key points. He passed out a detailed document listing the forty two specific changes the IT team would make to the system.

Checking the time, he had rushed through the presentation too quickly. He decided to finish with the cost-and-time savings the upgrade would achieve. But Janet asked a question and all six women started talking before he could answer. He had lost control.

He turned to Caroline for help, but she shook her head.

After another minute of chaos, Janet stood up and spoke. "Your time's up, but I see many unanswered questions, and you weren't writing down our recommendations. To ensure you get all our ideas, I want everybody to review your list and add their own recommendations. Caroline can set up another meeting next week when you can give us your feedback. Let's get back to our work so we can get out of here for the weekend."

Back in his office, Welch decided he wouldn't be working late. Walking past the executive parking lot, he admired a classic yellow Corvette convertible. Next to it was a brand new red Mustang muscle car. *Some executives reliving his youth.*

Welch remembered the good old days growing up in Texas when Roadrunners, Barracudas, Impalas and Goats (GTO) ruled the road. Every guy in the mid-west knew about a 327 or 383 and the original Hemi 426, all in cubic inches, not liters.

Welch had learned to drive in a used Corvair. It couldn't complete a high speed turn without the back wheels passing the front wheels. Flying home one night, a little old lady ran a stop sign and wrapped his little car around the massive front bumper of her Oldsmobile.

Fate is a hunter, but it missed Welch because of a little bit of luck, and enough common sense or fear not to push the edge of the envelope too often. *You don't get to grow old by being stupid all the time.*

Welch had pumped iron last night, so tonight was aerobic exercise. While on the stationary bike, he noticed a really big guy at the front desk. A blonde wearing a raincoat, standing behind him. He saw it here all the time; they spent $700 for a year's membership to lose weight and lasted about three weeks. *I don't know how to become a VP and make six figures, yet I see VPs that don't know how to lose ten pounds.* Welch finished his workout, showered and headed to the grocery store.

The first grocery cart hooked hard to the right. He kicked the cart and grabbed the next one which was marginally better. Inside the store, he systematically went down the aisles remembering what he needed. At the fresh produce section, he stopped to get some tomatoes.

She was standing by the cucumber bin, gently caressing one in her hand. No clothing could hide that figure, and she wasn't trying to hide anything. Welch stared like a schoolboy. She looked like that woman he had seen earlier in the gym. *I guess women that look like that buy groceries too. I've just never seen one here before.* She looked directly at him, smiled and dropped the cucumber.

He instinctively rushed over to pick it up. As she bent down, her skirt rode up and he caught himself staring at her legs. He was still staring when she looked into his eyes and the words "Thank you." flowed from her wet lips.

He responded weakly, "You're welcome." As they both stood up, his eyes struggled to work their way back to her face. It was a long journey with several detours. She had a face that still looked young but not too innocent. Her red lips smiled, and her eyes twinkled. She liked being in the game.

"I'm Sandra, my friends call me Sandy."

Welch's brain realized she was talking to him, and he needed to respond. "Hi. I'm Greg, my friends call me Greg." *Stupid response.* "I see you're buying food in the organic produce department. You look healthy. Come here often?" *No. I don't believe I said that.* He watched her caress the cucumber in her hands as the still conscious part of his brain realized he was babbling.

She gave him a 'what are you talking about look,' but then responded. "I find ways to get my exercise. Do you think I'm in good shape?" She rubbed the cucumber up the curve in her waist and across her breast.

"You look in great shape."

"Thank you," she replied with a submissive smile and her head slightly bowed.

He realized he was supposed to say something. "Ah, come here often, to shop I mean?" *It's better than what's your sign?*

"No, I'm new in town." *Why do men always love this line? Do I sound like I need a big strong daddy to take care of me?*

Let me show you around, No, too forward. "This can be a confusing area to learn your way around, in traffic and all." *Ah, she's new in town, lonely, maybe no boyfriend yet. Maybe she's looking for someone to show her around.* "Where are you from?"

"Pennsylvania, but now I'm working at the KitCat Sports Grill. Have you ever heard of it?"

"No, but it sounds nice. I'll just have to pay it a visit." He felt his confidence return. *I wonder if she's a dancer. At a sports bar? Nah, must be a bartender or waitress.*

"A visit would be nice, how about coming by tonight?"

That was quick. "Sure, what time do you get off? Work, I mean. When are you going to be there?"

"Oh, I'm not working tonight. You can meet me there in an hour. How are you at remembering directions? It's a little ways up the Parkway…"

In retrospect it was so obvious, he would ask himself "How could I be so stupid? What was I thinking?"

Any woman watching the conversation would know exactly what was going on and know the correct question was, "What was he thinking with?"

Welch rushed home and ran into his apartment to write down the directions while ignoring all the implications of his actions. *Was it left then right at the light or right then left at the second light? Does that count the* *light I stopped for at the e*xit? He dashed back to the car and grabbed his groceries, put the cold stuff in the refrigerator and left the rest in the bag. He changed into his favorite red shirt, brushed his teeth, and combed his hair. Jumping back in the car, he raced down the road to I-287 and hit New Jersey's weekly summer disaster—Shore Traffic.

New Jersey, the most densely populated state in the Union, has only one major highway that lets the Northern half of the state go 'down the Shore'. The Garden State Parkway averages 1.1 million cars a day, and today was double the average. Welch crawled along with traffic in his old gray Mercury Cougar, praying the car wouldn't overheat.

I got the car from my father. He sold it to me on his death bed. It was a cash deal, he wouldn't accept my check. Even when the Mercury Cougar with its big V8 was new, the performance was mediocre and the handling terrible. All the weight was over the front wheels, the opposite of the Corvair. With over a hundred thirty thousand miles, it was an accident waiting to happen.

He sweated in the heat and cursed his misfortune as he sat in traffic. While sitting in the car fantasizing about Sandy, a wave of guilt flowed over him. He reminded himself that he and Linda could date other people. His mind jumped to a girlfriend from not too long ago, Jean Taylor. The association was head-to-toe sexuality, enhanced with silicone implants. Considering her naturally endowed beauty, the implants must have been a psychological crutch.

He recalled their meeting on a ski trip to Killington, Vermont. Jean was from old money up in Boston, and her father was a judge. The family name was Winfred, but she kept the last name of her second husband even after her third divorce. Welch was sure she drove them all insane.

She had a PhD. in Psychology, which he found appropriate since he thought she had a multiple personality disorder—or multiple personalities disorders because they were all pretty screwed up. He never knew who he was going to date when he picked her up. A weekend with her was the equivalent of three nights of speed dating.

Welch knew he shouldn't complain since he always got to drive her Jaguar F-TYPE Coupe to her country club for the polo games. She believed the riders were "death defying daredevils charging around on horseback." To someone from Boston, maybe they were daredevils, but to someone who grew up working on ranches in Texas, watching rich men ride horses in an open field was all rather dull.

Only one thing was duller, their sex life. As beautiful as she was, sex with her had all the passion of taking Novocain at the dentist office. "Put your head back, turn left, a little to the right, a little more, that's the spot, hold it, a little longer, now you can spit, that wasn't so bad was it, we'll continue in ten minutes, but first, I want to critique you on what you did wrong and how to do it better next time."

They did it all, but it was all the same—no fire, lust, or joy, and absolutely no passion or intimacy. She was a great novelty, but he could not find a reason to keep going back.

As much as he hated giving up that Jaguar, he broke up with Jean after meeting Linda. Being a modern sensitive man, he didn't just say, "I'll call you tomorrow," and then never call; he told her he was leaving via email.

Even with all the electronic dating services, it was difficult to find an attractive, mature woman with her head on straight. He knew women had the same complaints about men. All the good ones are taken. All the single women are religious fanatics. All the single men are sports fanatics. *Where do all the good ones hide?*

Welch didn't know, but he was driven to keep on searching, just like all the other singles stuck in traffic as they drove to their parties down the Shore.

Chapter 26

Welch finally made it to the Parkway North. A few cars behind was the dark Chevy. The sun was red and low in the summer sky, but the air was still hot, humid and hazy. A heavy thundershower had passed over, and the road was slick. Traffic was bumper to bumper on the four lanes going south toward the Jersey Shore. Going north, all four lanes were heavy but moving fast. Welch accelerated to seventy five as he maneuvered into the fast lane.

Along this stretch of highway, there was no divider, only a fifty foot field of grass with an occasional tree separating cars moving past each other with a relative speed of up to a hundred fifty mph. Welch was only thinking about the cars in front of him, and Sandy's body.

The dark Chevy pulled into his passenger side blind spot.

Santana's "Black Magic Woman" came on the radio. He reached down and cranked up the volume.

Bang!

His car was spinning. If the pavement wasn't soaked, he would have been knocked across the divide, smashing into oncoming traffic. With bald tires on wet road, he was hydro-gliding down the

Parkway. The car had performed a slow 180 degree spin. He found himself looking at the car that just hit him.

Welch went into reflex mode and started pumping the brake. The black car tapped him again. He turned the wheel to execute another one eighty, but he wasn't that good.

Over-steering, the car skid off the road. The two left wheels hit the soft ground in the middle divider, pulling him across the divide toward the oncoming traffic.

Turning the wheels away from traffic, he went into another spin, sliding past a tree. He slammed on the brakes and controlled the car as it slid to a stop on wet grass. His hands started to shake as his brain went off reflex and tried to return to think mode.

"Relax. The car with two men, where is it?" he yelled to himself in the excitement. In the rearview mirror, he saw the car cutting across the grass divide. *What the hell. Why?*

"Call the cops! Where's my phone?" still talking to himself. It wasn't on the center console, and he didn't see it on the floor. The black car was coming closer.

Welch hit the gas and pulled into the left passing lane, now going south. Swerving to avoid cars, he tried to merge. Looking back, they were gaining on him. Traffic was heavy and not moving over fifty.

Checking his side view mirror, he saw the other car driving on the shoulder. "Never a cop when you need them." Welch pulled onto the shoulder and accelerated to eighty, passing cars in the passing lane.

The road narrowed for an overpass and the shoulder disappeared, forcing both cars back into the fast lane. Horns blasted and tires shrieked as he cut in the highway traffic. *Great, now I've got six cars out to get me.*

Traffic slowed and they were bumper to bumper. The little old lady Greg had just cut off was waving with one finger. The old man in the next lane was praying no one would hit his new Cadillac. Traffic slowed to forty. "Great, only in New Jersey can you have a low speed car chase."

He wondered if the men in the black car could see him in the heavy traffic. Changing lanes, he moving to the right. Traffic continued to slow. *If we go any slower, they can get out of their car and walk up to me.* He locked the car doors.

Crawling along, they were a few hundred yards from an exit when Welch came to a complete stop. It was not a good option to sit and wait. He pulled on the shoulder to go for the exit. "Are they following me?" In his rear mirror he saw the black car racing behind him. He hit the gas.

Welch saw the exit coming, and knew he was traveling too fast. The road ahead was a dead man's curve. He had taken it at fifty, but now he was doing seventy. The other car was closing in as he entered the turn.

Moving to the inside of the curve, he slammed on the brakes. The car decelerated as it slid across the road. He floored it to straighten out. There was not enough power and not enough traction. He continued to slide. The wheels smashed into the curb.

Hubcaps went flying. Momentum lifted the right wheels off the road. His side-view mirror was decapitated by the guard rail, but he managed to keep the car from flipping.

Welch realized he was excited yet calm. The driving was giving him a sense of control. The fear subsided as his energy focused on the task. Keeping his foot to the floor, he entered I-287 heading north. He patted the dashboard, "Stay with me baby, and I'll take you to the carwash, my treat."

The setting sun painted a peaceful twilight of soft colors across the sky. Traffic was still packed going south but light going north with him. He saw a car swerve across the highway in the rearview mirror and kept the pedal to the metal.

"Now what? I could use a little help here. The police station, I know where it is." *Can I get there before the car catches me?* 'Black Magic Woman's' instrumental came on the radio. "It's all happening to fast. Relax, get in the groove, focus." Looking at the open highway flying by was hypnotic. He felt in control.

Cowboy wasn't expecting the bad turn on the ramp and almost lost it, even with a big downshift. Swinging out onto I-287, he saw the Mercury taillights in the distance and the open road ahead. A car chase was what he lived for.

Cory saw a crazy look on Cowboy's face as they fed off their adrenaline. Cowboy reached under the steering wheel and flipped a switch. There was a loud clank, then the engine screamed as the GMC Supercharger came to life. Acceleration slammed Cory back in his seat.

Welch's speedometer was top-end at hundred fifteen. It was suicide on tires with over fifty thousand miles. He put the distractions aside and breathed slowly. *Relax, don't over-steer.*

A car in front; he gently changed lanes to fly by it. The highway curved, he used three lanes to keep the car under control. "Relax, listen to Santana, deep breaths, let the force be with you. I can do this, less than two miles to go."

The dark car's headlights flooded Greg's mirror. He carefully changed lanes. The Chevy banged his rear side. He pulled directly in front of the dark car so he could only be hit from the rear. The Cowboy changed lanes, and tried to spin him again. Welch fought to maintain control.

The dark car pulled alongside to hit him again. Welch slammed on the brakes and the other car shot past him. He rode the brakes, taking the exit at sixty. Hitting the horn, he slid through a traffic light. Looking back, the other car was coming down the ramp. "Who are those guys?"

He turned onto a two lane road going under I-287. On his left was the county golf course and on his right was an open area with a mile of soccer fields and baseball diamonds. A sharp S curve was coming up fast, then he would be home safe at the police station a few miles away.

He tried to slow down, but the brakes had faded.

He grabbed the shift and dropped into low. The engine screamed as he entered the curve, making the first turn but not the second. He landed in the ditch.

His mind was racing. "Relax, think, put the car in park. Start the engine, now in drive." The engine revved, but he was not moving. "Try again, gently, try reverse, low, nothing. I'm stuck." One rear wheel was spinning in the air, but the other wheel remained motionless in the ditch.

Headlights were coming up fast. He jumped from the car and started running for his life through the open field. Looking over his shoulder, the dark car had pulled into a parking lot and was driving on the soccer fields, coming after him. He turned, heading for the nearest tree line. Welch didn't look back, running with everything he had.

The Chevy was behind him. He heard the engine roar and the headlights lit up the night.

Hitting the tree line, he continued as the black car stopped behind him. He was in the woods before they got out of their car. Welch kept running. It was dark, and he could barely see to zigzag as he ran through the trees.

Out of breath, he could not maintain the all-out pace. He ran across another road into the woods and turned left. Traveling parallel to the road, the ground was rocky and dangerous to run on in the dark. He ducked down behind a large tree to watch the road. Breathing deep to calm down, he sat motionless and waited.

He was sweating all over and had to concentrate to keep his knees from shaking. Five minutes felt like an hour. *Is it safe?* He waited a little longer. An old van, a white Ford and a little Toyota SUV went by.

Slowly standing, Welch felt the cool night air on his face. Quietly brushing the leaves and grass off his clothes, he scanned the area for any sound or motion. He took a step then stopped. Someone was walking on the road.

From behind, he heard another car and saw the headlights coming into view. He knew by the sound of the engine it was the dark car, its high beams silhouetted a large man walking along the road. The Chevy stopped a few feet from Welch. He watched the large man put his hand up to block the headlight glare. "Turnoff your high beams, stupid. I can't see a damn thing now."

"Nothing here to see or shoot," the Cowboy replied as he stepped out of the car holding the shotgun. "Now what we going to do?"

"You're going to put that shotgun away before someone sees us. This is a covert strategical strike, not an open war."

Cowboy shook his head then tossed the gun on the driver's seat. "Gots to take a leak." He stepped to the side of the road, walking directly toward Welch standing motionless in the dark. As he relieved himself, his eyes adjusted to the night. Looking up, he stared at the silhouette in the dark.

"There he is!" he yelled and pulled the knife from his boot. He stepped in taking advantage of his reach with the knife in a slashing motion. Welch leaned back while attempting an off balance sidekick. The knife missed, but the weak kick connected, stopping Cowboy's momentum.

Attacking with a lunge, Welch sidestepped the charge, but could not counter with bad footing on loose rock. He was in trouble with one opponent in front and the other rushing to join the fight. It would be two against one in five seconds.

Welch stepped back to escape into the night. The Cowboy charged, but stumbled on the rocky ground, landing on one knee

Welch sprang forward delivering his front kick into the Cowboy's face. The man went down immediately with blood pouring from his broken nose and split lip. Welch saw the big man at the edge of the road pulling a gun from his belt. Welch stepped back in the shadows and merged into the night.

Welch moved along the edge of the road to maintain visual contact with the enemy. He watched the big man kick and curse the driver before dragging him back to the car. The car drove off as he lingered in the dark.

Welch felt compelled to tell the authorities, but tell them what? He was involved in a high speed road race? Maybe the police were already looking for them or him. *Not a good idea to turn yourself in. But they started it. And two guys with guns tried to kill me, and it was probably a second attempt? I have to tell somebody.*

Monopoly Games

Chapter 27

Welch made his way through the woods, avoiding the roads and open fields to reach the police station. He checked out the parking lot for a dark Chevy before he entered the building and stood in a small, claustrophobic waiting room. A cop looked down at him through a large Plexiglas window.

Welch was tempted to say 'I'm looking for Sara Connors' but figured the cop had heard those lines before.

"I'd like to report an attempted mur… no, a hit and run." *Keep your story straight.*

"Is anybody hurt?"

"Ya, me!" *Calm down.*

"Have you been drinking?"

"No sir." *But I could sure use one.*

"You look okay. Do you require any medical attention?"

"No, I don't think so." *But you might want to check the hospital for someone with a broken face.*

The cop grabbed some forms and was about to slide them through the tray door. "When did it happen?"

"Look, I think the guy waved a gun at me." He suddenly had the cop's attention. "It happened about half an hour ago. My car is two miles from here, in the ditch alongside the road."

"Is it a silver gray Mercury?"

"Yes, did you see them…. or something?"

"No, we just ticketed your car for illegal parking."

"You what? Do I get points against my license for that? Anyway, it was a black or dark blue car, a Chevy."

"What year?"

"I don't know. They all look alike."

"So it was some year, some color, are you sure it was a Chevy?"

"Yes, I think. It chased me and ran me off the road. Since those maniacs with guns may still be out there, don't you think you should at least look into it?"

"So you're saying he didn't actually hit you. Do you want to file a complaint?"

"Hell yeah! What the hell do you think I walked here for, pleasant conversation?" Welch realized he just stepped over the line and shut up.

"Don't get smart with me boy." The cop then turned and yelled over his shoulder. "Hey sarg, got the owner of the Merc that was called in. Says he was run off the road and wants to make a statement."

Boy, Welch bit his lip. *Did he call me boy? Am I in Mississippi? I'm older than you cop.*

Welch was checked for weapons then ushered through a steel reinforced security door into an office area and seated by one of the desks. A patrolman with stripes on his shoulder sat behind the desk. Welch showed his driver's license and A3E slot key for identification. He gave the cop the version of the story he had decided on, starting at the traffic light by the I-287 exit.

"Two men pulled up beside me and pointed their guns at me. I took off and they chased me. I was driving here when I missed the turn. The car was following me, so I ran across some fields, and it still chased me and almost ran me down. You can go look at the tire tracks on the soccer field."

Welch gave the best description he could on the car, but there was very little he could tell the cop about the two men. "One was big and fat, and one was tall and ugly with a bloody broken nose, and had a pump shotgun."

"Can you identify them in a lineup?"

"I doubt it, maybe."

"You didn't happen to get a license plate number?"

He closed his eyes. "There was no plate on the front of the car. That would mean they're from out of state, or lost their front plate, or just covered it up, or removed it. That wasn't very helpful, was it?"

When the questioning was over, Welch asked if he could use the restroom and make a phone call to AAA. His cell phone was still in the car, he hoped.

When Welch stepped out of the bathroom, he saw the sergeant talking with two tall men in dark suits; one of them was on his smartphone. They all stopped talking and stared at him. Welch looked down and checked his fly.

The sergeant called out, "Sir, these two men would like to ask you a few more questions, make sure we get all the facts. Why don't you use the office space in that room?"

"Sure, no problem." Welch hoped he could get some real help from them. He assumed they were two detectives and wondered if they'd found the other car and some guns. *Maybe I should tell them about Chicago, and then they'd know I'm not crazy.* He fell in between them as the three walked into the room.

"Oops, this looks to me like an interrogation room and not your office." *The mirror on the wall gave it away.*

The two men were tall and WASP with short hair, wearing dark suits, white shirts, and dark blue ties. Welch wondered if they were interchangeable. They motioned for him to sit, and he cautiously pulled up a chair; it screeched as it slid across the floor.

One of them sat on the other side of the table and started reading Welch's statement. The other guy leaned against the wall and smiled. *Is this going to be a good cop bad cop thing?* Welch fidgeted impatiently while he waited for the man to finish reading.

"It's Gregory Welch, am I pronouncing that right?"

"Yes, and you are?" *Is English your second language?*

He looked at Welch as if he was measuring him. "I'm Allen and this is my partner, Jack." Jack nodded and smiled again. He had nice teeth. "You live here in town and work at A3E, is that right?"

He nodded yes.

"What do you do there?"

"I'm a manager in the Standards Development Group. It's my responsibility to ensure that a standard developed by the A3E is fair, open and balanced." Welch could have gone with his ego-inflating, canned elevator speech, but he could see they were not at all impressed, so he shut up.

"Standards Development, okay." He made a note on the paper. "Can you tell us where you were earlier tonight, before the incident with the dark colored car?"

"Home, and driving around." Gulp, Welch pulled at his collar. *Did they see me starting to panic?* "Why do you ask?" Welch broke eye contact and starred at the papers on the desk.

"It's important that we tie up any loose ends," Allen replied. "Do you have anyone to corroborate your story?"

"Corroborate my story?" Welch didn't like where this was going. "Do I need a lawyer? I feel like I'm being accused of something."

"Are you feeling guilty about something?"

Welch rolled his eyes toward the ceiling. *The old Jedi mind trick. These guys are good, better just shut up.* "No." There was a silent, pregnant pause that was carried to term. Welch had been in sales, so he knew this one. The first guy who talks, loses. A long, slow thirty seconds ticked by.

"Mr. Welch, help me understand this. From your angle in the car, how could you identify the weapons, but not their faces?

"I was focused on the guns pointed at me." Welch forced himself to be still.

"But you gave one man a bloody nose."

"It was dark."

Silence.

"That will be all for now."

"Greg, one last thing, Jack interjected. "You said you manage the Standards Group, right? So you work with companies making Standards, right? Are you working with any companies right now?"

"About a hundred on any given day."

The two agents grinned at each other. Allen turned to Welch. "We have your home and work address. We'll be paying you another visit soon."

"Great, I'll serve milk and cookies." As Welch walked away looking over his shoulder, he could see Jack was already on his phone again.

****

Cory was on a high. The chase had been his biggest thrill since he was airborne. It scared the hell out of him, but that just made it a better adrenaline rush.

He was also pissed. His quarry had escaped, and it was Cowboy's fault. But Cory was the hunter and would win the game. *It would be a great win, a bowl game win, a Super Bowl victory.* The opponent was damn good, and that's what made the challenge so exciting.

He was afraid he would have to dump the Cowboy at the hospital emergency room to stop the bleeding. The man could barely drive back to the motel. His nose was flat on a puffed up, ugly face. Cory walked to a nearby CVS and purchased bandages, a neck brace and aspirin.

With his army training, he did a good job of stopping the nose bleed. In his anger, he wished he could have done it by tying a tourniquet around Cowboy's neck. Cory used the hotel ice machine and put ice packs on Cowboy's face. Both eyes were swollen shut, and he would be unable to drive for a few days.

Cory, who learned to drive in an Eldorado, had never driven a stick shift and learning with that hot rod in New Jersey traffic was not a good idea. After grinding gears and stalling out half a dozen times in the motel parking lot without ever getting the car into second gear, he ran out of patients. Slamming the door, kicking the bumper and spitting on the window,

243

he returned to his room to wait until his wheelman had recovered.

Cory felt empty sitting in the motel while Cowboy slept. Hidden in the lining of his suitcase was his beautiful white nose powder. He would take a good hit, then hop a cab back to the club where he had hired the stripper.

Sandra and her sister Sheila would make a good package. Both were for him. Losers like the Cowboy had to pay for their own entertainment. Tonight, Cory was going to party big time. Tomorrow he would resume the hunt. Chuck would be pleased.

Chapter 28

An hour after leaving the police station, a Triple A tow truck pulled Greg's car out of the ditch. After the truck left, Welch noticed the rear tire was flat. Thankful it was the only damage done, he changed the tire and removed the parking ticket. Turning the key, a loud bang scared him half to death.

Pulling over, he looked under the car to see that the muffler was about to fall off; one more repair bill to pay. "At least the muffler's under a lifetime warranty. But they'll charge me a hundred bucks in labor."

He parked his car at the far end of the apartment complex, and moved through the shadows looking for any suspicious people or cars. He checked the bolt on his door before entering, then locked it behind him. He turned on the air conditioner and took a straight swig of vodka out of the bottle before mixing himself a cocktail with organic cranberry-grape juice.

After his second drink, he stopped peeking out the windows. Inspecting the door lock again, he leaned a chair against it then took a long hot and cold shower. He double-checked all the window locks before going to bed but couldn't sleep. After a midnight snack, he fell asleep on the couch by the air conditioner with the TV on.

****

Shields left his office and went to the secure production area. The guards at the door recognized him as planned. The first guard, following procedures, asked to look inside his briefcase. He complied, signed in, and entered the secure area.

The lights were on, but the production area was deserted. There was no second shift working tonight. Shields realized he could save on the electric bill if the lights were turned off at night.

Using his slot key, Shields opened the first lock. He announced his presence with the intercom and Mona buzzed him into the control room. Steven looked up to see who was joining them at that late hour. Seeing it was the company President, he stood and gave the proper greeting.

"Good evening Mona, Steven. Sorry to disturb you. Please just go about your business." Shields said as he walked directly into their space while maintaining strong eye contact. Both looked down and away.

"Mona, doing your homework I see. That's making good use of your time. You're graduating next year, right?"

"Yes sir, finally,"

"Well, be sure to send me an invitation to the graduation. Now if you'll excuse me, I've got to do a little homework myself. That's the way of the world today." Shields noticed Steven was playing with the same E-gaming toy his son had, and shook his head. "I'm going over here so I can concentrate and get my work done. If there are no interruptions, I should be out of your way shortly." He figured that should give them the hint.

Shields walked to an empty terminal in the corner with the screen facing away from the technicians. He placed the briefcase on the desk, further blocking their view, then looked over his shoulder as he entered the password he had memorized. The room was cool, but sweat started to form on his brow as he slipped a flash drive out of his coat pocket.

Another quick check to make sure no one was watching, and he plugged the device into the computer while it booted up.

He glanced up at Mona again. His hands trembled on the keyboard as he entered the commands that took him to the files he needed. Shields smiled and almost laughed out loud, realizing *this job is making me paranoid as well as rich.*

As he waited, a queasy feeling hit his stomach and his mind went back to the boat, replaying the incident with the sharks. He started to tap his foot. The feeling of helplessness on the boat with Chen still bothered him. But with a quick click on copy, he regained a sense of control and convinced himself that he was as powerful as the pirates.

He moved to the next file. Watching the information transfer, he thought of the money transfer. *Money,* he whispered the sweet word to himself. Shields wasn't sure what he would do with a slush fund that big, but it sure felt good to have it. *Is this how Chen controls the sharks? How can I use my wealth to build more power and influence?*

"Mr. Shields." It was Mona, and she was walking over to him.

Download complete was blinking on his monitor.

Chuck stood up to block her view and hit his knee on the table leg. *Shit, shit.*

"Mr. Shields, I'm sorry to interrupt, but I see you're working on the computer."

She leaned to her left, but his briefcase blocked the screen.

"What is it?" he said defensively, causing her to recoil. "Sorry, I had something else on my mind. *Can't this woman take a hint? "So* what do you want, Mona?"

"Sir, I'm sorry. Did you bump your leg?

"I'm fine."

"I see you're working late and wondered if I could do any of your research for you. I have to be here for another two hours. I don't know what you need, but I have full clearance and thought I could help."

Shields sat on the edge of the desk to better block her view. "No Mona," he said then paused because he had momentarily forgotten the lines, he had rehearsed for such an interruption. "Look, don't worry about me. I just need to look at something for our planning. The Air Force is considering some more modifications. We have to determine what that involves. You just go back and do your homework, that's the most valuable thing you can do for me. Go ahead; I'm almost finished."

She walked back to her desk and textbook.

Shields let out a sigh of relief and rubbed his bruised knee. When no one was looking, he removed the flash drive and slipped it back in his coat pocket. Then he opened another file since he couldn't get up and leave immediately. After the appropriate wait, Shields turned off the machine and rose from his seat. Mona looked up from her textbook, but Steven never looked up from his toy. Chuck gave her a nod and a little wave. "Don't get up. Keep studying, see you soon," and he headed out the door.

Mona thought about the CEO of a company working at 10:00 at night. *God, I wonder if all this studying is worth it, if I'm going to be working like that for the rest of my life.* But still, she admired his work ethic and rated him acceptable as a boss. Steven's comment summed up his views with, "Shields must be a real asshole to be the CEO and have to work at this hour of the night."

The guard, following standard operating procedures (SOP), inspected Shields's briefcase while he signed out. As soon as he walked away, the guard went back to the World Federation Wrestling matches on his portable TV.

Back in his own office, Shields sensed his heart was beating fast and felt light headed. He poured himself a scotch to relax and celebrate his achievement. "To my continued success and good fortune" he toasted himself. *It was all too easy. No wonder so many government secrets get stolen; no wonder this country is falling apart. I'll keep the flash drive in my home safe until it is time for the transfer. It obviously isn't secure around here.*

Then he thought about the drive in his home with his family, and imagined the sharks swimming around his house. Now that he had done it, he wondered if he should have done it. Pouring another drink, he worried that his action would put his family in danger. Chuck was the protector of his home; he could never let it happen.

Those feelings and concerns sat in the back of his mind as he took another sip of scotch. Shields didn't like to think about those feelings, so he pushed them aside, but he knew they were there. He focused on the knowledge that his superior intellect would let him succeed and protect his family.

****

Morning sun broke through the windows. Welch realized he was no longer sleeping and sat up. He remembered the car chase, the police station, Sandra. No, it wasn't a dream. Cautiously getting up, he peeked out the window and saw children playing in the parking lot. He quietly laughed and shook his head at the absurdity that this was the same world he had lived in last night.

Now he knew it was deliberate. *Just because you're paranoid, it doesn't mean nobody is out to get you.* He didn't know what he was supposed to feel, or do. Should he be afraid, relieved, excited? *All of the above. Is this the new norm?* Not sure, he procrastinated with *live in the moment* and *one day at a time.*

He tried to call Linda. He wanted to tell her he loved her, and life without her had no meaning. He wanted to ask forgiveness for how he took her for granted, and he wanted her to know that he put her on a pedestal. But no one answered, and though he knew better, he felt annoyed that she was not there for him.

He started to worry, then rationalized his concern. *I know she turns off her phone when she's working or at the gym. She wouldn't answer if she were driving.* He didn't leave a message.

Later that afternoon, he followed Sandra's directions to the Kit Cat Grill. It wasn't there. "Surprise, surprise." On the way home he pulled off the road by the I-287 exit ramp and walked back to the dead man's curve. He found his side view mirror lying on the shoulder. He picked up one of the hubcaps, but the other was long gone.

He stopped by the gym for a workout, but his heart wasn't in it. It occurred to him that the big guy at the front desk last night might have been in the Chevy. The woman could have been Sandra. He checked at the desk, but no new members had signed up last night.

He reminded himself, *the gym isn't a good place to meet women.* He did remember meeting one hot number at the gym, a very sexy little divorcée, blonde, five two, and could still fit into her college cheerleader outfit. She worked as an elementary school teacher in one of the wealthy school-districts.

The two of them were having a nice evening of wine and sushi until Welch made a political comment. After time in the Army, he had some opinions about when America should put boots on the ground. To her, his view was tantamount to cowardly treason. Much to his surprise, she was an extreme Neocon; her copy of Mein Kampf gave it away. *Never discuss religion or politics with a woman until after you go to bed with her.*

****

Sunday morning Shields went to church with the family, followed by tennis at the club. Years of private lessons on the family court, and his height gave him an advantage. He had won the club doubles championship three years in a row, but then his partner got cancer and Shields hadn't seen the guy since. Now he was having problems finding a new partner for the club tournament.

He felt most of his buddies at the club were poor team players. "Doubles," as he explained, "It's a team sport. My partner has to get out of the way when I can make a shot and get the shot if it's out of my reach."

Sunday afternoon Shields loaded up his Gulfstream with the company war council, and headed for Canada. The temperature in Ohio was reaching 100 degrees, and the heat wave was forecast to last all week.

Ballot results were coming in, and several strategic decisions had to be made. What better place to do it than in the cool mountain air at the St. Louise Lake Hotel by Banff National Park. Throw in a few rounds of golf with a couple of government clients, a Japanese partner, and presto, you've got the perfect business conference with one big write-off.

Immediately after takeoff, the men got down to business. It started with a presentation by Reisberg that had been approved by Shields. "Gentlemen, I have good news. Our sources monitoring the Federal Communication Commission are saying the telecoms and major players have not expressed interest in the new frequencies now available. Their strategy, and all their resources are focused on Wi-Fi, and they are going after the TV spectrum to get more bandwidth."

Reisberg held up an official looking document and read slowly for emphasis, "Multiple reliable sources confirm that over the next ten years, all airwave TV antenna reception in the US will be discontinued. Only cable or satellite delivery will be available. Those TV frequencies will become dedicated to cellphone use only. The Bells want to end all residential landline phones in the US. Only cellular and Wi-Fi will remain. Congress is on board with big carriers." A dramatic pause followed as he placed the document on the podium.

He clenched his fist and raised his intensity, "We all know Wi-Fi services have all kinds of security problems. More important, it has a maximum point to point range of only about sixty miles. By using the new available spectrum, our radios are completely secure and have more than triple the range with only a nine volt battery. Gentlemen, we have the opportunity and potential to become the next monopoly in communications."

The jet cabin went silent followed by a burst of applause and excitement. Shields let everyone talk and enjoy the euphoria while he made a mental note to himself. *Hold private meeting with financial people to issue more stock. Use my Bahamas bank account to set up a straw company and buy up the new stock offering, driving up the price. Yes, my arrangement with the multinational will catapult me onto the world stage. It's a Grand Slam. I'll be on the cover of many magazines.*

Shields gave everybody another minute before bringing the group back to the current issues. The balloting was the last remaining hurdle. Most of the ballots were in and nobody had blown the lid off their plan. The most common reason for a negative vote was because the engineers that were paying attention realized they were not being given all the information they needed to understand the parameters.

If they had all the information, it wouldn't take long to figure out the standard ballot process was a sham that created a monopoly. Some real double talk had to be crafted as a response to their negative ballots.

Most people, engineers included, aren't looking for a lie, and most people only find what they're looking for. For anyone who did find the dirty little secret, they would have to be persuaded to come over to the Dark Side. The phones would be manned, and promises would be made.

There was work to do, but the numbers looked good, and Shields was confident everything was going according to plan. After assigning new responsibilities to his people, he had the pilot contact the hotel to reserve a tee-time. Returning to his seat, refreshments were served as they worked until they landed.

With light from a setting sun in the clear mountain air, Shields played a quick nine holes with Thomas Dumont, who had arrived that afternoon. They were joined by their respective legal representatives involved in the detailed negotiations for the Taiwan facility. Shields played a great game, but still could not beat Thomas. He was sure he was being hustled.

After the game, when the two men were alone in the bar, Thomas spoke, "Mr. Chen has asked me to check with you on the additional information you are providing to close the deal."

Shields felt annoyed that someone was being sent to check up on him. He took a breath to measure his response, sat up straight to stare down at Thomas, then quietly responded, "You can tell Mr. Samuel Chen I have all the information. I can give it to you now, or I can fly out and hand it to him personally as soon as we get the financials resolved on the facility sale. There are major tax concessions important to my business operation that I want. Your accountants know what they are. As soon as all this is put to bed, he can have his 'additional' information."

He paused, but then continued in a louder, impatient voice. "And tell him and his freaky friends to get the rest of their money ready for transfer. As soon as we sign this deal, I'll be at the Atlantis the next day for the rest of my share of our agreement."

"That's good," Dumont responded in a reassuring voice without blinking. "I don't know all the details you're talking about, but I'll relay the message exactly as you told me. I'm sure that's what Chen and his associates wanted to hear.

"By the way, I was told they have excellent facilities at this resort so I'm going to the gym to pump some iron and get a massage. Catch you later at the restaurant. Let me buy your boys a bottle of champagne to celebrate. "

Shields felt better after his little outburst, and was sure he had put Dumont in his place. Things were going according to Shields's plan, and that meant he was in control. The money would soon be in his account and all his problems would be over. His future was looking good, as he always knew it would.

Chapter 29

Wyoming is a big state, and Manderville, Wyoming, is a small town far from the Interstate Highway system in time and distance. Folks said it was in the middle of nowhere and next to nothing. The town had two trailer parks, one old, the other older. Enchantment Village, the older park, was now predominantly Hispanic.

Rodriquez, Spanish on his father's side, returned home to Enchantment after his medical discharge from the Navy. He lost a leg from the knee down in an accident off the coast of China. V.A. benefits and his wife working enabled them to survive and raise four children.

The oldest son, Adam, was now serving twenty to life for bank robbery and manslaughter. The oldest daughter had committed suicide after multiple arrests for prostitution and drugs. His other daughter, married and divorced with two children, was a waitress at the Cross Roads Diner on Highway 789. She would visit her parents but never leave her kids alone with them.

There were whispers of child molestation, but the town was not ready to believe such things. The father was a good Christian and a patriotic American war veteran. It was alright for a veteran to drink a little too much. He still went to church with his wife every Sunday and she taught Sunday school.

His youngest son, Matthew, had been shielded as a child by his two older sisters. He enjoyed going to church and there was talk of him going into a Catholic Seminary. But after high school, he was Born Again and left home to join the Air Force.

His fundamentalist affiliation gave him the discipline to work hard and the network to get ahead in the military. While on assignment with NATO in Spain, he had met and married Maria from Barcelona. To obey her husband, she left the Catholic Church and joined his fundamentalist denomination.

After a promotion, he was transferred to Colorado and assigned to the Command Communications Division responsible for Strike Force Code Authentication. The officer over him, if a tactical nuclear strike was ordered by the President, would authenticate the commands. Then he would release the codes, timing, and target information to the unit selected for package delivery. It could be by sub, land base or Aerial Platform.

The Aerial Platform concept is not new. It was used extensively during the Cold War as a standby first strike or for retaliation. It consisted of several squadrons of B-52 strategic bombers flying at fifty thousand feet and loaded with fifty megaton Hydrogen bombs.

If a surprise attack was launched against the United States, these bombers were in no danger of being destroyed on the ground. They were already safely airborne and ready to fly over the North Pole to destroy their targets in Russia and China. All that was needed to start World War III was the coded authorization to attack.

The B-52 squadrons have all been grounded since the end of the Cold War. However, the US still maintains two small Aerial Platforms, now designated the APII Strike Force. The Navy and Air Force maintain a modified F-15 or carrier based F-18 Super Hornet carrying a cruise missile armed with a thirty megaton hydrogen bomb.

That's two planes flying at fifty thousand feet, twenty-four seven off the coast of China and North Korea with other countries in range. The same operation with two in the air is also going on over the Middle East and Eastern Europe.

Like all nuclear weapons, the system was considered 'failsafe' because it cannot be fired without two sets of Top Secret cryptographic codes. The first set was used to take flight control and onboard weapon systems operation away from the pilot, and give it to a command center. A copy of these codes were kept on file at Shields' secure facilities. The second set of codes, kept at Command Communications in Colorado, was the nuclear arms release code required to launch the missile.

The entire operation was separated from the total nuclear war protocol to prevent any possible confusion with the authorized strike. The system gave the president a near instantaneous secret nuclear strike capability, controlled in size and limited in the number of people with prior knowledge.

Matthew's job was to babysit the Air Force Captain who babysits the nuclear release codes. If they were called on the Red Phone, and the call was authenticated, their job was to transmit all the needed intel to the designated platform. That platform would then target and fire the weapon.

If the platform was aerial, its home base would be given the release code. Then the base would fire the missile remotely by communicating the coded target instructions and the second code to arm and fire the missile automatically without any action required from the pilot.

Twenty-four on, twenty-four off was a long shift with not much to do except for training exercises and the occasional war game, so Matthew spent much of his time reading his Bible. He had found a church of his denomination not far from the base and went weekly with Maria and their newborn son.

He also attended a men's prayer group with other servicemen who shared his apocalyptic views of the Second Coming. The group leader encouraged the men to talk about their work and how they could contribute to the 'End of Days.' One night after a meeting, Mathew had a dream— he knew it to be a premonition.

An Arab war with Israel became a nuclear world war and all nations were destroyed. From the ashes of the global holocaust, his son rose to become the King and sit at the right hand of God to rule Earth for eternity after the Second Coming.

Mathew knew this was a prophecy and shared the story with his church leaders. They introduced Mathew to Daniel Larson, a visiting church member and donor.

Daniel was born the son of a poor Croatian farmer. As a young man he had trained as a weightlifter and wrestler and won honors on a national level. While he still worked out religiously, he became a KGB agent after graduating with a language degree from a British University.

As a new agent in Eastern Europe, he had tried to restart the Red Guard and lost the tip of his finger when a blasting cap went off while being attached to a timing device. He became one of Russia's best intelligence agents, and was transferred to the United States. With the collapse of the Soviet Union, he'd found himself out of a job.

He'd been in the States long enough to know there was a strong demand for military and business information. Using his many skills and contacts to become a corporate spy and information broker, he freelanced in the capitalist global market. This new line of private work paid much better than the communists ever did. Even as the KGB worked to reconstitute itself, Larson and his contacts grew their network as they organized in the new world order where power was still the ultimate goal.

After several meetings with Larson, Matthew was convinced he could contribute to God's will, the Second Coming, and his son's ascension to the throne of Heaven. He could ensure Israel was not destroyed by a surprise attack in the coming apocalypse.

If a nuclear weapon exploded in an unpopulated area of Israel, then Israel could win the war by launching a nuclear counterattack. Mathew now understood God's purpose for him in this world, and Larson assured him that's what the nuclear firing codes would be used for.

The task was simple. When Matthew was given the go signal, he would enter the secure room, kill the officer, then remove the codes from the safe. He had access to the combination. The authentication and fire code was in a plastic container and would have to be broken. Then, he would simply take the elevator up to ground level and out the door to call Larson and give him the codes. Alarms would go off when the dead officer did not report for the shift duty change, but so what? Matthew would live forever in heaven and his son would be King.

Chapter 30

Welch watched his rear view mirror for the dark Chevy as he drove to work Monday morning. Cautiously pulling into the parking lot, he was determined to do something, only not sure what. While surveying the area, he noticed a large man in a dark suit getting out of his car. Welch started walking toward the building as the other man did the same. As their paths converged, *False alarm,* Welch recognized him as another employee in the building.

Nursing coffee at his desk, everything looked the same. All he could do was prepare another document detailing the events in Chicago and Friday night's road race. To that, he added his conversations on the mountain with Howard. He emailed himself a copy to give it a time stamp, then printed it and added it to the growing file. There was no point sending a copy to his boss, since it would be regarded as a conspiracy theory and treated as fake news.

Later that day, Caroline called him into her office to discuss the balloting upgrade. She handed him four copies of his list of recommended changes, each copy marked up like a Christmas tree with red ink. Back in his office, he consolidated the information and found Janet's team had made fifty changes to his proposal.

He called Albert Jones, the IT tech support manager who worked with him. Welch would meet with the engineers to learn what they needed to follow the established procedures. Next, he would flowchart and design the screens and links on paper. Then, Albert would bring it to life in the digital world.

Together, they reviewed the changes Janet and her crew wanted. Albert shook his head in disappointment and laughed, "Glad I'm in IT and don't have to deal with politics."

"Lucky you, not one of these managers asked me a single question about the upgrade. I can see some didn't even read it. They just took their red pencils, put their two cents in, and gave me a list of fifty changes. Maybe five or ten are reasonable. Some are a total waste of time, like the background should be blue instead of green. The rest are flat-out wrong. So much for ownership.

"And on top of that, Ms. Bostrom, our resident Grammar Nazi, gave me a C- because I left a participle dangling. No gold stars for me, but Georgette did give me two smiley faces."

"Greg, look on the bright side. At least it wasn't the Affordable Healthcare website."

"Might as well be for all the support I get from these people,"

"Greg, do you ever read their reports? Do you ever support Janet or her team?"

"But..."

"No but. She's the boss and bosses need to know you have their back."

"But I get the work done on time and in budget. Doesn't that count for something?"

"Not really. Trust is more important."

Welch responded with a frustrated laugh. "Okay, you're right. But it's not the gender, it's the system. This organization is a war on common sense, and it's stupid that I have to politely put up with this crap. I'll need two months to undo the damage, explaining in writing why their suggestions aren't the greatest idea since sliced bread."

"Look at it as an opportunity to show you're a team player."

"I hear you. I know I'll have to thank them for their effort and keep a dozen of their suggestions, because if I reject them all, I'll be considered more uncooperative then I am already. The background will be blue, or maybe periwinkle with lavender stripes, or metallic blue with glitter and polka dots."

"Or maybe cobalt with mauve and azure."

"I have no idea what that is."

Welch had worked with women before and thought he worked with them very well. He liked having a few females around to dilute all the macho testosterone, which was always destructive in a business environment. But this social club he was dealing with had gone to the other extreme. There was no balance, and he didn't get any support from his boss on how to adapt to this strange new world. *Sounds radical, but maybe civilization needs both men and woman to work together to make progress—just a thought.*

Later that afternoon, he saw Caroline in her office and went in to talk about his concerns with the RCC initiative. The conversation didn't get too far. Janet had received a call from someone complaining about Welch's attitude during a phone call. Caroline said that Janet would be placing him on probation. It was a procedural step before Janet could fire him.

"Was it my calls with John Gordon and the RCC vote?"

"You will be told all the details as soon as the proceedings start."

"Have you ever talked to Janet about my conversation with Howard, and all the other stuff going on with that initiative?"

Silence.

"I'll take that as a no. Do you believe me? I would feel a lot better if somebody believed me. A little support would be nice." Welch was about to bring up the weekend road race and weapons encounter, but she interrupted him.

"It's got nothing to do with the RCC. It's a Miss. Barbra Lockhart in the Utilities Power Grid Group that called to complain. You're lucky she refused to make a written complaint or a sexual harassment charge. You would already be out of here. Besides, it's not a matter of what I believe. I have a job and want to keep it. I work with Janet and her friends' every day, and she runs a good department here. You have no idea how much better things run now than before she started."

"So I've been told, more than once. She hired her friends, and got new computers, and we have a network just like the rest of A3E and the entire corporate world. Of course things move better and faster now because of what she did. But in the real, for-profit, corporate world the question is, what have you done for me lately, not twelve years ago. This department is still out of date in hardware and software."

"An A3E member has submitted a complaint, and I'm not going to get into a fight with the membership. They're like doctors and lawyers, they stick together."

"And we stick apart."

No response to Welch's comment made discussion difficult.

"The only thing that's going to come out of all this is Janet is going to fire you unless you stop this vendetta right now."

"I don't know any Hardlock or what's her name. The point is something wrong is going down here. I tried to fix it, and now I'm going to get sacrificed because I'm doing my job. Wait a minute, you said Miss. I've only talked on the phone with one woman lately and she was asking about 802.12 wireless electronics. You said the caller is from Utilities which doesn't make much sense. Besides, all I did was transfer her phone call."

"Well! You need to learn how to talk on the phone and do your job without pissing people off!"

Welch sat back in his chair. That was the first time he had heard her use such language or even raise her voice. "So help me. Please." He pleaded. "You're my boss. Help me with this RCC mess and Hardcock. I don't want to sound paranoid, but can you see this has got to be a set up."

"You are paranoid. Forget about the RCC. There is nothing you can do."

Welch stood up. "I take it you just don't want to get involved." He walked out of her office knowing he had just burned another bridge.

Back in his office, he closed the door and sat at his desk holding the rage inside. Tonight would be a very long night. He also knew Caroline was a little bit on target, and that's why he didn't have anybody on his side. *That's the reason I'm stuck in this Godforsaken job. And I'm fighting just to keep it. Some people are satisfied with their station in life. I'm not, but I never figured out how to take the train to the next station.*

Welch tried to think how he should handle the situation and remembered his old mentor and longtime friend, Andy, who was born in Hungary.

When Andy was six years old, his father woke him up in the middle of the night. The family slipped out the back door of their farmhouse with Andy holding his mother's hand, and his father carrying a sack with all their belongings. He could see the fear in his mother's eyes as they walked through the empty fields in the dark. His father told him he must not make a sound as they ran up to a fence. He shivered in the cold wet dirt as they crawled under the barbwire.

The Russians had invaded and crushed the Hungarian Revolution. Andy and his family escaped to freedom. They made it to the United States on the last boat to Ellis Island. He remembered his mother holding him up to see the Statue of Liberty.

From then on, Andy's life became the standard American success story. Boy makes good and goes to college. The summer of his senior year, Andy traveled around Europe. After partying in Paris, he went to visit the place of his birth. He talked to the neighbors and the old folks were glad to learn his family survived the escape. One old man cried. He was still in the house of his birth. Neither he nor his children had ever traveled more than twenty miles from their farm.

Andy graduated and married his college sweetheart. He got a good job and progressed through the corporate ranks to become Welch's boss. In the corporate world, Andy was always calm, friendly and professional. After a corporate 5K race, he started training and running with Welch. Road work strips all pretense away, and they became good friends.

Welch tried to emulate his style with only modest success. One trick was to find the smallest piece of agreement and say, "You would agree that…" It established common ground to defuse any us vs. them attitude. Second, it confirmed the idea as fact so you could move on to the next idea. Third, it got people in the habit of saying "Yes."

Another good trick was the old, "I understand what you're saying, but I'm not sure I agree with your conclusion." What a great way to tell somebody you thought they were full of shit.

Welch remembered sitting in the President's Office when the CEO told Andy to resolve a problem by doing steps 1, 2, and 3 immediately.

"Sir," said Andy, "I understand what you want, but…"

"Don't pull that crap on me. Just do what I said."

"Very well sir, but when I finish, may I come back to your office and tell you I just made a terrible mistake?"

Andy moved on to Wall Street and the big bucks. He continued up the ladder and became a Senior VP. Welch and Andy didn't travel in the same circles any more, but Welch liked Andy's circles better.

Like all people, Andy had his idiosyncrasies. Under that calm, cool exterior, one saw little spots of turmoil. He would not wear a seatbelt, and he smoked despite his wife's nagging and their running. He admitted he didn't enjoy smoking, but "nobody is going to make me quit" was his attitude.

Welch called and Andy's admin picked up. "Andy, please."

Pause. "May I ask whose calling?"

"Tell him it's Greg Welch. It's a personal call. I'm a friend.

Pause. "Sir, he's no longer with us."

"Oh, well can you give me his new number?"

"Sir, he passed away. It was a heart attack about three months ago.

Welch's initial reaction was anger at his friend for smoking and anger he wasn't around to help him. Slowly, the loss set in. *Damn you. Why did you have to go? Did all that money make you happy, was it worth it? You will be missed, very much.*

Later in the afternoon Welch got an email telling him to report to Janet's office for the review board. Fear and anger returned. Unemployment was death; who was he without a job. The world outside his office continued, but in his office the world had stopped. He closed down to protect himself.

If he won the lottery, so many problems would go away. He and Linda would travel around the world. He would buy a Porsche 911 and Linda would sit next to him on the hood with the Golden Gate Bridge in the background. He would give the finger and take a selfie with the other hand. He would send it to Janet and everyone who ever cut him.

Chapter 31

As soon as Smith at Computer Security intercepted Greg's email to file, he called Shields. It was still early on the Pacific Coast, and the sun was just breaking over the mountains. The light from a clear blue sky poured through the picture window in Shields's Presidential Suite. He was getting out of the shower when the call came, and he did not take it well.

"I told Cory to expedite one trivial detail! If he can't do it, I'll have to find someone who can. Smith, you have to make sure there are no hard copies in his office and clean the hard drive. Can you get inside and handle it?"

"I have contacts in New York that can be there in a few hours. They have experience at gaining access to corporate facilities like A3E. Once in, I'll coordinate the cleaning of the hard drive, but you have to find out where all the hard copies are filed, and give us the location or we will have to tear the office apart to find it."

"Okay, I'll give instructions to Cory, and he can coordinate with you as soon as I put this together. Give him all the support he needs. If there are any problems, I want to be notified immediately. I am holding you personally responsible for keeping up your end of the deal."

"Remember that our original agreement was just for the technical work. Additional services will require additional fees."

"You will be covered as long as you do your job."

"Good, I'll take full responsibility for my part. Just don't blame me for somebody else's screw-up. Chuck, before you move on this, realize you are upping the game here. This is an organized group of professionals you'll be dealing with, and this is serious shit."

"I have no choice. Other people screwed up, and I have to fix it." Shields hung up. He quickly called Cory to issue his new instructions. "I can't wait any longer. Forget about accidents, we don't have time. Let me make this real simple. You've got forty eight hours to get your man and hold him. Call Smith now to coordinate the details. When it's over, dispose of the mess. Don't come back to work if you fail." *How can I build my empire if these people don't do their part? Why does this guy Welch continue to fight when he has already lost? You're expendable. This is much bigger than you.*

The hotel staff came in as Shields finished the phone conversation. He got dressed before his team arrived for a working breakfast. Waiters served an assortment of fresh fruit and delicious hot rolls while the chef in the suite's kitchen took orders for eggs, crepes and Canadian bacon. The morning business agenda included gearing up for production in Mississippi, starting an advertising campaign, and negotiating a license with the Japanese firm.

While the others were eating breakfast, Chuck worried if Cory could handle the job. The track record so far was not good. After breakfast, he pulled Dumont aside. "I know you're looking forward to a nice fat finder's fee when this job is complete. Before that can happen, I have a few loose ends to take care of, and I think you or some of your associates can help."

"Happy to help, what can I do for you?"

"A manager at A3E is asking too many questions and needs to be removed. I have people working on it, but they're just amateurs for this kind of work. I need a professional to help them out, and was wondering if you can recommend anyone."

"To use an old cliché, I'm honored that you came to me for help. We do have an excellent resource; works out of Washington and can get the job done."

"Good. I need him to work with my man to insure we clean up any paper trail left behind."

"He prefers to work alone, but I'm sure you can arrange a contract with the conditions you require."

"Okay, you call your man, and I'll call mine to explain the new rules. They can work together to insure the job is carried out correctly."

"Mr. Shields, one more thing. I have some good news for you. I spoke with the buyers last night to make them aware of your concerns. Seems you have them over a barrel. They have their own timelines and cannot delay anymore. They have directed me to instruct their negotiators to accept your demands. Assuming you have the additional information, we can get the property deal done today."

"Cut the crap Dumont. You know damn well what 'additional information' they're talking about, the blueprints. Got it right here. As for the codes, give me a date."

"We expected you would be prepared, so we deposited a million in your Bahamas account to show good faith. There is a courier waiting downstairs to get the data to our tech people for verification. I'll come to your office and sign the papers this Thursday. Clear your calendar for 10:00. As for the codes and frequencies, we want to buy that day. That should wrap everything up so have an account ready for the funds transfer. Of course, you're still welcome to come out to the islands and spend a few days with us."

Shields looked down at the floor, deep in thought, but responded, "Thursday is fine."

"Chuck, don't worry. You won in the negotiations. Trust me, the only thing this deal is going to do is make you rich, and that's what you want. Now, there is a courier waiting in the lobby, and she is looking forward to seeing you."

He took the elevator down and hurried past the front desk toward the lobby.

"Chuck," she called out to him.

He turned to see Tina standing by the entrance to the bar. As he approached her, she turned and walked over to a table in the empty room. Unsure of himself, he stopped in front of her. She put her arms around his waist and pulled him in to feel the warmth of his body. "I've missed you."

"You're the courier?"

"Yes, a girl has to earn a living somehow. I understand that you have something for me."

The line was too easy. "I've got a lot for you. Come on up to my room."

"I'd love to, but I was referring to the package they want me to transport, and I have to leave immediately to meet your deadline. Besides, look over there. They don't trust me. I have an escort."

Shields turned and looked behind him. Standing by the door was the big bodyguard.

"Chuck, when I get this taken care of, I'll have some time off. We can meet and I'll bring my resume so you can interview me. How does that sound?"

"Why is he here?"

"Chuck, hello. Stay with me. They don't trust me. They trust you; you're a partner. You're in with them, right? Tell me now if you're not." She paused for a response, but got none. "Then give me the data. I can get it out of the country. Besides, I've got Carlos over there watching me."

He started to take the envelope out of his pocket, but she hugged him. As she kissed his cheek, she grabbed the package and slid it into her purse. "I know we'll see each other again soon. It's in your stars."

She casually strolled into the lobby with Carlos following her. Shields, and half the men in the lobby, could not take their eyes off of her as she left the building. The doorman flagged down a cab and the bodyguard got in with her.

"What the hell is going on?" He took the elevator back to his room.

There was a lot to do before the corporate jet brought in today's golf guests. They included the Ohio and Pennsylvania state politicians who controlled their police, fire and civil defense spending for new equipment. There was anti-terrorist money and stimulus money that needed to be spent.

To clear his head, Shields looked out the window at the golf course below and the snowcapped mountains in the distance. *Now this is the way golf should be played. Courses should be surrounded by deep forest, with clear mountain streams and towering peaks or a rugged ocean coastline, not housing developments.*

He wanted to protect these great resources from ruthless land developers. As he looked out from his suite, Shields decided to join and contribute to a good environmental conservation group like the Sierra Club. *These beautiful golf courses have to be protected from developers for future generations.*

****

Welch sat at his desk reviewing the status of the RCC ballot. If it got eighty percent, which looked inevitable, only one thing could stop it— the Executive Board of the committee. Their primary function was to ensure that the negative votes had been addressed. This final review had resulted in only two ballots being overturned.

In one case, an engineer voted 'No' because a design flaw could burn out a substation switching system. On further investigation, turned out he was right. The only attempt to build a monopoly was over fifty years ago, in the marine cable systems. The plot was discovered, and the proposal defeated on the first ballot, but no punitive action was taken.

Professor Howard, as the committee Executive Board Chairman, would block any attempt to overturn the ballot. Welch would have to go over Howard's head to the Board of Directors, making him a whistleblower. Probably an unemployed whistleblower, maybe even a dead one. He wondered if he should give up or compromise, but suspected it was too late.

If the RCC initiative became a Standard, some companies would go ballistic when they realized it created a monopoly. It would be a black eye for A3E. Welch knew he better CYA, because Janet would be looking at him to take the fall. But he would be fired or dead, or dead and fired long before then.

His friend Karen knocked on his door. "You look down. Want to go for a walk?"

He looked up. "Can they fire a person after killing them, or do they have to fire them first?"

"I think there're some labor laws against that. Come on, let's get you out of here. You need to get some fresh air."

"Sure, but only for a little while." Part of Welch wanted to be alone, but part of him wanted someone to talk to.

As soon as they got outside, Karen started speaking, "I heard you're going on probation. Everybody in the department is talking about it."

"I didn't know I was so popular. The probation is just a front to keep me quiet. There is so much more going on, you only know the half of it."

"You mean the problems with the RCC? Word gets around. Oh, and you're right; you're not that popular."

"How do you know about the RCC?"

"Office gossip. There are very few secrets here."

"Guess I'm just not in the grapevine; is there an app for that? Maybe I should start hanging out around the water cooler. Do we still have a water cooler? So what does this grapevine say about who's spying on me?"

"Can't help you there. Don't know anything about that."

"I didn't think that would be in the gossip columns. What's new by you?"

"Let's just say me and a few others are watching this very closely, since one of us will probably be next."

"You? Are you really worried about them coming after you? You do good work."

"Yes, but I got a really bad review last month."

"I'm sorry. Is it because of me? Like you're aiding and abetting the enemy? Do they think we're conspiring to overthrow the empire? I don't want to get you in any trouble. We can stop meeting like this."

"Stop. I can take care of myself. I know I'm being set up because Janet wants her own people in. But I don't care. It's all a game anyway. It's not the end of the world."

"It's not? You sure about that?"

"They don't like my work, to hell with them. I'll find another job or stay home with the kids."

"Don't you care why?"

"I couldn't care less; what difference does it make anyway?"

"I admire your values, you've got guts.

They walked a little further. "Karen, thanks for everything. Your support means a lot to me. Anytime you need anything, I'll do everything I can to help you."

"Don't worry about me, I'll be fine. But did you really go mountain climbing on a business trip? Nice move." Then she gave him a puzzled look. So why do you climb?"

"Because I'm good at it."

"Aren't you afraid?"

"Yes, but I feel safer up there than around here."

They walked back to the building in silence. She smiled, gave him some kind, reassuring words, then walked back to her cube. He realized how fearless she was, and he knew, with her attitude, she would be all right. He didn't have to worry about her.

He returned to his office thinking the new revelations about Karen made no sense. *I'm in trouble because I don't play the game with the boys or the girls. Maybe I threaten them and their cushy jobs. But why Karen? Could Janet and her inner circle of friends be as paranoid as I am?*

Janet doesn't want to lose her job any more than I do. We just go about it differently. She hired her friends and builds alliances that support her. That strategy makes a hell of a lot more money, and she's the boss. Should I just play her game, kiss ass, and look like I'm cooperating?

After work, Welch headed for the gym which let him postpone any decisions. Understanding Janet's strategy was good, but he still needed to figure out what he was going to do. He had an appointment in forty eight-hours to be put on probation, if he was lucky.

After a hard workout, he returned to the apartment for his dinner routine. He could have selected an excellent bottle of wine for under thirty bucks, if he had one. Tonight's selection was his best mediocre bottle for under ten bucks.

Welch thought about how he defined himself in his work and his future at the company. He needed to make some decisions. *But never decide today what can be put off until tomorrow. Cast your fate to the wind.* Quotes and clichés compulsively rolled through his mind as he looked for a signpost or inspiration on how to live his life. *Power corrupts. Live in the moment. All you need is love. To be or not to be. Whatever.*

He flipped the TV remote endlessly from channel to channel. Pouring another glass of wine, he continued to ask himself how he got into this predicament, afraid he knew the answer. He was a fuckup, hurting himself and everyone around him. He remembered the Spanish girl from college.

He treated her poorly and hurt her badly. They were young, he was insensitive and stupid. He really didn't know any better, and thought he was just being cool. But now he knew about love, sorrow, and how much he had hurt her. And there were others. *Sometimes you dump them, sometimes they dump you, but somebody always cries.*

He wanted to be a nice guy and team player; but how could he without selling out? He could not just give in. *But if I get fired…*

He sat on the couch and finished his bottle of wine. Nodding off, he thought he heard a door squeak and got a funny feeling. *I'm not alone.*

Slowly getting up, he grabbed the empty wine bottle by the neck and walked into the bedroom where he exchanged it for his nun chucks lying under the bed. Walking through his apartment, he turned off the TV and the lights, checked the doors, and looked out the windows. He sat and listened for any sound, but only heard the distant traffic.

Sleep overtook him, and he dreamed he was back in the army, riding in the rear of a 'deuce and a half'. Overhead, 155 mm flares lit up the sky while he looked for his equipment. He knew he was not prepared for combat. The truck drove into a dark tunnel, and he could see the names of soldiers inscribed in the bricks on the wall, like a row of tombstones. He was looking for his helmet when he woke up.

All was quiet, he walked to the bedroom and quickly passed out on the bed. He overslept and knew he had dreamed more, but could not remember them.

He arrived late for work, but it didn't concern him. In a little over twenty-four hours he would go before Janet's review board. Closing his office door, he didn't know what to do so he spent the day, like most days, doing paperwork, answering phone calls, and daydreaming. He had no new ideas, and no one bothered him.

Around four o'clock, the call came.

"Mr. Welch, a friend in the Standards Department suggested you would be a good person to talk to."

"Okay, that's nice," *Hope it's not for phone sex.* "And whom will I be talking with?"

"I'm Charlie Baker, member of the Standards Group, and I'm calling because there is something very wrong going on with the Communications Standard that we're voting on."

"Wait. Who recommended you talk to me?"

"Let's just say some mutual friends. But they said you could be trusted."

Welch opened the website to the ballot and found Charles Baker on the list of voters, but he had not cast his vote. With a few more clicks, Welch had his personal information.

"Mr. Baker, to verify your identification, may I have your address, date of birth, and where you got your degree, and mother's maiden name and school mascot?" *'Cause I don't trust you.*

The information all checked out. Welch was satisfied that Baker was who he said he was, but still concerned it was a setup. "Thank you, Mr. Baker, now please tell me what you think is wrong with what you're voting on."

Charlie laid it all out, and it matched Welch's knowledge and suspicions. Charlie had done his research and figured out the monopoly.

"Yesterday I contacted Howard, who denied the allegations at first, then he offered me a consulting job. When that didn't work, he threatened me with membership suspension. When it started to get nasty, Howard warned me that I would be libel if I initiated any slanderous rumors.

"I couldn't sleep. I was up all night, so I called some friends at headquarters. You were recommended as the man to talk too and that could be trusted."

Chapter 32

*H*ere *we go again. Again. It's Groundhog Day all over again.* Welch said to himself.

"Mr. Baker, you need to come here, like immediately."

"Sorry Mr. Welch, I'm stuck at home, sick and on bed rest. Doctor's orders. Let me suggest you drive out here after work."

Now why am I not surprised to hear that?

"It's only a two or three hour drive depending on traffic. So you should leave after rush hour. We can collaborate on a statement, and you can use it tomorrow at your probation review board. I can conference call in. I want to help, and I understand we can help each other if you want to fight."

Welch carefully considered the suggestion then responded, "Okay, I'll have a quick dinner and head up there after six. You'll see me around nine. This will be a late night. Are you sure you're ready for this?"

"I've been standing up to injustice all my life, and I'm not going to change. I see what's going on. Engineers are busy folks, but when this comes out, others will stand up to stop this kind of underhanded business."

"See you tonight." *Hope you're not trying to blow smoke up my dress.*

Welch hung up, turned off his computer and walked out of his office. The car had a full tank, and he wanted to be at Baker's house before dark. Weaving through traffic, he made good time on I-287 until the backup getting on I-80 West. The interstate was heavy, but moving, and a short time later his car exited onto Rt. 15, continuing to speed past Pickatenny Arsenal. The highway went up a long steep hill, and the hills continued as he drove by several lakes sparkling in the afternoon sunlight.

Driving through the rugged landscape, it was hard to believe he was still in New Jersey— green mountains rose from the boulder covered shores of blue reservoirs. Rocky peaks had high cliffs and deep gorges weathered by the elements. But Welch's attention was focused on the road, and he did not listen to the sound of nature calling him. His thoughts were on the vices of men, and he did not feel the peace from the landscape.

Taking the Sparta exit, he drove through the center of the small town to the Lake Mohawk Private Community. It was a three mile, man-made lake in a deep valley dotted with old summer cottages and new mega-mansions.

Turning onto Lake Shore Drive, he passed the old country club, built to look like a castle. He had been on these roads before, but missed the next turn and had to double back to find Reithner Drive. The winding road took him downhill to the lake and one of its private beaches.

A party was going on, and traffic wasn't moving. A Dodge Ram pickup negotiated the narrow road, backing up to launch a sleek inboard-outboard ski boat off the beach ramp. Welch squeezed the steering wheel and locked his jaw to refrain from hitting the horn as he waited. The element of surprise would be lost if he waited much longer. Welch jumped when he heard a loud bang. The young partygoers were setting off fireworks, and he watched skyrockets explode over the lake while he waited.

When the road cleared, he drove another three hundred yards before finding the address. He saw a Lexus SUV in the driveway, but didn't stop. He drove by slowly, scanning the area, and made a U-turn a hundred yards further down. Passing the house for a second look, he continued back to the beach area where he found a place to park.

Walking to the address, Welch could see the house was an old Tudor with scaffolding around the front, apparently getting a facelift. Mr. Baker's home was sitting in a small lot carved into the slope of the valley. The property did not fit Frank Lloyd Wright's "sublime integration of man and nature."

In the twilight, Welch faded from sight as he slipped into the tree line. Traversing the edge of the property, he moved to the back of the house. He could see lights on upstairs, but everything looked normal. Returning to the front of the house, he tried to look in the garage windows as he walked, but it was too dark to see anything. *Nothing, all too quiet. I should have asked if anybody else was going to be home.*

'Pop'. More fireworks exploded in the distance.

He ducked under the scaffolding at the front door and started to ring the bell, but stopped. He turned the doorknob, it was unlocked.

Shit. He took a deep breath, shook his head and stepped inside.

Standing in the foyer, he saw nothing unusual and softly called out, "Mr. Baker." He left the door open behind him as he walked into the living room and called out again. *Everything normal, so far.* Continuing into the next room, soft sunlight filtered through a small window illuminating the file cabinets and a large desk.

Trouble.

The lamp was knocked over and papers were on the floor. A docking station with screen sat in the middle of the desk, but no laptop was attached. *I'm too late.*

A large fancy letter opener lay by a pile of half opened mail. He heard a sound and grabbed the blade as he spun around.

Nothing. *Relax.*

The sun had gone down behind the mountain casting a shadow over the valley. Visibility was limited, but he remembered seeing a light on upstairs. He had gone this far, and nothing had happened, yet. He went upstairs, then paused to listen outside the bedroom. He pushed the door all the way open to make sure no one was behind it before cautiously stepping in.

On the floor next to the bed was the body dressed in pajamas and a robe. Welch's impulse was to apply first aid, but he could see the old man's face frozen in fear and knew it was too late. Pills were scattered on the floor; the empty bottle clutched in the dead man's hand. More medicine bottles were on the nightstand. He put the letter opener down then took the bottle from the man's frail hand. It was Baker's heart medication.

Welch gagged looking at the dead body, then remembered his situation had not changed. The review board meeting was still on for tomorrow, and all he could do was feel sorry for himself. *My last chance just died.*

He considered slipping out the back door, but remembered his fingerprints were all over the house. *Better call the police. Damn, I left my phone in the car.* He wanted to leave, but could not turn away. He stared at the dead body.

A tear filled his eye as he recognized the anguish on the old man's face.

"I'm so sorry Mr. Baker, guess they got to you first." He put his hand over the man's eyes to close them and whispered. "Time to sleep, Sorry I let you down. You shouldn't have gotten involved. But you wanted to fight them. Well, you gave it your all. You fought the good fight. We'll find a way, and get those bastards. I swear to God, I'll get'em for you."

A sound brought Welch's attention back into the room. There, he heard it again. Louder.

The closet door flew open. A man jumped out with a baseball bat swinging for the fences.

Welch leaped backwards, landing on the bed. The bat flew by him, crashing into the bedpost. Rolling off the bed, he was far enough away from the second swing. The man continued his charge, winding up for the third strike.

Welch stepped into his opponent. Grabbing the arm before he could start his swing, he used the man's momentum in a judo throw to flip him over his shoulder.

Looking down at the man on the floor, he recognized the bloated face. Welch decided not to wait around for his fat partner with a gun. Dashing out of the room to get away, he started down the stairs, already pulling the car keys from his pocket.

The lights went on. He looked up and stumbled, letting go of the keys to grab the railing and right himself. The keychain landed on the floor in front of him, and he swooped down to pick it up.

When Welch looked up, he saw the silhouette of a man standing in the living room between him and the door. His exit blocked, Welch looked around the room for something to grab, but there was nothing to use as a weapon. *Great, if this guy attacks me, I can use the car key defense.* Welch took a step towards the unknown intruder. He was about Greg's size.

"What do you want? Who are you?"

Silence. Welch took that as confirmation of a threat. The man stepped out of the shadows, and Welch could make out his facial features. He was Asian and wearing a black oriental cut shirt. The man moved closer. Greg saw his eyes and his cold stare. Welch's knees almost buckled as he stepped backwards. He knew that look.

The man in black threw a wheel kick over Welch's head to get his attention, "Come with me," and casually made a follow me motion with his hand.

Welch's knees started shaking, he had to do something. *It's now or never.* He nodded yes as he passed by the intruder. With all his power and rage, he thrust his key to the man's eye.

The Asian didn't even bother to deflect the strike, but simply turned and tilted his head. Welch's attack missed his face by a quarter inch, which was all the man needed. They were face to face, and the karate master looked bored by Welch's effort.

Before Welch could follow up with a second strike, his wrist was being bent and his feet were swept out from under him. He hit the floor, but let his momentum roll him over to spring up and counterattack.

He charged in with his front thrust kick low to the groin. Continuing his momentum, he fired a lunge punch high to the head.

The Asian calmly stepped back parrying the kick while grabbing the punch with his rear hand, using Welch's momentum to pull his arm forward and down. The Asian's lead arm grabbed Welch's arm above the elbow, performing an Aikido move. By holding the wrist and applying pressure behind his elbow, Welch was smashed into the floor, his arm bent behind his back. It felt like his shoulder was being ripped off.

"Okay!" *I guess it's never.*

"Next time I break your arm, don't make a sound."

He let Welch get up while maintaining a grip like a steel vice. In his hand was a short piece of heavy cord. Pulling Welch's other arm behind his back, he tied both hands together. Welch felt like a calf in a rodeo. The master had complete control and could inflict great pain simply by raising Welch's arms behind his back.

The Cowboy came down the stairs carrying his baseball bat and looked at Welch. "I should kill you," he said shaking the bat in Welch's face.

"I'm already dead," he replied with a blank stare.

They walked through the kitchen and stepped into the garage. Welch saw the dark Chevy, and the laptop in the front seat. The Asian opened the passenger door and flipped the seat forward motioning for Welch to get in the back.

"Guess I'm not riding shotgun."

"On the floor."

It was difficult with his hands tied behind him. The Cowboy threw his bat in the trunk, hit the garage door opener and got in the driver's side. As they pulled out, Welch fell flat on the floorboard. The Asian reached back and threw a blanket over him. "Not a sound or you die with great pain."

****

Ten minutes after the Chevy pulled out, another car pulled into the driveway and two men got out. They rang the front doorbell and knocked. Finding the door unlocked, they pulled their guns and went inside. A quick search found the body. They called Agent Allen, who was parked outside Welch's apartment.

Allen relayed their findings up the chain of command. "Kirk, we're in place staking out Welch's apartment and Baker's house, but I think we're too late. Welch is gone, and Baker's dead. Apparent heart attack. If Welch's body gets fished out of the river tomorrow, the press will have a field day with our failure to protect a witness."

"Allen, let's not get ahead of ourselves. We don't know for sure if they have him. But if they do, we'll find Jim Hoffa's body before we find Welch. I don't want to bring anybody in on charges only to have them lawyer up. We still have too many unanswered questions and limited evidence. There is a big piece of this case missing, but new names are popping up, and one of them is on the terrorist watch list."

Kirk's voice was getting louder, deeper and melodramatic. "Welch is our cat in Edwin Schrodinger's Box. We don't know if he's to be or not to be. Whether it's nobler..."

"Sir, excuse me. We could put out an APB on him."

"Look. This is bigger than our congressman. We're dealing with national security, and I'm meeting with the CIA tomorrow morning. I'll consider the APB after the meeting. Wait there in case he shows up. You can question and detain him for his own protection while the rest of this plays out. Call him and see if he picks up, but keep it low key and call me immediately if anything new develops. Remember, we're after some big fish here, and there is a tide in the affairs of men..."

"Will do." *You pompous fool.* The two agents returned to their car to stakeout the empty apartment and wait further instructions. It would be a long night.

****

Lying on the floor in the back seat, Welch's sense of dread subsided with relief that he was still breathing. *This is real. To stay alive, I need to be alert. I must stay focused.*

Trying to figure out what to do, he thought of TV shows and movies where this had happened. If he was in the trunk, he could pull the wires from the taillights, and a cop would pull them over. *But I'm not in the trunk, guess they saw that show too.*

The car accelerated onto Rt.15. With his ear on the floor, he heard the purr of the engine. It was big, and he felt the shifting of gears. *It's a stick, a four speed, no, five or more. This was the car that tried to run me off the road.*

What is it, dark color, a Chevy, what year? I should remember these things, and where we're going so I can lead the cops back to the hideout when they let me go. That's a weak assumption considering they've tried to kill me twice already. When CSI looks at the body, they'll wonder for weeks why it has no big toenails. So why are they holding me now? Because I have something they want. I'm a regular Colombo.

Figuring out where they were going turned out to be easy. In addition to listening to the GPS, the Asian was a back seat driver repeating the directions. "Turn here, get on the interstate going east, not here, over there." The car swerved as Welch bounced on the floor. They drove on for what seemed like hours, but was only about forty five minutes. "Follow the signs for the GW Bridge."

"Da what?"

"Just drive."

It doesn't take a rocket surgeon or a brain scientist to figure out where we're going: the Big Apple.

Chapter 33

A3E headquarters is open twenty-four seven to accommodate international operations. A night shift of ten technicians manned the computer room to back up the daily files and insure all systems are up and running. After 6:00 pm, only the guarded front door is unlocked and all who enter must sign in.

A cleaning crew of eight pulled up in a large van. Before anyone could exit the vehicle, two men approached the driver flashing fake badges and real guns. After a brief conversation, cash was given to the English speaking driver as a thank you for his cooperation and silence.

The two men returned to their car and quickly changed to fit in with the cleaning crew. The van driver signed in the crew and talked with the guard as the crew passed under the security cameras in the lobby. No one paid attention as two of the cleaners walked pass the cameras surrounding the IT Department and continued down the hall.

A quick check over their shoulder, and the two ducked into the unoccupied Standards Department but didn't turn on the lights. They entered the office they were looking for, closed the door behind them, lowered the window shade and sat on the floor. They looked at each other, realizing how small the office was. "This is a manager's office?" one laughed. They checked their cell phone signal, picked the lock on the desk drawers, then waited silently in the dark.

****

The dark Chevy took the George Washington Bridge over the Hudson River into the City. The Asian turned to the driver. "Show me the false teeth of our first President, and I'll show you the G.W. Bridge."

"What?" the Cowboy responded.

"Never mind."

"That's a good one." Welch said with a little chuckle.

"Shut up back there!"

Good thing I didn't tell him I've heard it before.

"Slow down here."

Welch braced himself for some quick turns as they made their exit onto the Henry Hudson Highway going down the East Side of Manhattan. Traveling over a mile, they turned into the public housing projects on the edge of Spanish Harlem and came to a stop.

Welch had found no opportunities or strategy to escape. He figured when he got out of the car, he would just start running and screaming. Even if his hands were tied, it may be his only chance. The Asian reached back and checked the knot binding Welch's hands, it was secure. As he struggled to climb out of the back seat, two men grabbed him and wrapped their large hands around his arms. The bigger of the two gripped his shoulder with his fingers against his throat while the Cowboy and the Asian walked on ahead.

Well it's now or never, again.

He brought his right knee all the way up, then drove his foot down into the side of the guy's knee. He heard the cartilage crunch. The man screamed and went down on the pavement. Welch did a one eighty driving his knee into the other man's groin.

Hearing the scream, the Cowboy spun around and saw the carnage as he pulled his weapon to fire, but the Asian ripped the gun from his hand. While Welch was driving his knee into the man in front of him, the Asian walked up behind him and lifting Welch's hands up behind his back,

Welch's head went down as he bent over from the pain in his shoulders. He was spun around, and a single finger was thrust into his solar plexus. Welch froze as his diaphragm spasmed, and he desperately gasped for air. He wasn't running anywhere.

"Don't do that again. My job is to bring you in alive and unharmed." He shoved the gun barrel into Welch's groin. "But just alive, I still get paid."

Welch nodded and looked around, wondering if he may have a better chance with his abductors. It was a hot summer night, and he was the minority in the neighborhood. Running down the street with his hands tied behind his back might draw a lot of unwanted attention. He heard loud music, but noticed most people were just minding their own business trying to get through a hot night. Nobody was paying attention to the three not from the Hood.

The Asian returned the weapon to the Cowboy. Even with his swollen face and neck brace, Welch could see the southern boy was clearly uncomfortable in the neighborhood. Welch wondered if he should have killed him.

Hands bound, Welch was escorted to the entrance of an apartment building guarded by local gang members. The Asian walked over and shook hands with the biggest man in the group. At the building entrance, the Cowboy spoke up, "No way I'm leaving my car alone around here."

"Shorty," the Oriental said, "Make sure nothing happens to the guy's car." Then turning back to Cowboy, "There, it will be okay."

Shorty instructed two guys in the group to watch the car. In true military fashion, the orders had been passed down the chain of command.

Shorty joined the three visitors as they entered the building and walked to the elevators, taking a slow ride to the top floor. They walked down the poorly lit hall to the next to the last door. The Asian knocked and stood back so he could be seen through the peephole. Someone unlocked three deadbolts and a chain before the door opened.

Welch was pushed through the door.

Chapter 34

Stepping into a short hallway, Welch recognized the standard apartment floor plan. He stopped to look in the kitchen, but was pushed into the living room/dining area. The lights had no shades and the glare bounced off bare white walls. An old Formica table covered with beer cans and pizza boxes set the ambiance of the humble abode. The other end of the room had a dirty green couch and several fold out chairs. The air conditioner droned in the background.

One large over stuffed brown chair had an equally larger over stuffed white man sitting in it. The man looked over at Welch, chugged the rest of his beer and stood up. Under his folded belly was a gun hooked in his pants. He looked at the Asian, and they nodded at each other. Welch noticed there was no love lost between them. The big man gave his prisoner a once over and smiled, "What do you know, it's Gregory Welch."

This is it. How do I play this one? Welch felt defiant, but calm. He shrugged his shoulders. "It's Mr. Welch, but you can call me Greg."

"And you can call me Cory.

"Hello Cory, think we've met, but haven't been formally introduced."

305

"Cut him loose." One man stepped forward snapping his wrist to open a switchblade.

The Asian, who had been leaning against the wall with his arms folded, stepped forward. "Wait." Spinning Welch around, he grabbed his wrist and pushed his finger into the knot. With a hooking motion, the knot opened. The rope burned his wrist as it was pulled away. Welch's arms fell to his sides. He shook his shoulders and tried to rub his arms to get the circulation going, unable to lift his hands above his waist.

Cory pulled out his gun, and laughed when he saw Welch tense up. "Hold this," he said, handing the gun to the man standing next to him. Cory looked over at the Asian. "Are his arms alright? I didn't want him injured."

"He's alive. I tied him loose."

"I beg to differ," Welch added.

"Shut up."

"Yes sir." Welch replied with mockery.

"I've been looking forward to finally meeting you on my terms." Cory extended his open hand and stepped toward him with a 'nice to meet you' smile. Welch knew what was coming next. Cory leaped forward with an uppercut to the abdominal.

Welch's arms were still too weak to block. He stepped back and exhaled to tighten his stomach muscles. A fist smashed into his gut. With a thud, he crashed into the wall behind him, making a large hole in the sheetrock.

Cory rushed him with another right to the gut. Welch turned and deflected the full force, but still smacked the wall again. He bounced back into a left hook aiming for his chin. He ducked low enough to take the force on his forehead avoiding a broken jaw. Cory's pinky ring drew first blood as it sliced into his scalp. Crashing down, Cory tried to knee him but missed.

I fall too fast for him. Lying on the floor, Welch felt like he'd been hit by a Mack Truck— a slow moving truck, but still a big Mack Truck.

Not that it was what Welch was thinking, but if it was a good karate strike, it wouldn't have knocked him backwards. The strike would have penetrated like a knife or bullet causing massive internal damage. Being knocked backwards was like a hard push. Even a freight train hitting a man at one mph would not do any internal damage, but would push him back.

"Get up." Cory screamed and kicked Welch in the chest. He tried to kick him again, but Welch rolled away. "Get up you little piece of shit."

Now Cool Hand Luke would have gotten up, and said something funny. John Wayne would get up, but not say anything. Marlon Brando would have said, "My old man could hit harder than that." Bruce Lee would have jumped up, licked his blood and spit it back in his opponent's face. Welch decided discretion was the better part of valor and stayed on the floor.

Cory bent down and grabbed him. Lifting him up, Welch was thrown into the wall. The sheetrock shattered, putting another hole in the wall. Shorty was getting annoyed. "Hey man, you fucking up my pad."

Cory rushed Welch like a football player, thrusting an elbow into his chest. Welch went down again. "Get up! Is that all you've got? You're not so tough, now are you?"

Looking up from the floor, Welch smiled, "Well if you had just asked me, I could have told you that and saved us all a lot of time."

It was funny peculiar, not funny ha. Welch couldn't move, but he had no sense of pain. *Numb yes, pain no.* There was nothing left to fear. He was resigned to fate. *I'm already dead.* That didn't mean he had to give up. He remained defiant and determined to fight. *Stay focused.*

Cory grabbed a metal folding chair, raised it over his head, and was about to take a swing at Welch.

Suddenly the Asian was standing between the two of them. "Wait. We have some questions to ask first. Then you can have your fun."

"Right. Pick him up."

Two men grabbed Welch up and placed him in a chair.

"I go first," the Asian said as he sat down in front of Welch. He grabbed his arms and put his hands over Welch's wrist. "Now, I'm going to ask you a few questions."

"Shoot...I mean go ahead. I enjoy a good conversation."

Welch looked at the Asian's hands. The knuckles were fused together. The man could punch through steel.

"Look at me. Look in my eyes and maintain eye contact. First question, what is your name?"

"Gre-gor-y Wel-ch," he said, enunciating slowly. "How am I doing so far?"

"Do you know who I am?" Ignoring Welch's remark.

"Not a clue. We haven't been formally introduced. Our host has no social etiquette. "

"Do you know why you're here?"

"Surprise Party?"

"Do you know why you're here?" His grip tightened.

"I'm guessing it has something to do with work, but not sure what. Can you go a little slower with some easier questions?" A thumb applied pressure to the back of Welch's hand. He knew his bones would start breaking. "I'm betting it's the radio communications standard. Can we do multiple choice?"

"Do you know a man by the name of Thomas Dumont or Larry Larson?"

"No. Should I?" He responded and suddenly realized the Asian was measuring his pulse and watching his eye dilation as a lie-detector.

"Do you know Mr. Samuel Chen?"

"Is he your daddy? Sorry. Guess I just don't get out that often. Besides, I'm not very good at names."

"The Lucky Lady?"

"Never met her, but I think I'd like too.

"Okay. He's all yours," the Asian said, letting go of Welch's hands. "Note I gave him to you uninjured."

Ignoring the Asian's remark, Cory grabbed Welch's arm as he sat down beside him, then slammed the arm down on the table. "Now it's my turn, and I play the game a little different."

"Like Monopoly."

"You know you're kind of a disappointment to me." Cory was working himself up again. "I was expecting a better challenge."

"So sorry to disappoint you. Life can be a bitch like that. I'll do better next time." But Welch could see Cory wasn't listening. *I get no respect.*

"Give me that little switchblade," he said to Shorty. "Hold him down." The two men grabbed Welch. "You're going to give me what I need."

"Deodorant and breath mints?"

"Funny guy. I'm going to ask you the questions now. If you don't give me the answers I want, I'll cut off your fingers. One at a time."

"How many questions? More than ten?" He tried to think. "But I'll spurt blood and bleed DNA and maybe HIV all over you."

"Right", Cory snorted as he tried to think that one though. "Cowboy, give me your lighter. Now hot shot, give me what I want, or I'll burn your fingers off. One at a time."

Welch shook his head. *Me and my big mouth.*

"Cowboy, get a pencil and paper, there's a pen in my jacket. Now Welch, or Greg, listen up. The tech guys need a clean access to your computer through the front door. What's your password?" With a click, a bright yellow flame popped out of the lighter.

Welch couldn't remember what it was. "Let go of my hands. I won't try anything, I need my hands to remember my password. I have to go through the motion."

Cory let go. Welch pretended to type it out on a keyboard while he recited the password. Cory laughed, but he understood what Welch was doing.

"Now, where are all the hardcopies of your emails to yourself about the RRC?"

"What hard copies? I don't know what you're talking about."

Bang!

A back hand to the face, and Welch's nose was bleeding.

"Lower right hand drawer of my desk, in the back. A folder marked file copies." *Shit, there goes my bargaining chip. How did they know? I've been hacked?*

"Now that wasn't so bad was it?"

He's going to do it again, Welch ducked.

Bang.

Another back hand blow to the forehead, and Welch was on the floor. Cory got up and stepped over Welch as he pulled out his cellphone. He looked at the phone then moved to the window. Shaking his head, he shouted. "No damn signal."

"Use mine. My service gets a signal here." Shorty threw over his phone.

Cory pulled a piece of paper from his pocket, looked at a number and entered it on Shorty's phone.

****

In the A3E building, a cellphone vibrated in the pocket of the man sitting on the floor. He opened his phone. "Hello." He listened and repeated back everything he heard, but wrote nothing down. "I'll call you back in less than thirty minutes. Don't do anything until I confirm he's telling the truth, and we have it all." He snapped the phone closed.

The heavy set man stepped outside Welch's office and closed the door behind him. He stood guard while the little guy turned on the computer and went to work. Going in with the password was a better way to enter the poison software than trying to circumvent security from BC Smith's office.

Just hitting delete did not remove data from the hard drive. Using a flash card, he imported a program used by the NSA to wipe secure Intel from data storage. He found the emails he wanted on the hard drive and instructed the program to overwrite the fields seven times.

Then, he added his own touch by 'spoofing' over the cleaned addresses so a standard search program would jump over the 'overwrite' as if nothing was there. Only by going directly to the address, would the overwrite show up. While he waited for the program to finish, he opened the desk file cabinet having already picked the lock. After going through several folders, he found what he wanted and put the papers in his pocket.

****

Cory handed the phone back to Shorty and smiled, "He'll call us right back." Cory walked back to his chair and looked down at Greg still laid out on the floor. "Get this piece of shit out of here. I don't want to look at him anymore."

Okay, here we go. "Wait a minute. I was wondering. Does anyone have a phone I can borrow?" Three men put their hands on their phones.

"What? You think you're going to make a call?"

"No. I wanted to get a group selfie."

Silence. *Tough crowd.*

The other two in the room, TJ and Grunt, dragged Welch into the bedroom.

Welch laid on the floor alone. It was time to go to work. He ignored his cuts and injuries; circulation had returned to his arms. The room was furnished with a dresser and two mattresses on the floor. He checked the window, no fire escape, no balcony, no way out.

He would have to go through the wall. The closet was on the opposite side from the door. Stepping into it, Welch sat down on the floor and placed his foot about six inches from the corner. A kick would make too much noise, so he pushed his foot into the wall. The sheetrock cracked and gave way as his foot went through.

Reaching in, he ripped out several pieces of sheetrock enlarging the hole. He reached in again and found no wires, studs or insulation, just another layer of sheetrock. Repeating the process, he kicked out the second layer of sheetrock until the hole looked big enough. Going head first, he wiggled through to the bedroom of an unoccupied apartment.

He ran to the front door, unlocked it, and slowly looked out. The stairs were on the other side of the building. He would have to go past Shorty's apartment to get to the stairwell. Then what, he wondered? He couldn't just walk out through the front lobby. They would see him, but he couldn't hide in the stair well. *Just stop on some floor and knock on doors asking for help? Sounds like a Plan B. Hope I can find a Plan A.*

Locking the front door, he felt trapped as he fought off old feelings of paralyzing anxiety. He shook it off and focused his attention on solutions as he walked back to the living room. He opened the sliding glass door and stepped onto a small balcony. He was on the corner of the twelfth floor. The balcony to his right was Shorty's. Going down the outside of the building didn't look like a safe option.

Catty-cornered to the apartment building was another structure under construction. The steel frame was just one floor below and to the left. He considered. *I could jump. It's doable. Are you nuts?* The front door to the stairs was the only way out. *I'll go with plan B.* Suddenly he heard yelling from Shorty's apartment. *They know I'm out, the jig's up.*

****

Cory got his call back fifteen minutes later. "Mission complete. Before we move out, double check with your hostage. Make sure there are no more copies, or computers that need fixed while we're still in the building," the voice said.

A military man, Cory liked that. It felt good working with professionals. "Stand by." Cory turned to Shorty, "Tell your men to bring the wimp back in here."

The two troops went back into the bedroom and discovered their hostage was missing. First, they looked under the mattresses. There was only one place left to look, and that was the closet. It had a small hole in its wall. TJ started through the hole, but got stuck at the shoulders.

The other man raced back into the living room, "He got away." Everyone ran back to the bedroom and saw TJ's legs extending out of the closet. Cory smacked Grunt in the back of the head.

"The next apartment," Shorty yelled, and they all started running for the front door.

Welch had decided on the Plan B stairwell exit, and ran to the front door. He opened it just as Shorty and the gang opened their door into the hall. They all stood looking at each other. *Well this is awkward.*

Welch jumped back inside the apartment, slammed the door and locked it. Running into the bed room, he saw the head protruding from his hole in the wall. He dashed back into the living room as they broke through the front door. He realized climbing down the balconies was his only chance to get out alive.

He went out on the terrace and over the railing as they ran into the living room. Looking down one floor at the steel construction, Welch saw several sheets of plywood making a platform supported on the steel girders. He considered the odds of making the small platform verses climbing down. His eyeball calculations of force and distance were not distracted by his fear of heights. Shorty, with the others behind him stepped out on the balcony and reached for Welch. He jumped.

Chapter 35

When Welch was young, he went sky diving. It took four seconds for the chute to deploy. He had jumped twice and had no idea where eight seconds of his life had gone. Now, Welch had no idea where nine and a half seconds of his life had gone.

The plywood platform had a little bounce in it to soften the landing. Welch was lying on his side, and his ankle felt funny. He knew it was going to hurt in the morning, if he lived that long. Someone was yelling. He jumped up ignoring the pain. The plywood was sliding under his feet, and he fought for his balance. *Gotta get out of here.*

He stepped on a steel beam. Looking down, he saw only darkness. Unable to tell if the flooring was ten or two hundred feet below, he instinctively put his arms out for balance.

At the far end of the building was a construction crane. There had to be a stairwell or ladder there. Welch took off in that direction. But his foot was on something rolling. He struggled to maintain his balance. Lying at an angle to the girder corners was a pile of five foot long steel rods for reinforcing the concrete. Regaining his balance, he looked back.

Cory was going ballistic. He had drawn his gun, but knew he couldn't shoot Welch. They had to confirm all the documents were destroyed. "Go get that son of a bitch." He grabbed TJ who had finally crawled through the hole in the wall and joined everyone on the balcony. "Go on, get him, you let him get away."

"Hell man, no way. I'm not jumping off no building. You can just go f…."

The barrel of Cory's gun was jammed into TJ's mouth. "He made the jump, now you make the jump, and I'll be right behind you. Or I'll just throw your sorry ass over right now, you too Grunt."

The two men stepped over the railing and jumped, landing with a bounce on the plywood. TJ got up slowly, but Grunt stayed down rolling around holding his knee, grunting in pain.

Welch stopped and looked back. *That platform was the one bridge I should have burned.*

Cory turned to the Asian who simply smiled and said, "After you."

Cory stuck the gun back in his belt and rolled his gut over the railing. "I'm coming to get you, and I'm gonna kill you." He yelled "Geronimo" and jumped off the deck. Cory landed on the platform and executed a perfect paratrooper roll returning to his feet, but the platform buckled under the impact of the big man. One section of plywood broke off and fell.

The remaining plywood started sliding off the steel beams. Cory grabbed a beam and pulled himself up, ripping the gun out of his belt. The weapon, plywood, and Grunt fell twenty feet to the concrete below. The Asian couldn't follow Cory without the platform to land on.

Welch heard the crash from the falling deck and turned to look back; TJ was chasing him. *If I run, they'll chase me down. If I make it to the bottom, they'll just be waiting for me. Time to make a stand.* At a beam joint, Welch turned and picked up one of the steel rods.

TJ, running behind him, grabbed a bar. He assumed a fighting stance while trying to twirl the heavy steel rod in his fingers, screaming "hiya" karate sounds. The steel rod was a hundred times heavier than the dry bamboo TJ practiced with in his dojo.

Welch held the steel in a tight curled wrist grip and smashed it against TJ's rod, knocking it out of his fingers. Welch stepped forward thrusting the rod like a bayonet on a rifle into his opponent's chest. TJ collapsed on the girder, rolled off, and fell with a thud on the concrete below.

Welch's eyes had adjusted to the light, and he saw a two floor drop to the concrete slab below. Looking up, Cory was charging toward him in a state of rage with a steel rod held like a rifle. He was too big with too much momentum for Welch to fight head on. *Fight smart.* Welch jumped to the side onto the girder at a right angle to avoid the frontal attack and countered with a jab.

With one hand, Cory swung the rod to his side with enough power to block Welch's thrust. The impact knocked both men off balance, and both almost fell off the steel. Like two men in a log rolling contest, they fought to remain upright.

Cory turned to charge, swinging the rod like a baseball bat to take Welch's head off. Welch ducked and thrust low with a blow to Cory's leg. The strike slowed him down, but his fury blocked the pain as he continued his assault. Welch was stepping back as Cory continued swinging the steel rod. The big man pressed the attack.

Welch had to find a new strategy or get killed. He threw the bar at Cory's head, forcing him to block it. Welch spun around and started running along the beam, withdrawing to find a stronger tactical position. Seeing his prisoner run, Cory yelled and threw the heavy steel rod like a spear. It flew over Welch's head. Cory ran after him.

Welch was looking at the crane platform in front of him when he stepped on a steel rod and lost his footing. He landed face down, his breath knocked out of him. He grabbed the beam to keep from falling to the floor below.

The big man stopped at his feet. "I'm gonna kill you with my bare hands." But he just looked down at him. Welch was already down so Cory couldn't hit him with his fist. He couldn't walk around him, and he was too fat to bend down while balanced on the narrow steel beam. Like an angry child, he started kicking Welch's feet. Cory suddenly smiled, stepped back to a steel beam cross section and reached down to pick up another rod.

Karate has only a few basic moves, (block, kick, punch) but part of the art is doing them from any position. Holding onto the beam with one hand, Welch twisted on his side. Sliding closer to his opponent, he snapped a sidekick up into Cory's groin. It was a weak kick with no penetration, but it distracted Cory. It allowed Welch to slide closer to the fat man. He pulled his knee up to his stomach, and delivered a strike straight into the opponent's kneecap. He heard the bone crack.

Cory screamed in pain as Welch kicked his knee a second time, but rage still controlled Cory's mind. He dove to tackle his opponent like a loose ball. Landing on top of Welch, the huge mass crushed him into the steel. They started to roll.

Welch grabbed the beam as Cory grabbed him around his neck. Welch couldn't hold on for both men, and they rolled off.

Falling, Welch's brain shutdown as tunnel vision closed off his world. Cory, a paratrooper with twenty jumps, went into freefall. It was so exciting, so beautiful flying free.

The roll continued until they crashed into the concrete floor below. Welch landed on top. Cory's massive body cushioned his fall.

Welch regained awareness as he fought to get his muddled mind and limbs to work. He felt the body under him with a massive arm wrapped around him.

Welch kicked to break free, then realized the body wasn't moving. It wasn't breathing. Relief flooded over Welch as he recovered from the shock. *I'm alive and I'm still standing... well almost.*

He could hear someone yelling from the balcony, "Hey Cory, you alright down there?"

"No asshole, he's dead!" *Stupid, stupid, idiot.* "When am I going to learn to keep my big mouth shut?"

On the balcony, the Asian turned to Shorty and the Cowboy, "We have to get him. I have a contract." They ran through the apartment into the hall going for the elevator.

"Wait, stop." Shorty ran back in his apartment and opened the cabinet over the refrigerator. He pulled out two AR-15 assault rifles modified to go full automatic and extra clips. He threw one gun to the Cowboy. The three of them headed for the elevator.

Welch was trying to think. *Focus, now what?* He checked the fat body for a gun, some keys, anything. All he found was a big roll of bills, so he stuck it in his pocket. "What the hell."

Welch could see two bodies as he looked across the concrete floor. TJ was dead with the open chest wound. Grunt was semi-conscious and moaning softly on the Concrete.

Lying on a sheet of plywood next to the body, Welch saw the handgun. He grabbed the weapon. It was heavy, cold, and deadly. He breathed a sigh of relief and felt stronger; he could protect himself from danger. With little effort, he could kill them. The realization was both a fear and a rush.

The gun was the old Army Colt 45. Although no longer the standard issue, Welch had fired the weapon in the military. He stuck the gun in his belt and ran for the stairwell.

Halfway down, he realized that someone would be waiting for him at the bottom. He listened carefully but didn't hear anyone following him down. On the fourth level he grabbed a crowbar leaning against the railing. On the third floor he threw it down the stairwell. It clanked on the bottom, then silence.

Quietly, he made his way down to the second floor. *Now what?* He quickly walked to the back of the building. He looked over the edge and saw a large pile of sand. Holding the gun in one hand, he jumped down into the soft dune, and rolled to the ground.

"There he is, over there!"

The noise came from his left so Welch took off to the right, running between the building and a chain link fence. He saw his escape route was a dead end as he raced forward. The construction site had been fenced off. Gunshots behind him blasted through the night and a bullet whizzed over his head.

On his right was a small stairwell leading to a basement door. He jumped in for cover, hit the door and it swung open. He fell through the doorway, dropping three feet into the basement. The dark room was large and empty. It had no windows, only the door he came in.

He was trapped. Slamming the door closed, he tried to find a lock, but the room turned pitch black. He opened it again to let in some light. A gunshot told him to close it.

He heard men yelling outside and backed away. He stepped to the side about ten yards while keep his gun pointed at the entrance. He laid down flat on the damp concrete, ready for the assault.

Two shots rang out as the door was kicked open. A beam of light flooded the other side of the room as Welch lay motionless in the dark. Cowboy jumped in and sprayed the room with the AR on full automatic. The noise was deafening in the closed space.

Cowboy, firing from the hip, had never emptied the clip of an assault rifle on full auto. The recoil pushed him backward raising the barrel. The first three rounds hit the concrete floor, the next two rounds hit the back wall, and the rest of the clip fired harmlessly into the ceiling.

Welch remained still on the floor. He aimed at the center of mass, and slowly squeezed off a killing shot. Nothing happened, the safety was on.

Despite what is viewed on TV, an AK47 or M16 (or a modified AR15) on full automatic will empty its magazine in less than three and a half seconds. Instead of taking cover to lock and load a second clip, the Cowboy continued to stand there fumbling to insert the new clip.

Welch took another breath, and pushed the safety off. He carefully aimed again and fired twice.

The Colt fired a high mass, low velocity slug knocking Cowboy backwards into the wall behind him. He yelled "I'm hit!" and collapsed. "Why did you shoot me?" He whispered, but never got an answer. The life drained out of him as he slowly and quietly died on the floor.

Killing gets easier.

A controlled three round burst came from behind the door. Before Welch could react, a man dashed into the room diving into the darkness as the door closed behind him. The door opened again. Welch saw the rifle barrel and fired. The door closed, but Welch had given away his position.

Five shots from the other corner of the room struck the floor around Welch. He rolled left. The room was black. Neither man made a sound. Now, it was a waiting game.

Welch's round that had gone through the metal door struck Shorty in the arm. The slug still had enough force to shatter the bone. Blood spurted out, and it hurt like hell. Shorty knew he had to get the arm bandaged soon or he'd bleed to death. It was time to take care of Shorty.

He wrapped his shirt around the wound and quickly walked to the front of the building. Two gang members were sitting on a bench guarding the Chevy.

They all went back up to the apartment. The stockpile of drugs, cash and guns was stashed in two large duffel bags. They headed for a safe house three blocks away.

The waiting game continued in the basement. Welch had a strong motivation to be still; he didn't want to die. He figured it was the Asian that dashed in the room. All their karate and working out now meant nothing. The guns equalized everything. Lying on the floor, he wanted the gun to be bigger so he could hide behind it, needing its magical protection.

He tried to see in the darkness and hoped the Asian's night vision was no better than his. Time passed and the cold from the floor was beginning to get to him. He tried to relax and breathe softly. *Wish I was in warm water; swimming could level the playing field- no karate, no gun. I would be warmer. Stop, stay alert.*

He thought of the old throw-out-something, get the other guy to fire at the sound and give away his position trick. *Those idiots never checked my pockets. I still have my wallet plus the big roll of bills. I could throw the money, but as Jack Benny would say, 'I'll have to think about that.'*

Something hit the floor in front of him. He aimed at the sound, but held his fire. *He's trying the same trick; great minds think alike.*

They waited in silence. Welch ran different scenarios through his mind. *He thinks he's the hunter, he'll be the aggressor. Or he waits till morning for the light to see me.* The waiting continued.

Minutes seemed like hours, and the concrete floor was getting colder. Welch tried to stay focused. Something hit the floor in front of him. He flinched, almost firing the weapon. A few inches from his gun, he could barely make out something white, a tennis shoe. The Asian was barefoot so now he could walk around quietly. Welch tried to flatten out to stay low.

Do I hear him walking, or is it my imagination? His eyes played tricks on him as he peered into the darkness. *Was that him?* Slowly reaching out and grabbing the shoe, he looked and listened. *Yes, I hear or feel it again, a vibration in the floor.*

He tossed the shoe in the direction of the sound. It hit something and fell to the floor. Both men started firing. Bullets went over Welch's head as he aimed for the flash and pulled the trigger, then silence.

He waited.

Welch heard breathing then the sucking sound of an open chest wound. Slowly, he stood up, standing sideways to hide behind his gun.

A sudden blast shattered the silence. A bullet tore at his shirt. Welch emptied his clip as he hit the floor. When the shooting stopped, he only heard his own breathing. He waited another five minutes before he got up again.

Opening the front door, light revealed two bloody bodies. The dead Asian had another clip in his pocket, but his weapon was a Beretta. Welch took the gun and stuck the 45 in his belt. Cowboy had car keys in his pocket, and a wad of bills. Walking to the door, he looked back into the darkness.

"Last man standing."

Chapter 36

Welch stuck his head out the door, all was quiet. He walked around the building holding the Beretta just in case. The streets were deserted, and he walked to the Chevy. Slipping in behind the wheel, he started the car and listened to the engine purr. He checked around the seat and glove compartment for more ammo, knowing the Colt was empty. Welch found nothing, and decided he better move on.

It had been a long time since he drove a stick, and the car stalled twice before he got the feel of the gears. Welch drove a few blocks until he got his bearings and found a numbered street sign.

Driving through the sleeping city, he crossed 138th Street going downtown. At 125th, he turned right, passing the Apollo Theater. He was in the center of Harlem, one of the safest neighborhoods in the City. He knew his way to the West Side Highway and back onto the George Washington Bridge. Its steel superstructure was a beacon of light, showing him the path home.

He saw the dawn breaking with the faint glow of morning light as he looked back at the Manhattan skyline. In front of him, the Palisades Cliffs dropped 500 feet to the Hudson River below.

Crossing the great span, he remembered all the Governor Christie blocking the bridge jokes, but his focus was on the road going home. On the Jersey side, he followed the signs for the Turnpike. Morning rush hour traffic was starting, and he resisted the temptation to open up the car's engine.

As he took the exit off of I-287, he remembered his car was parked 50 miles away. "Oh hell!" Being only a few minutes from home, Welch continued and cautiously drove through the apartment complex. Everything looked quiet. He parked a block away and walked back. As he approached his door, two men jumped out of the shadows.

"Greg Welch."

He spun around pulling the Colt from his belt, then remembered it was an empty weapon. The two men ducked behind a parked car, pulled their guns, and yelled "FBI" while waving their identification.

"Who?" They looked familiar. "What do you want?"

"FBI, put the gun down now."

Welch took a step back then lowered the gun when he saw their badges. Being cautious, he put the gun in his belt, walked up to them with his hands held high, and inspected their ID's.

"FBI, no shit, thanks for not shooting me, but aren't you a little late? May I see a second photo ID please?"

"We met you at the police station last week, remember?"

"Oh, that's why you look familiar."

"Shall we go inside? It's important. We need to talk, right now," Allen stated more than asked. His partner called the Captain to report their missing person had been found.

"As tempting as it would be to say get a warrant, I'm a little too tired to mess with you so come in. Here, it's not loaded." Welch said as he handed the agent the 45. "I have no more use for it."

He reached for the door then remembered he didn't have his keys. In a sandwich bag buried by the steps was his spare. It worked and the door opened. "Have you been waiting long?"

"As a matter of fact we've been waiting all night. I've been trying to reach you on your cell. We would like to know where you were."

"Gee, did you miss me? It's a real bitch when you don't know what's going on. Overnight? I hope you guys get overtime." Welch looked around to see if anything was missing. "Have a seat. I've got to make coffee, want any? "

They remained standing, "Now would you mind telling me where you were last night?" He stated, not asked, in a louder voice.

"You first, why do you want to know? How about telling me what the hell is going on around here? Bet you know a bunch of people are trying to kill me, or else you wouldn't be here."

The two men looked at each other, then Allen spoke, "It's really very simple Mr. Welch. You seem to have stumbled into a federal investigation, and your name keeps coming up in conversations we've been monitoring."

"Well excuse me for interfering. I'll try not to let it happen again."

"Don't get smart, or we'll have this conversation downtown. Your failure to cooperate is withholding evidence and considered a crime."

"Hold it right there! If you say you've been monitoring me, that means tapping my phone, right. Then why the hell didn't you protect me? They've been trying to kill me since I was in Chicago."

"We weren't monitoring you at that time and not aware of your involvement then," Allen said defensively. "We didn't learn of that till after the fact. But now it's the reason you're not under arrest. Then last night we lost contact with you before we could bring you in.

"You have to understand there is a lot of red tape, and bureaucratic approval required before information like wire taps can do an inter-agency transfer and be analyzed. We got the intelligence passed down to us and acted on it as fast as we could."

"So somebody knew something was going to happen, and bottom line, I just got delayed in the bureaucracy. Rockford was right, the Feds are useless."

"Look smart ass, the only reason you're not getting locked up to be interrogated is we're chasing some bad characters, and don't have any time to waste on you. They can get away."

I'm a waste of time.

There was no point in venting anymore, so Welch told them his story. The two agents turned on a recorder, took copious notes and called the Captain twice. Their questions told Welch they already knew part of his story, but they were not showing their hand. When he asked questions, they told him they couldn't comment on an ongoing investigation.

"So I'm thinking all this shit happened because I tried to stop somebody who wanted to make a lot of money by making a monopoly from a Standard. But you're the Feds. So there must be something more, like national security implications that you're not telling me. How do I fit into that?"

Allen thought carefully then responded, "Let's just say your persistent involvement caused the other side to show their hand, and that enabled us to put the pieces together. Of course any mentioning of this would be denied."

Greg reluctantly told them about the Chevy when asked how he got back to the apartment. He 'forgot' to mention the wad of bills.

"You killed some people, even if it was in self-defense. We'll need you to sign a statement and testify in front of a grand jury even though you seemed to have put down all your corroborating witnesses."

"Sorry, next time I see a collaborating witness trying to shoot me, I'll just threaten them with harsh language." Welch realized they needed him, and he had an opportunity to negotiate. He started acting polite. "Excuse me sir, you want my cooperation. To do that, I could use some help from you. You would agree we can help each other. Yes?"

Allen nodded in agreement.

"First, I'm probably getting fired today because of, as you call it, my persistent involvement. The boss mistook my patriotism for a bad attitude, what a silly mistake. My credibility, not to mention my cooperation on the witness stand is not so good if I'm unemployed. You would agree their defense attorneys will make it sound like sour grapes, you know, the disgruntled employee thing.

"I'll be a more impressive witness on the stand as an employee working in cooperation with law enforcement. *That sounded pretty good.* You agree it would be good for all of us if you can explain to my boss I was assisting you guys, and you need me to stay on the job. At least for a little while."

Agent Allen knew that Greg had a point and started his own negotiations. "You've got balls." He knew the Agency's objective was to get the big guys at the top of the food chain. He would need Greg's testimony.

It was time to play good cop. Alan was sure the Captain would be willing to make a deal. "We may need you to tie up a few lose ends. So as long as you give us your complete cooperation and keep your attitude under control, I can make a few calls.

Someone will talk with your superiors about your employment. I'm sure your company doesn't want any unnecessary publicity, but you must play by our rules and don't piss anybody off."

"You're setting a high bar."

"Listen Welch." Allan was getting exasperated. "A long investigation with a lot of senior people and countless man hours got compromised last night. Some really big fish may get away because of this fiasco, so don't push it. We need your full cooperation, or you will be out in the cold, and we can make it very cold. You understand?"

Welch didn't like being threatened, but he got what he needed so, this time, he was smart enough to shut up.

"*Moi?* Okay that's fair. We've got a deal. I'll hold up my end of the bargain." Greg extended his hand, and they shook on it. "Tell my office I'll be in tomorrow, and I'll be good, cross my heart. I've got to have a nightcap and get some sleep. Care to join me… for the nightcap?"

They all went back to the Chevy, and the agents took the Berretta They did a quick search finding the shotgun and bat in the trunk. They took the guns and told Greg not to move the car. "Someone will be back for it."

"But I don't have a car. You don't want me to touch that set of wheels? My car's parked by the beach in Sparta, and the keys are somewhere on

Baker's living room floor. How am I supposed to get to work tomorrow and be a good employee?"

"Okay, we have two men up there. One of them can drive your car down. We've got to run."

"One last thing," Welch added. "Seriously, thanks for your service. I know you guys have been stressed out lately with all that's going on." They shook hands, and he waved good-bye as they sped off.

Back in his apartment alone, Welch took three aspirin and made himself a screwdriver without orange juice. He wished he could afford to keep Jack Daniels in the house, but knew he would drink too much if he did. Making himself comfortable on the couch, he reflected on the past twenty-four hours. He had killed a few people, but didn't enjoy it. *Now at least I know I'm not a psycho-killer.*

He had to admit it was exciting, and he had learned a few things about himself. Like he was stronger than he gave himself credit for. And, he didn't get any pleasure from the deaths. *I'm not looking forward to doing anything like that again anytime soon.*

He was alive, so it was a good day, but he'd be sore tomorrow. He was just too tired to think any more. *I'll finally get a good night's sleep.* And he did.

Chapter 37

Welch slept all that day and through the night. Waking the next morning, he felt mentally rested despite his physical bruises. The FBI had parked his car outside, but he still had the keys to the Chevy. Feeling a need to reassert himself, he drove it to work. Everyone in the department stared. He needed to talk with Karen and find out what the grapevine knew.

Before he could find her, his boss walked into his office. Caroline started to speak, but stopped as soon as she saw his face. She shook her head. "Go home. Your probation review has been postponed. Take a sick day."

Welch didn't ask for a new review date. On the way out, he saw Janet in the hall. He gave her a friendly hello, and she shot him a dirty look. *I don't know what the Feds did, but I love it. Having more power than your boss, priceless.*

Not worrying about unemployment is better than not worrying about getting shot, but don't let this power go to your head. With my newfound notoriety, I should build some kind of relationship with my boss and Janet that keeps them happy, and me employed.

Sitting at home that afternoon, Welch's face swelled even more despite the icepacks. He realized his leg and shoulder pain were hurts that would be around for a very long time. When he returned to work the following day, his computer was gone. The reflex action was to assume he had been fired. Caroline told him the FBI had it, and he was to go to their Newark office.

"When you get back, I want you to tell me what the heck is going on."

"I could tell you, but then I would have to kill you." Her look of surprise quickly turned to anger. "Just kidding. I'll tell you everything. Do you have a National Security clearance and need to know?"

The drive up the Turnpike to Newark didn't take as long as it took to find a parking place. Downtown Newark is a vibrant metropolitan area. It's the residential neighborhoods that needed work. Unable to find a parking place on the busy streets, he pulled into a parking lot. He hoped the FBI would reimburse him for parking. *A3E sure as hell won't.*

Welch met with his good friends Jack and Allen to make a formal statement, look at mug shots, and endure another round of questions. He told them all he knew, including his suspicions about John and Shields. They asked questions, but didn't act at all surprised at his answers. Welch guessed his paranoia was on target.

"You have my computer. I documented the incidents, if you want, I can pull it up if it's still there." They walked down to the computer lab, and he was handed rubber gloves to wear. Welch booted up his

PC, but he was using a different keyboard. His had been 'bagged and tagged' for evidence.

"It's not here." He showed the lab technician where he it should be. They were not surprised that it was gone. Welch asked for a note so he could get a new computer if they were going to keep his. Allen told him to 'knock it off'.

At work the next day, Caroline invited him to the cafeteria for coffee. She paid, and he realized she was trying to make peace.

"The FBI was here again yesterday. They asked more questions about the RCC and about you."

"And you told them?"

"That you're irritating, obnoxious and honest, but it seems they already knew all that."

"Thanks for confirming it, I think."

"They also interviewed Janet. Don't worry, she's not going to rock the boat. You're safe for now. She's in damage control to protect her department."

"And her reputation," he added.

The next day Welch got a call from John. The RCC ballot was being postponed.

"Gee, that's too bad, is there anything I can do to help?" he said trying to control his sarcasm. Welch went on to remind him that an initiative can't remain in limbo indefinitely. *All your balloters will start dying off or maybe go to jail.* "If it's going to be postponed more than a month, you must consider withdrawing it."

He lied. The Department had initiatives take a year between ballots. John told Welch he would get back to him with a new date, then hung up without thanking Welch for his offer to help. *And after all I've done for him.*

Welch fired off an email thanking John for keeping him abreast of his ballot postponement. Then he saved a copy to file and printed a copy to start a new paper trail.

****

Thursday morning, Shields got to work early, and went directly to the secure area. One nightshift engineer was sound asleep, the other was sitting at a desk, half asleep with a donut and coffee. Chuck walked by him going directly to the safe and opened it.

Knowing what was in the safe, the Engineer began to worry. "Sir, what's up?"

Shields turned with his piercing stare. "You're not on the 'Need to Know' list so just eat your donut." Standing in front of the safe to block the engineer's view, Chuck found the dated folder and slid its contents into his coat pocket. Putting the folder back, he closed the safe and smiled. He had made millions of dollars in less than thirty seconds. *Should I have demanded more? I bet I can get a better deal the next time they want the codes. The price has doubled, take it or leave it you damn pirates.*

Game face on, he turned and walked pass the rattled engineer. "Relax, there's no nuclear war. Go back to sleep."

Sitting in his office, he read the paper and waited for the call confirming Welch had been disposed of. It never came. Unable to reach Cory or Thomas, he tried Smith in Chicago, but the phone had been disconnected. He was getting worried. He was not in control.

Langstaff, who had contacts in the Standards Department, made some calls. He learned that Welch was out, but the FBI was in Janet's office. Being in the dark was maddening, but Shields still had appointments to keep and wanted everything to appear normal. In a few hours, he would make the biggest deal of his career. He was racing the clock to get a slush fund that would set him up for life. Sitting in the office of the Director of Human Resources, Judy Green, he wondered how he ever got into this predicament.

Looking around, he remembered Judy had the smallest office on executive row, was not a VP, and was the only woman on the floor other than the secretaries. He could not focus on what she was saying as he stared at the psychology books on the shelves behind her.

The meeting was supposed to be about the sales commission plan for the new product line. Shields didn't want to give his profits to the sales force just for being order takers. Judy had a different agenda and wanted to talk about the Myers Briggs Management Training Program. He had no interest in it, but would probably let her do it just to keep her quiet.

"Mr. Shields." It was Doris. "I apologize for the interruption. I need to talk with you."

He shook his head in irritation and stepped into the hall with her. "Now what?"

"Sir, the FBI are in the building and on their way up to see you."

Shields's first impulse was to jump out the window, but he knew never to operate on impulse.

"Go back to your desk and tell them I'm not in. If that doesn't work, stall them as long as you can."

Continuing down the hall, he stepped into Biggs' office. A bald, overweight, sloppy dresser sipping a thirty-two oz. soda, he was the corporate legal counsel. Biggs was on the phone, so Shields motioned for him to get off his call while he stood in the doorway watching his secretary. He saw two men and a woman march up to her desk then walk right in to his office. *They have no right to do that. Who do they think they are?*

Shields pulled a twenty dollar bill from his wallet and turned to Biggs as he hung up the phone. "Here is your retainer. You're now my private lawyer."

"Mr. Shields, I'm a corporate tax attorney. What am I supposed to do with twenty bucks?"

"Three FBI agents are here, and they want to talk to me. You've got to stop them. How do you think it will look if I'm arrested? What will people say?"

"Chuck, I don't know what's going on, but I'm not the best person to help you with a personal legal problem. I can give you some recommendations for attorneys if you tell me the nature of the problem."

"Too late for that."

The three agents walked into the room. Louis Carter, a new man on the force, was from the local office. Dirty Joan smiled with anticipation as she whipped out her cuffs. Captain Kirk recited his favorite lines with a most dramatic flair, "Charles Claiborne Shields, you are under arrest for bribing an elected official and attempted murder. You have the right to remain silent, you..."

"Wait," Shields blurted out the only thing he could think of, "I have information about spies and terrorists!"

The agents shot each other a quick glance and smiled. Joan had to look away so she wouldn't start giggling. Kirk continued with his most contemptible sneer. "Tell it to the judge. You have the right to an attorney..."

"If you arrest me, they'll get away. This company has top secret military work. I know who the spies are, real international spies trying to steal my secrets. I can get them for you. But you have to give me a deal!"

It was what the agents were hoping to hear. Joan bit her lip as she quivered with excitement. This was not the first white collar executive the Captain had ever arrested, and he was used to making deals. The agents knew their case was weak. The massacre in New York had shortened their timeline and eliminated a couple of potential witnesses. There weren't many left.

Much of the evidence was from NSA wiretaps, and a good lawyer might get it thrown out of court. The agents looked at each other. "Okay, I'm going to read you your rights, then you start talking. This better be good."

"That's my attorney. Biggs, do something! That's an order. I own this company. I'm the President; I'm not a crook."

"Excuse me, gentlemen, Miss, I'm Mr. Shields' attorney, and we cannot make a deal to discuss subversive or clandestine operations against the company while my client is under arrest. Mr. Shields has stated he will cooperate with information relevant to national security.

"I suggest you immediately contact your superiors and explain your situation. After you leave, we will be happy to meet with you at your location, and give you this important information, only if full immunity is granted to my client."

"Alright, wait here while I make a call." The agents walked into the hall and smiled while speed dialing their phones. They had not counted on legal counsel being present, but Kirk could handle the lawyers.

For now, they needed to keep it quiet. When the time was right, the testimony by the CEO of a national defense corporation would bring down their congressmen. The agency would get to prosecute a domestic spy case, and hopefully, nab some international terrorists. The agents knew this would make the six o'clock news and front page above the fold in the *New York Times*. It would be great for the FBI as well as their careers.

As the Feds left the room, Biggs picked up the phone and dialed his friend, a top criminal lawyer.

Shields was so impressed with Biggs' actions he forgot he was the one being apprehended. "Way to go Biggs. You've earned your retainer. I can't believe those government bureaucrats would jeopardize the security of this great nation just to make an arrest like that."

Biggs looked up at Shields and shook his head. "I don't know what's going on here, but you're going to need a lot more than twenty bucks before this is over." Biggs turned his attention back to the phone. "Joe, its Biggs. Drop whatever you're doing and just listen."

The agents re-entered the room. "Okay, we'll keep this quiet for now. You two in one car and follow us downtown. Let's go."

"Not so fast," Biggs piped in, "We'll give you an office to wait in, so you don't have to worry about a flight risk. We'll go downtown at two this afternoon."

Kirk, expecting Biggs' statement, quickly responded. "No! I'll give you ten minutes to lawyer up, and then we all go downtown, even if I have to drag you there. And it will be in handcuffs for everyone to see. And we will read you your rights and arrest you right now."

"Alright, we accept your offer," Biggs replied after listening on the phone. Shields was arrested and they read him his rights. "Now gentlemen, if you will please wait outside for ten minutes while I confer with my client."

"Excuse me," Shields interrupted as he looked at his watch. "Is there any chance we could postpone this for twenty-four hours. I have an important meeting today."

Silence, as everybody stared at him.

"How about just till this afternoon? We'll meet you downtown." Shields added while checking his watch again.

"You've got to be kidding," the Captain finally said. "Nine minutes, we'll be waiting down the hall."

"Have Doris get you some coffee and donuts. You like donuts, right? But go wait in the conference room and not in my office."

"Please close the door on your way out," Biggs added.

"Joe, did you hear all that? Now we're alone, you're on speaker. When we have to leave, we can continue on my cell in the car." Biggs turned his attention back to Shields. "You've got the best white collar criminal defense attorney in the state on the phone. I'm going to let him take over, Joe."

"Mr. Shields, good morning. But let's not waste time with formalities; we can discuss my fees later. We have very little time, and I have lots of questions. First, let's hear your side of the story. Start with why you are being arrested."

"The FBI said it's bribery and attempted murder. You can't let them do this to me!"

"Attempted. Alright, who do they think you attempted to kill?"

"I didn't try to kill anybody. I'm the Boss. It must have been Cory going rogue. This whole thing is Welch's fault. He started it!"

"Okay, slow down. We'll get back to that in a moment. Now, I want you to tell me, who did you try to bribe?"

"Recently?"

Chapter 38

"Times up," Kirk said as he returned to Biggs' office. "Who are these two guys?"

"They're my associates," Biggs replied. "They'll be going downtown with us.

"I don't care how many people follow us downtown, but inside, he gets legal counsel, not counsels.

Biggs started to object, but Shields interrupted. "Gentlemen. Can we just get out of here?"

Shields, the three agents and three lawyers headed down the hall to the elevator. Kirk was puzzled by Shields' last comment, and wondered why he was in such a hurry.

As Shields passed his office, he spoke up, "Excuse me for a second. Doris, I need you to cancel all my appointments for the day. Do it right now."

Kirk had an 'Ah ha' moment. Time came to a stop.

The 'ding' of the elevator opening could be heard in the background.

Doris replied. "But sir, Mr. Dumont and his associates are on their way up." The elevator door opened behind them.

Hearing the name Dumont, two agents went for their guns as they spun around.

Dumont, surrounded by an entourage of corporate suits, stepped into the hallway.

"Hands up!" Kirk yelled pulling his weapon. "You're under arrest."

Dumont was faster. Jumping behind an accountant, he pulled a plastic gun and put a bullet in Carter's chest. His second shot hit a lawyer stepping between him and Dirty Joan.

Kirk could not get a clean shot with all the civilians running and ducking for cover.

Dumont aimed at Kirk and pulled the trigger.

The plastic gun jammed.

Joan got off two quick shots as she dove for cover. They missed as Dumont jumped into the stairwell. Kirk radioed 'officer down' as he tried to stop the young agent's bleeding.

Joan pushed her way through the crowd of suits and chased Dumont down the stairs. She burst through the door on the ground floor, ducking from the sound of gunfire.

Racing to the sound, she saw the dead security guard on the floor. His gun was missing. She ran out of the building to the waiting limos in visitors' parking. Only the drivers were there. The sound of a motorcycle pealed out in the distance.

Dumont was gone.

****

That night, local news WPIC reported two security guards killed, and a federal agent in critical condition. At least one executive was seriously wounded in the gun battle. The perpetrator was still at large.

Three more lawyers and four accountants were being treated at the local hospital. Two had heart attacks, and the others were being treated for trauma and serious injuries.

A local reporter got a live interview with one of the secretaries at the scene. It aired on the evening news.

"It was horrible, just horrible, and all the screaming. I've never seen anything like it in my whole life. Lawyers, accountants, running everywhere. Paper flying in the air. That handsome young agent was shot. Blood was all over him. I pray for his soul.

"Guns were going off. It was so loud. Thank God I'm alive. People were crying and trying to hide everywhere they could. Two very rude men crawled under my desk while I was still sitting there. And some accountant was hiding behind my potted rubber plant. My boss tried to jump out the window, but it was safety glass, and he just bounced off.

"Everyone was terrified. The carpets are all stained and probably ruined. The smell of... you know, will never come out. Oh, it was just horrible."

Chapter 39

It was late afternoon when Welch got the urgent call. He was told to walk out the main entrance of the building. "Don't stop to talk with your boss. The FBI will take care of it. A police car is coming to pick you up. Go."

As he stepped outside, a state trooper pulled into the lot. The officer, wearing a serious expression, was a big man with square shoulders in a trim blue uniform. No one was going to talk their way out of a ticket with this guy. "Mr. Welch, get in the back seat. Buckle up." As the car pulled out of the lot, the trooper hit the gas, lights and siren.

"What the hell's going on?" Welch asked.

"Don't know sir, but it must be important. My orders are to get you to Newark ASAP. Excuse me while I concentrate on my driving," he said ending the conversation.

Welch tightened his seatbelt, sat back, and enjoyed the feeling of power as cars moved out of their way. As they sped through traffic to the federal building, Welch started to wonder. *Now what have I done.*

Someone was waiting for him at the front entrance, and he was rushed into the building past security. Stepping out of the elevator on the fifth floor, Welch met his two favorite agents, Allen and Jack. They shook hands and quickly ushered him down the hallway to a private room before he could ask any questions.

The room was ghost green with no windows and a large mirror on one wall. Electronic equipment sat on the shelving of the opposite wall. A man was sitting at the table in the center of the room. He had the same build and similar suit as the other two agents, but older with distinguished gray hair and a disarming smile.

"Please be seated. I'm Doctor Hamilton with the Central Intelligence Agency." Welch looked over at his FBI friends and they nodded an approval.

After forty minutes of non-stop rushing, Welch felt someone had put the brakes on as he watched Hamilton move in a calm, relaxed manner. He made direct eye contact yet gave a pleasant sincere smile. There was no pretend 'I'm your friend' or controlling 'I'm in charge' in his nonjudgmental expression.

Welch felt comfortable with the apparent honesty and hoped it was genuine. Hamilton opened a folder on the desk and lifted the papers from it. "Greg, I have the transcript of your testimony and would like to ask you a few questions."

"Doc, go ahead."

"Think carefully and try to remember as best you can. It says here you were questioned by an Asian man. Do you remember his name?"

"No... Don't remember him ever giving me any name, but he asked if I knew who he was."

"Yes, I see that in the transcript. Did he mention anything about a Lucky Lady?"

"Not sure if I remember that. But yes, I think he did."

"Anything about boats or the Caribbean?"

"Sorry. Was that who, what the Lucky Lady was?"

"Do you remember the name of anyone else that night?"

"I'm not too good with names and we really didn't do any formal introductions. I was under a little pressure, you know. Wait. I remember he asked if I knew a Thomas Dumont, or something like that."

"Are you sure of that name?" Hamilton asked as he scribbled some notes on the transcript.

"Yes, positive." Welch couldn't think of any witty comebacks. "I do remember that was one of the names he asked about. He asked about a few names. Another one I remember for sure was a Samuel Chen."

"Interesting, you're positive?" His facial expression changed to a dead-serious stare.

Welch nodded. "Absolutely."

Hamilton remained calm but displayed a worried frown as he reached across the table and picked up the office phone. Looking straight at Welch, he tapped in a number. "Hello, Doctor Hamilton here. Holding. Yes, I'm on a secure line, priority one. Rush please." He looked up at the wall clock then down at his watch.

Hamilton turned and talked into the phone. "Are you ready? It's a go. Send a hunter to the Lucky Lady. We only have a few hours. Go with whatever resources you have. It must be stopped. One way or the other. Thank you."

He put the phone down and looked back at Welch with a smile. "You've been most helpful; we appreciate your cooperation. I understand that you and your handlers have a working arrangement and that your cooperation and confidentiality is complete?"

Welch looked over at Allan and Jack. "Yes, we have a cooperative arrangement. Me and my handlers, we're all good buddies here."

"Very good," Hamilton replied as he stood up. "Thank you for your help. Have a nice day Mr. Welch." He reached out and gave a quick handshake then turned to the two Agents. "Remember, Dumont is still at large. We want him, and you need to get him before he slips away again." Hamilton turned and promptly left the room.

Welch turned to the two men. "So you're my handlers. What gives with the CIA?"

"Some activity connected to the investigation is outside the United States, so we're required by law to pass it on to our associates. Nothing for you to ever be talking about. Ever." That was all Welch was going to get out of them.

"I get it, but now that we're such good buddies on the same team and all, I still want to learn the secret handshake and maybe get a decoder ring?"

No response.

"Do I at least get a lift back to the office?"

Later that night, Welch felt good enough to go to the gym for the first time since he got banged up. His workout was strong, but not compulsive. Back at his apartment, he drank his protein shake, then nuked a Lean Cuisine. After dinner, he relaxed, poured himself a glass of wine and watched the news, fantasizing he would see himself.

Welch wondered if the information he'd provided would make any difference. To what, he didn't know, but it would be nice if he had saved the world or at least helped it a little bit. He was pretty sure he had, and it made him feel optimistic. He was certain the events had changed him, and he knew that was a good thing.

Feeling good, he called Linda to tell her how much he missed her. The call did not go well.

He apologized for not calling more often and for other things. They talked for a long time, and she reminded him that he once told her they should date other people. Welch knew that meant she was seeing someone else. Biting his lip to hide the pain, and the anger, he said he wanted to see her again to have the conversation in person. They agreed to spend a week together to decide if they had any future, but couldn't agree on where.

After hanging up, he realized it was a stupid mistake not to go anyplace she wanted—he was learning. Going online, he sent her a dozen red roses, a box of Godiva Chocolate, and a gift certificate to her favorite lingerie store.

Not satisfied, he wanted to tell her how he felt, *it's time to take a chance and double down,* but was afraid he'd mess things up even more. Deciding to send an email, he quickly concluded a hundred page statistical marketing analysis was easier to write than a love letter. He carefully constructed the email, but was never satisfied that it conveyed his feelings. It was a frightening but liberating experience. He deleted his comments on the FBI, then added an 'if not' protection clause for himself.

Dear Linda,

I want to continue our discussion and ask the questions I was afraid to ask. I have made mistakes, but I have learned from them, even if I had to learn the hard way.

Some recent events in our relationship have caused me to look at how I want to spend the rest of my life. My most beautiful, loving memory is with the wonderful woman I worship and adore. I fell deeply in love with you and it was the best. If you have any similar feelings, if you want me making breakfast for you for the rest of your life, let me know where you stand.

If not, my rich, beautiful feelings will go back to the best memory file. If you have any questions or want to talk, or just need time, let me know.

Love

She quickly responded.

Just read your e-mail and all I can say right now is "wow." I will send a more thoughtful reply shortly. I also have wonderful, loving memories.

Until then,
Linda

Not what he was hoping for. *I'm the pilot, and I'm going down in flames. The control tower is yelling. "Eject, eject!" But I continue holding the stick, trying to pull out of the dive.* The second email followed later that night.

Your email overwhelmed me, and it has not diminished. I thought about it but then, as usual, my practical side jumped in.

I saw the old movie, Cafe Society last week and it made me think of how sometimes I think of you and how you are doing, and perhaps you do the same with me. And yes, occasionally, what life will be like if we stay together. It does seem like an impossible situation to me for a number of practical reasons. We have a very strong connection, aka chemistry, that started out in Anaheim and it developed into love.

Some of it was lust of course but much of it for me was how we both felt about the world. We traveled well together (of course that's all we were able to do), had adventures that were fun and then we had to say goodbye for a while, until the next visit.) I realized how lonely I was.

So I'm thinking that the I love you offer isn't good for us to do right now. There are other thoughts, but I will save them for another time.

Will you tell what recent events and relationships have made you look at how you want to spend the rest of your life? (I have a friend with cancer and that affects how I want to live my life.) I do really love being in contact and look forward to continuing this discussion when we meet.

Bang! Crash and burn. He gave it one more shot, hoping he was hitting the right buttons.

Linda,

You said you were lonely. So was I. I tried to understand how not holding you could make me feel so alone. (I'm a one woman guy), and why I fell so hard for you. I also considered locations and all the wonderful places we went together. I quickly concluded that even if you lived in North Dakota, my feelings would be the same.

Could it be sex? After all, you are the most intense, erotic, passionate, sensual- No judgement, only peace. Not exactly the reason but what it (you) did was transcend the physical so I could see beyond it to caring, sharing, giving, trusting, commitment and love. And it scared the hell out of me. So I said we should date other people (you know I never did).

Can sex and love be separate? I don't want to separate them, but even if I could only hold your hand, I would still love you. I was beginning to understand it all, but I guess I've run out of time. No excuses.

Love is eternal, but life is not. I don't want to put my beautiful memories and feelings in a box just to make new memories. I want to be with you.

That's about it from here. See you soon.

Love

There was no response, confirming what he already knew. Trying to relax with his glass of wine, Welch started obsessing on Linda, so he closed his eyes and thought of Gayle to change the subject—then Tina and Susan, Pam and Laurie. He carried them with him as each was a part of who he was today. They would always be the best part. *Don't know if it's a strength or a weakness, but it's all I got, so I'll go with it.*

He would use that love to get it right the next time. He wouldn't make the same mistakes, again. Welch was sure of all the things he should not be, but not clear on exactly what he should be. *Maybe just myself. Yes. An epiphany.*

As he sat on the couch, Welch realized all his questions and prayers weren't going to be answered tonight. *Life is a tangled chain of disconnected links, or something like that.* But he understood the sun would come up tomorrow, and that was new for him.

He refilled his glass as he thought about the events of the day. *Despite tonight's setbacks, I'm moving in the right direction. Wow, what a concept. I like it.*

Sleeping, he soared with eagles and flew over a field of windmills. He forded a stream of clear, cool water. He was walking down a long, dark hall. Perceiving movement to one side, he turned and saw his reflection in a mirror. Everything was alright; he could go on. So he slept comfortably, not remembering what he had dreamed.

Chapter 40

A crescent moon hid behind thick cloud-cover over the Gulf of Mexico. High winds and passing rain squalls gave a bumpy ride to the C131 military transport at 12,000 feet. Its bay door opened, and six Navy SEALS jumped silently into the night's black abyss.

Far above them, military satellites tracked their target and relayed coordinate data to a Navy E2C Hawkeye. The surveillance aircraft, with its radar dome sitting on top of the plane like an oversize beret was assigned to US drug smuggling operations. Forty five minutes ago, the CIA gave it a new mission priority to triangulate and coordinate a top secret operation codenamed Orion.

Two super hornets with anti-ship and anti-aircraft missiles had just entered a holding pattern, circling at twenty-two thousand feet directly above the transport. An EA-18G Growler electronic warfare aircraft arrived on station. It carried an array of tactical wing pods loaded with the most sophisticated radar and radio signal jamming equipment.

The Growler started jamming the second the SEALS left their plane. A Coast Guard Cutter and a nuclear, attack sub, the closest US combat ships in the area were over forty miles out, but steaming full speed to the drop zone to provide additional backup.

Somewhere below the free-falling SEALS was the Lucky Lady. In six minutes she would enter Cuban waters where two Russian-made destroyers of the Cuban Navy were waiting to escort her to Havana. Their radar was tracking the C131. They had orders to fire as soon as the American plane reached Cuban airspace, but suddenly it banked hard right. Seconds later, it disappeared as the ships' radar went blind.

A squadron of Russian MIG -21's took off from Havana Airport, only to be painted by American radar and have their own radar and communications jammed. The jets were told to turn back or be shot down; flying blind, they had little choice.

The six SEALS in freefall oriented themselves, lining up in a preplanned formation. They searched for their target using enhanced nvgs, (night vision goggles). The team used the enhancement feature to pick up the heat signature of the Lucky Lady. Sergeant Walkowitz, the senior man and team leader, positioned himself second in the lineup. With many jumps and combat experience, he relaxed in freefall and mentally assessed the situation now that he had a peaceful moment to himself.

Never had he jumped in such horrible weather, so the mission was obviously critical. A line drop onto the boat from a chopper would have been his preference, but they would not have reached the target in time. Likewise, a Rigid Hull Inflatable Boat (RHIB) for an aerial boat insertion was not an option. They had to do it the old fashion way.

If the yacht crossed into Cuban waters, the US Navy would sink it with his team onboard. This was a rush job under CIA control. He didn't even have time to assemble a full team. Walkowitz's unit had just returned from a mission in South America and half his men were given passes. Tomorrow, they planned on field testing new navigation equipment off the Florida Keys. But this came up.

Two new SEAL graduates were available on base and quickly assigned to his unit. They had not yet been deployed overseas, and Walkowitz was concerned that this was their first combat mission. The new group took off and arrived over the target with only minutes to spare.

While his team had relaxed in silence, Walkowitz listened on the radio as his command scrambled to secure resources and backup redundancy for the mission. There was no time to get all the reserves they needed. He wished the backup support helicopters (helos) with Rescue Swimmers were in place, even if they were only trainees out of Jacksonville, Florida.

Landing on an armed yacht, traveling at sixteen knots, at night, in high seas, with strong cross winds was no easy feat. If the jump time or coordinates were off by a hair, they would miss the target completely.

The whole team would be treading water until the Rescue Swimmers arrived.

Last, he wondered why after all this effort, his orders were to capture—not kill? Did this mean there were high value intelligence targets on board or civilians? What was the ship's layout? How many onboard and how well were they armed? He didn't have much Intel. The fog of war was dangerous enough; he didn't feel good going in with so many unknowns before the shooting even started.

Walkowitz could see nothing in the black sky below, but it was time to go to work. He said his soldier's prayer, "Oh dear God, please don't let me screw up or die," before deploying his chute at twelve hundred feet. There was little time to maneuver if they were not directly in line with the target. At one thousand feet they broke through the cloud cover.

He was checking to ensure all his men had deployed their chutes when he heard Taylor's shout in his headset, "Target below. Right where she's supposed to be." Taylor, a decorated combat veteran, moved up to point as they continued their descent in single file to land on the small moving top deck a few seconds apart. Taylor had done two night jumps like this, one in training and one against pirates off the coast of Africa—but not in conditions like this, and never onto such a small ship.

Standing on the yacht's top deck, a guard was trying to light a wet cigarette. He was armed with an M82A1 Heavy Sniper's Rifle, and night vision goggles. Drenched from head to toe, he looked up cursing the rain just as Taylor started his flare out to brake for landing.

The guard raised his weapon, but Taylor drew faster. A short burst from the SEAL's HK416 cut him down. To accurately aim and take out his target, Taylor had sacrificed himself by letting go of his chute control lines.

Caught in the crosswind, he missed his landing spot, slamming hard into the boat's side railing. Breaking his arm and dislocating his shoulder, he tried to hold on to the rail, but his chute dragged him under. Tangled in the silk and lines, Taylor struggled in pain to keep his head above water. His emergency beacon automatically deployed upon contact with the saltwater.

The SEAL's gunfire was silenced, but the falling bodies and slugs passing through the deck drew some attention. Standing on the bow looking for the Russian ships, the second guard with the AK47 ran up the ladder to investigate. He also saw a parachute and raised his gun, but was stopped by a short burst of fire from Walkowitz, already standing on the deck. He stood guard while Berman, the third man to hit the deck, helped catch the others as they landed.

The guard lying near the SEAL's feet suddenly rolled over with a revolver in his hand. Walkowitz realized the guards must be wearing body armor, and posed a danger to his team. His training had already put two bullets in the gunman's head. He consciously repeated the procedure on the second guard.

As he watched for movement, he told himself he had to kill them to protect his men. *All armies are different, but all soldiers die the same.*

He also told himself he had to get out of this business, he was sick of killing and wanted to go home to hold his children before he lost his soul.

The yacht's captain, an old military man, and the first mate were on the bridge trying to figure out why the radar screen had gone white. The captain's suspicion was confirmed when he heard the bullets passing through the deck and saw the movement outside the cabin.

He immediately drew his pistol, but reconsidered his options. He dropped the gun and started yelling "I surrender!" first in English, then German and Spanish. The first mate was not so cerebral. He drew his Glock and fired as the first SEAL burst into the cabin. Two hollow point slugs hit the SEAL in the chest cracking his ribs. The impact drove him backwards, and he fell on the deck.

His body armor saved his life, but it was the first time the big man had ever been knocked down. He cursed loudly to express his displeasure.

The second SEAL tossed a concussion grenade into the cabin and stepped back while the first mate continued shooting. The grenade blast didn't damage the cabin, but the shock wave burst the eardrums of the two crewmen and woke up everyone on the boat.

When the two SEALS re-entered the cabin, the captain and mate were rolling on the deck and crying in pain. Their hands were quickly bound behind their backs.

Walkowitz entered the cabin and saw the area had been secured. He yelled, "Are we all accounted for?"

"We're all down!" was the reply from Flynn, the last man to land on the deck as he entered the crowded cabin with the others. "Taylor is MIA."

Walkowitz understood but ignored the last statement, staying focused on the mission. Taylor's fate was now in the hands of God and a Rescue Swimmer. Walkowitz grabbed the ship's wheel and spun it around as he pushed the throttle forward hard. The boat turned sharply away from Cuba and headed north.

"Flynn, guard the prisoners. Tex, keep the boat on a Northwest bearing or sink it." "Faulkner, Berman, come below with me! Orders are don't shoot unless it's life threatening!" he reminded the team, then added, "This boat is still hot, be careful!"

Below deck, everyone had been awakened by the blast of the grenade and violent course change. Chen's first thought was an attack by pirates or drug smugglers. He ran out of the master stateroom carrying his AK47 and a 44 Magnum in his belt. Tina Hall came out of the adjoining stateroom carrying a bottle of Beefeater's Gin.

Standing in the dim lit hallway, they watched three crewmen come up from the engine room, the leader carrying a sawed off shotgun. They ran headlong into three heavily armed men in black, coming down the stairs.

As they all crashed together in confusion, Walkowitz held his fire and kicked the gunman in the groin. Then he swung the butt of his assault rifle into the side of his head, knocking him out cold. "Surrender! Hands up or I'll shoot!" He yelled at the others, first in English and then in Spanish, Farsi and Polish.

Hearing the commands, Chen realized the intruders were American military. He flipped the assault rifle to auto as shouldered his weapon, drawing a deadly bead on the cluster of SEALS.

Tina wielded the gin bottle like a club, smashing it into the back of Chen's head. She pushed the gun barrel up as the weapon fired. Grabbing his ponytail and pulling him backward, she kicked the back of his knee. As he went down, she grabbed the pistol from his belt. Chen slammed into the deck with a loud thud as she drove her knee into his chest.

When he yelled in pain, she stuck the barrel of the revolver in his mouth and turned toward the SEALs.

"Don't shoot! British Secret Service."

"Put down the gun," Walkowitz yelled as he covered her with his weapon.

Cautiously walking up to her, he expressed his surprise. "A bloody Brit! Who do you think you are, Mrs. Bond? What the hell are you doing on this side of the pond?"

"I could ask you yanks the same bloody questions. I didn't call for your help."

He ignored her statement. "Are there any more of you?"

"No, but there's a fat little man handcuffed to the bed in my stateroom."

Walkowitz grinned as he tried to picture it, but let that one slide.

"Now do you mind keeping this bloke covered while I finish getting dressed, then we can sort this all out."

Monopoly Games

Chapter 41

The storm was getting worse as the Sikorsky MH60 Romeo Helicopter entered a holding pattern five miles behind the Lucky Lady. The copilot was checking the fuel gauge when the warning light went on. They knew a SEAL was in the water.

Kelly, the pilot, adjusted his heading, and the Sikorsky locked in on Taylor's emergency beacon. The Romeo model was the newest shipboard helo in the fleet, replacing the older Bravo. They had essentially the same airframe and similar engines, but the avionics package was all new.

The pilot and copilot sitting forward were senior men with extensive combat and rescue experience. They had been on a routine training mission near Miami when they received an emergency call to land at Key West Airbase. They topped off and headed south. Their craft, Romeo 159, was sixty five minutes closer to the Lucky Lady than the fully manned Romeos taking off from Jacksonville further north.

The third crewman riding in the back was Curtis Miller, a recruit-in-training to be a Navy Rescue Swimmer. Miller had two years of college at a state university, but found it boring and frustrating. With no sense of direction or motivation, he dropped out to start his own business as a graphic artist. Six months later, he was deeply in debt and had to admit financial defeat.

Deeply hurt by his business failure and the many 'I told you so's', he enlisted in the Navy SEAL program. Now with a strong sense of direction, he excelled through five months of Basic Training and BUD, graduating at the head of his class. But during Hell Week of SEAL training, one bad step put him on his back, and ten minutes later, he was washed out of the program.

Although depressed by the failure, he had learned his worth and could live with a temporary setback. Seeing his college background and training record, the Navy asked him to join a less glamorous, but elite, small group of men called Rescue Swimmers.

Miller had been in the program for months. He was excited to be on a real mission, using his training to rescue a lost SEAL.

The training had required him to memorize every nut, bolt and wire on the forty two million dollar helicopter. Since the primary function of the helo was antisubmarine warfare, he was SONAR trained to identify, target, and kill every make and model of submarine on the planet. Plus, he could ID eight species of whales by age and gender.

In combat, the helo intel would be assimilated with its fleet SONAR/radar, weapons, and navigation data. The information was coordinated in real time with all craft to create the Navy's integrated air/sea defense system.

As they approached Cuban Airspace, the helo dropped under a hundred feet to avoid radar detection and conserve fuel. As their aircraft approached the beacon signal, it dropped to under seventy feet before turning on its powerful floodlights.

Miller, wearing his gunner's harness which secured him to the Romeo, opened the side door to start his visual search and was hit with a sheet of cold rain. He had already 'changed out' to his wetsuit. Shrugging off the cold water, Miller looked down at the white capped waves on a dark rolling sea.

It was a bumpy ride as Kelly worked to steady the chopper in gale force winds. Miller was thankful to be tethered to the helo. Leaning out the door with his night vision goggles, he searched for his lost SEAL.

"Approaching target, radio position 100 yards." The voice of the copilot came through Miller's headset. He swung the stretcher outside the door and tested the hoist. The equipment worked, but the stretcher banged violently against the chopper in the wind and rotary wash. Miller held it steady and continued his search as the seconds went by.

Looking at the white caps rolling under him, he knew they had already traveled 100 yards when he heard the pilot, "Coming around for a second sweep. Keep your eyes open back there." Miller ignored the comment as he stared down through the rain into the angry black void below. He saw the light beacon and a bobbing object before it went behind a wave.

"Survivor in sight, two o'clock, 40 yards!" The captain responded with a course correction, slowing his air speed and dropped altitude. Miller watched until he was directly overhead.

"Pop smoke!" Miller yelled.

The pilot did, then came around again, this time heading directly into the wind.

"Hold position," Miller commanded.

Kelly was good, Miller was right where he needed to be. But the captain and copilot could not see their man in the water from their position directly over the SEAL.

"Request verbal control," Miller added. Following standard procedure, he would make the final adjustments to guide the chopper's hoist directly over the man.

Miller could see the injured man was badly tangled in his chute. Taylor was alive, but in serious trouble. He raised his good arm just as a massive wave dragged him under. When his body came up, it was struggling under the chute. He would not last long. The next wave would take him down for good.

Navy regulations are explicit. A Rescue Swimmer can't enter the water unless a second Rescue Swimmer is onboard to handle the lines and hoist. The stretcher must be pulled down by the rescuer to prevent it from being sucked into the prop wash, downing the helo. Plus, if the SEAL in the water can't hold onto the line, he's most likely dead, and there is no point in endangering the life of a second person. But Miller saw the man was still alive and drowning as he watched.

The other Bravos had an ETA of thirty seven minutes. Taylor wouldn't last another thirty seven seconds.

Miller unhooked his safety line and yelled, "He's alive under his chute. I'm going in!" Before the pilot could respond, Miller took off his helmet, grabbed his two-way radio and jumped.

The captain started cursing like a sailor. The copilot unbuckled to go back and maintain visual while operating the hoist.

Miller kept his eye on the target to orient himself as he hit the water a few feet clear of the parachute. He did not come straight up but swam underwater to his target. Not the correct Navy procedure, but necessary this time to save a life.

The chopper floodlights did not penetrate the black ocean. Miller swam blind with his arms spread wide until his shoulder hit the man's legs. He grabbed hold as he realized the body was not moving.

Six month of intensive training paid off as he propelled the SEAL upward with a powerful kick. Miller breached the surface lifting Taylor's head out of the water. But they were forced back under by the wet parachute nylon.

He pushed up the chute with one arm to give the SEAL some breathing room. Grabbing his knife with the other hand, he ripped a large hole in the chute. Miller swam through it, dragging the man behind him.

As the co-pilot lowered the lines and hoist, he hoped a large rogue wave would not knock them out of the air. The stretcher, swinging in the violent wind, dropped in the water a few yards from its target.

The stretcher was not visible in the high waves, and the roar of the Romeo was deafening. Miller struggled to swim, towing the SEAL by the back of the collar, dragging the chute through the high surf. Miller found the stretcher and rolled the man onto it. He applied several quick rescue breaths to get air into the man's lungs. Taylor responded with a gasp and a cry of pain.

Miller held on to the stretcher as he struggled to cut away the tangled chute. It bobbed violently in the rolling waves. Securely strapping his man in, he signaled for the copilot to hoist him up.

He avoided the chute as he remained in the water until the stretcher returned, then slid in. The copilot extended a hand to help Miller in, then shook his head before returning forward to his seat.

Miller put on his helmet with communication gear, locked in the winch, closed the door and yelled, "Secure!" into his headset.

The Romeo banked and accelerated to return to American Waters while Miller applied first aid. The copilot notified Command of the recovery and computed a course setting. The captain contemplated his dilemma. Should he report his rescue swimmer for disobeying Navy regulations, or recommend a medal for bravery?

All jamming stopped as the SEALS on the Lucky Lady set a course to rendezvous with the Coast Guard cutter and sub. She would be escorted to Guantanamo where a team of CIA interrogators and computer scientists would take over.

Chapter 42

It had been two weeks since Welch was called to the FBI headquarters. The summer heat had broken and there was a slight chill in the morning air. Since the CIA meeting, he had worked hard to patch things up with A3E senior management. He remained quiet instead of argumentative. He was polite instead of cynical, and supportive instead of combative.

The changes were easy when 'you don't sweat the small stuff' and everything in the office was small stuff. There was no need to feel defensive if your ego doesn't feel threatened. Much to his surprise, his most work still got done without all the stress.

He knew he still had an issue with authority, but tried to act like a team player. Caroline even complimented him on his new attitude, showing patience and sensitivity to her team. Unfortunately, his relationship with Linda was not improving.

His workouts at the gym were more intense, and he felt stronger. He was drinking a little more, but didn't think it was a problem. He knew it was under control.

The only problem at the office was boredom. Every day was boring. Every meeting was boring as he smiled and bit his tongue. Every hour was boring as he sat in his office doing his paperwork. After all that had happened, having your bosses like you was a boring goal.

Janet stuck her head in his office. She did not look happy, but then she never did. "Gregory, the upcoming trip to the International Standards Conference in Europe, you're coming too. Apparently, your FBI friends want you there. Call them.

"Here's your letter with my signature approving you as a member of the U.S. delegation. The conference details are on the website. And Welch, don't let your silly games interfere with my business plans. Do you understand me?"

"Yes sir… yes, Ms. Winslow." *Your priorities don't sound very patriotic.*

She walked out of his office. Welch picked up the signed paper on her stationary. He would make copies and file it. Reading her directive, he realized the event was the week he had hoped to be on vacation with Linda. His first thought was that he could take her with him to Europe, but then he remembered their trip to Chicago. She was not happy about being shot at. He needed to call Allen before deciding what to do.

If there was any danger, he didn't want her along. But if he just canceled their plans, or said 'you can't go with me,' that wouldn't go over well. It was a lose-lose proposition. Welch closed his office door and called Allen. He was annoyed no one answered and left a message asking to be contacted before he left the office.

The remainder of the day was quiet as he worked on the changes to the ballot system and waited for a return call that never came. He did get an email from Ms. Wilson, the consultant. She would be in New Jersey next week and wanted to take him to a non-Indian restaurant for lunch. She hoped to continue their discussion on Zen and improving international relations. Welch was sure the timing of her visit and the sudden invitation to the International Conference was no coincidence. It was going to be an interesting lunch.

Walking to his car after work, he saw the man. The guy was standing with his back to Welch about a hundred feet away. He stood out because nobody just stands in a parking lot. Welch watched in his rearview mirror as the man got in his silver midsize Ford and followed him.

"It's easy to see you're being followed when you're paranoid enough to look for it," he said out loud to no one. The car, which Welch took to be a rental, stayed a safe distance behind as they moved through traffic. He thought about doing a 'Steve McQueen' car chase, but he was not in a 427 Mustang and decided to set up a simpler confrontation.

His adrenaline rising, Welch slid his bootleg Eagles tape into the player, and turned up the volume. Humming the words, he thought about their meaning, "This could be heaven, this could be hell."

As he approached his apartment complex, 'The Boys of Summer' was playing and it reminded him of her. Welch considered driving around the block to hear the end of the song, but thought that might look a little suspicious.

He pulled in the complex, watching the second car follow him. He double checked to make sure there was only one car and only one person in it. The Feds always traveled in pairs.

Welch exited his car as the man pulled into a nearby parking space. Welch didn't want to get shot in the back, and he would be a stationary target unlocking his apartment door. Instead, he continued moving and followed the narrow sidewalk to the end of the building.

He rounded the corner, out of sight, then put his back against the wall with his lead hand open and pulled back to his ear. He hoped he was right, because the next person walking around that corner was getting hacked in the throat.

Waiting, his biology was in fight mode, but his brain started to think, and it started to question why. *This is stupid, volunteering for a fight. Does he have a gun? I could get killed.*

If he had more time to question himself, the outcome might have been different. But the man came around the corner carrying a large handgun with silencer and high capacity clip.

The gun was held shoulder high, blocking Welch's strike.

Welch grabbed the man's hand as the weapon fired. The man tried to push the barrel in his face.

The gunman attempted a head butt. Welch stopped his momentum with an elbow to the solar plexus. The strike hit body armor as the man grabbed Welch's hand before he could dig his fingers into his enemy's throat.

The gunman attempted a judo throw. Welch stayed low to keep his balance and countered with a knee to the groin. The man tried a leg sweep. Welch bit him as they slammed together.

Each used all their strength and skill to overpower the other. They fought for the gun.

Welch sidestepped and used his assailant's momentum to smash him into the building. The body armor absorbed the blow. The gun fired two more rounds near Welch's face. His ears were ringing, the compression disoriented him.

The opponent attacked with another head butt to the temple. It jarred Welch's skull. He lost focus.

Stumbling, he fought to remain upright. The gun fired as the barrel moved closer. Welch went backwards fighting to keep the gun out of his face.

The gunman drove in for a takedown. They hit a low iron fence and flipped over it.

Falling into the bushes, the gunman let go of Welch's wrist to break his fall.

Welch stayed focused on the kill with every synapse under his control. With his freed hand, he gouged out the assailant's eyeball.

The gun fired as the big man's body convulsed in pain. Welch spun around the man and grabbed the gun barrel with his free hand.

He pulled the hot barrel into the man's throat with all the force he could generate. The man's body struggled until the windpipe collapsed. His movement stopped. Welch continued the pressure until he was sure there was no breathing.

He gripped the gun with his finger on the trigger and stuck his head out of the bushes. There were no other attackers.

After catching his breath and scanning the parking lot, he rolled the lifeless body behind a large bush and stepped on the sidewalk.

Welch grinned as he held the lethal weapon in his hand and looked at the red dirt by the body. He won.

Down the street, two women pushed baby strollers. They were watching their children and did not notice him. Holding the gun under his arm, he pulled out his phone. This time Allen picked up.

"It's Welch. We have a situation. I've got a dead body here."

"What body? Where are you?"

"In front of my apartment. No one saw the fight. I have his gun; it's a big one with a magnum clip and silencer, like a real professional. Get your butt over here."

"Are you by the body? I need you to do something. Does the body have an ID, or did you notice any distinguishing characteristics?"

"If you call a really big fucking gun a distinguishing characteristic, then yeah! Look, I was really busy and wasn't looking for any God da… Shit, hold on."

Welch came back a few seconds later. "No ID, must be in the car. But yes, there's a distinguishing characteristic, he's missing the end of a finger on his left hand."

"Congratulations Welch. You just bagged a most wanted, aka Thomas Dumont. Stay where you are. Don't move. We'll be right over to take care of the cleanup. Good job man."

"Wait a minute! Did you set me up? Were you expecting this? That this guy would come after me for messing up his business plans?"

"No. Not at all. Don't be paranoid. We would have given you protection.

Yeah right.

This was an unanticipated move, not their normal style. His organization must have told him to clean up any loose ends."

"But I'm the loose end! And what the hell is normal style? Didn't we go through this once already? Will this organization send another clean up man?"

"Not likely. Dumont was your only connection, and you cleaned him up. Welch, relax. We're on our way. You've done a great job for your country." Allen hung up.

Welch felt a sense of pride, and he did relax as dopamine flooded his brain. He had been victorious, and people were congratulating him. He wondered if there was a reward for getting a most wanted. *Or was this just the patriotic thing to do? Was that being cynical, or naïve, or both?*

It felt awkward just standing around covered with dirt and blood. Welch figured it would be less conspicuous if he waited in his apartment. At least he could clean up and take some aspirin, or pour himself a drink. Those head butts hurt like hell as the adrenaline rush died down.

He walked to his apartment and unlocked the door. Looking over his shoulder where the body was hidden, Welch experienced a repulsive feeling travel through his body. *What's happening to me? A dead body, an organization, what have I been dragged into? I didn't ask for this.*

Welch stepped inside and locked the door behind him. He tossed the gun on the couch. The room was hot and stuffy. It was hard to breathe. He turned on the air conditioner, walked into the bathroom, and saw himself in the mirror.

Powder burns were on his face, and his shirt was covered in blood. He ripped it off and threw it on the floor. Welch compulsively washed and rewashed his hands and face until they were red before going into the bedroom to put on a clean shirt.

He went to the kitchen and poured a triple shot of vodka then knocked it back. It both burned and felt good. He scooped two handfuls of ice into the glass and poured himself another round. After double-checking the door, he settled down on the couch next to the gun. Removing the clip, he cleared the chamber, removed the silencer, reinserted the clip, and rested the weapon on his lap.

Welch sipped his drink, then put the cold glass on his red forehead. He closed his eyes and breathed deeply to relax. His mind drifted, and he saw her standing in front of him. She was as beautiful as ever, just as he had last seen her so long ago. He reached out and ran his fingers through her hair. Gazing into her eyes, he saw a deep sadness.

He reached out to comfort her, but she looked away. Welch struggled to understand what was wrong. He studied her features, and they began to change. He saw the face of another woman he had once known. Changing again, she became a collage of lovers from his past before returning to Linda.

Welch realized he was in a dream, but willed it to continue.

She spoke, but he could not hear her. She turned to walk away. He tried again to reach out to her as she looked back over her shoulder. Knowing he must not lose her, he followed her into a crowded railroad station, waiting room. Then she was gone.

Although he could not see her, he knew that he would always be looking for her. One day, he would find her.

Welch heard the doorbell ring. He opened his eyes and looked around the empty room.

"Greg, its Allen, FBI. Are you there? Open the door."

Recognizing the voice, he took a swig of vodka then stood up.

"Just a second," he replied, knowing they would love to kick in the door. "I see we're on a first name basis now," he added as he tucked the gun under his shirt.

Unlocking the door, Welch stepped to the side as it opened, then he took another sip of his drink.

"Come in."

THE END